Table of Contents

Fundamentals of Engineering

Core Studies for BTEC First in Engineering

Peter M Roxburgh
Laurie A Roe
Anthony Szary

Business Education Publishers Ltd

1993

©Peter M Roxburgh, Laurie A Roe and Anthony Szary 1993

ISBN 0 907679 52 8

First published in 1993

Cover Design by Caroline White

Graphics by Gerard Callaghan

Published in Great Britain by Business Education Publishers Limited,
Leighton House, 10 Grange Crescent, Stockton Road, Sunderland, Tyne and Wear SR2 7BN

Tel. 091 567 4963   Fax. 091 514 3277

British Library Cataloguing-in-Publication Data
A catalogue record for this book is available from the British Library

Printed in Great Britain by Athenaeum Press Limited, Unit 3, Mill Lane Industrial Estate, Newcastle upon Tyne

To Mabel, Mary, Jan and Alex

Introduction

This book is intended to be a major learning resource for students studying the BTEC First Diploma in Engineering. Its content covers the specifications of the following 90 hour units:

- Engineering Fundamentals
- Mathematics
- Science
- Information Technology

In addition the book contains a programme of intergrative assigments which cover the four units mentioned above as well as the specifications for common skills. These integrative assignments are the central core of the programme as they actively involve students in the learning process, integrating knowledge and skills from the core modules. The assignments involve the application of knowledge to meaningful tasks in a work-related context. They are about learning-by-doing, encouraging students to find things out by themselves and helping to develop their skills in realistic contexts. The benefits of using assignments to develop learning, as well as to assess it, are well documented and include the following:

- students are involved actively in the learning process
- students practise their skills in realistic situations
- skills and knowledge from a number of disciplines can be integrated
- students are usually more motivated
- students develop qualities of self-reliance, self-confidence and self-management
- students develop skills in problem-solving.

The programme of integrative assignments contained in this book covers the majority of the core unit objectives and the common skills for the BTEC First Award in Engineering and it can be supplemented by a programme of modular assignments, a series of phase tests or a project designed to be completed during a period of work placement.

Portfolio of Evidence. One feature of the book is that once a student has achieved an objective this can be recorded using the task data sheets for each of the assignments. These achievements can then be recorded on the module specifications and student profile which is given at the back of the book and will eventually build up until the student has met all the objectives of the course. In this way the book forms a portfolio of evidence and a log-book which the student should maintain and which a tutor can verify.

The *Programme of Integrative Assignments* available in this publication was assembled and managed using a Learning-Management-Support software package, called *Universal System*. Using this system it is possible to assemble a mixed programme of Integrative and Modular assignments with Phase and end-of-course assessments, or any permutation to satisfy a particular need. This may be achieved using modules drawn from any source or mixture of sources.

Universal System-software package was designed by P M Roxburgh and L A Roe

Mathematics

Science

A   **Oxidation**

1   Establish through experiments, the basic chemical processes involved in burning and
     rusting as examples of chemical reactions (interaction between substances which
     result in a rearrangement of their atoms) and apply this knowledge to a variety of
     practical situations. Cover the following: 112
     1.a Composition of air   112
     1.b Mass gain of metals such as copper, brass, iron and steel   112
     1.c Analysis of oxides   112
     1.d Effects of oxygen and water   113
     1.e Examples of damage caused by rusting   113
     1.f Preventative treatments   113

Information Technology Studies

Programme of Integrative Assignments

Module Specifications and Profiles

Engineering Fundamentals

A Safety hazards

1   **Study the 'Health and Safety at Work Act', using practical situations and layouts in the workshop/laboratory to identify the major responsibilities of the employee and hazards**

- the need for personal hygiene, cleanliness and tidiness in the working situation, highlighting possible hazards arising from untidy working conditions
- dangers associated with unsuitable clothing and hair
- importance of machine guards
- dangers associated with electricity in the workshop
- possible dangers from compressed air; noxious fumes and liquids; explosive gases and dust
- the need for eye protection against sparks and dust

It is very important that you acquire and practise safe methods of working and use your intelligence, initiative and knowledge to help to ensure the safety of the workplace and so minimise the risk of injury or disability to yourself or your colleagues. These brief notes have been prepared only as an introduction to health and safety in the workplace and in order to help you understand, discuss and develop the various aspects of health and safety. There are several statutory regulations which guide how you should dress and behave, and the way in which you should undertake various tasks. You have a personal responsibility to acquaint yourself with the details of these regulations.

1.a   The need for personal hygiene, cleanliness and tidiness in the working situation, highlighting possible hazards arising from untidy working conditions

There is a risk of contract ing skin disease from contact with a variety of fluids and liquids which are widely used in workshops and laboratories. This risk can be significantly reduced by washing thoroughly with soap and hot water at the end of each working shift. You can also protect yourself by using barrier cream. You should change and clean your overalls regularly. This will prevent grease and oil accumulating on them, and damaging your normal clothing and body.

It is important to make sure that each person has sufficient space in which to work and that your work space is kept clean and tidy. For example, it is dangerous to crowd too many machines into a confined space and the minimum work space for each person is specified in the government's health and safety legislation. Remember that it is your responsibility to keep the working area clean and tidy. Common safety hazards include spilt oil, and tools or materials which are left lying about.

1.b   Dangers associated with unsuitable clothing and hair

It is generally accepted that the most practical clothing to wear in a workshop is a boiler suit, which should be close fitting, without loose cuffs. You should always keep its buttons properly fastened. This should prevent loose clothing being caught in rotating machinery. In many workshop situations it is wise to wear protective footwear which has slip resistant soles and which is resistant to heat, oils and other chemicals. Shoes should also have steel toecaps to reduce the risk of an injury by a falling object.

Long hair can easily become entangled in rotating spindles when you are operating a machine tool, such as a lathe or drilling machine. If you do have long hair, then wear a cap. This will reduce the potential hazard and also protect your hair from grease, dirt and splashes of cutting fluid.

1.c Importance of machine guards

As an employee, you are responsibile for making sure that any guards which are provided for a machine are used in accordance with the instructions for that particular machine. Grinding wheels, lathe chucks, drills and milling cutters, pulleys and belts are all examples of dangerous machinery which should be used only when a suitable guard is in place. The Health and Safety at Work Act requires that the dangerous parts of all machinery be protected with guards.

1.d Dangers associated with electricity in the workshop

Using electricity in the workshop can be dangerous. You (or your workmates) could be electrocuted causing at best a slight tingling sensation. At worst you could receive a severe electric shock which causes muscular contraction. This could throw you across the workshop floor, stop your breathing, or even prevent your heart from beating. Electricity can also burn, and you should be careful to protect yourself and to prevent a fire.

Here are some guidelines which you should follow when using electricity:

1. Do not use faulty electrical equipment. Report any faults immediately.

2. Do not touch electrical equipment if your hands are wet: there may be a fault in the equipment.

3. Frayed wires are dangerous: report them.

4. Make sure that electrical connections are always made by a qualified electrician.

5. Make sure that electrically-driven hand tools are properly earthed and insulated.

1.e Possible dangers from compressed air; noxious fumes and liquids; explosive gases and dust

When using compressed air, be careful not to release it in a confined space. It can not only cause fright, but it is also potentially injurious to eyes, ears or nasal passages if released near anyone's face. Do not try to remove waste materials, such as swarf, using a compressed air line, since this can result in a piece of flying material blowing into someone's eye or into a piece of precision equipment.

If you are working with noisy equipment, always use ear protectors, such as plugs, valves or muffs.

Never smoke in a prohibited area: this may cause an explosion or start a fire from explosive gases or vapours which you cannot see.

Noxious fumes may also be invisible and consequently you should always use a respirator if the machinery or process you are working with is likely to produce noxious fumes.

1.f   The need for eye protection against sparks and dust

If you are working with machinery which is likely to produce sparks or dust then you should always wear eye protection equipment, which is designed to meet the particular combination of hazards that you are dealing with. Make sure that you are familiar with the following British Standards.

BS 2092	Provides standards for goggles, spectacles and visors.
BS 1542	Provides standards for face and hand shields, and helmets.
BS 2092	Makes recommendations to prevent penetration by dust, flying particles, chemical splash, or gas.
BS 1542 & BS 679	Provides standards for hazards such as glare, ultra-violet and welding flash etc.

2   Simulate the appropriate procedures which should be adopted in the event of workshop accidents

- mouth to mouth resuscitation, using dummies
- various types of fire – oil, electrical and chemical
- physical injury

2.a   Mouth to mouth resuscitation, using dummies

If there is an accident in your workplace you should be able to offer mouth to mouth resuscitation. To do this you should take the following steps:

1.   Lay the casualty on his or her back
   Turn the casualty's head to one side
   Clear any obstruction from the casualty's mouth
   Turn the casualty's head upwards.

2.   Place a folded coat, or something similar, under the casualty's shoulders
   Angle the casualty's head by pressing the forehead down and lifting the head up
   Pinch the casualty's nostrils closed (except in the case of a small child).

3.   Take a deep breath
   Cover the casualty's mouth with your own (for a child cover the nose as well)
   Blow gently
   Look for rising of the casualty's chest
   Remove your mouth.

4.   Take a deep breath while the casualty's chest deflates
   Repeat the blowing procedure six times quickly, then ten times a minute (for a child, twenty shallow breaths a minute).

5.   When breathing restarts, place the casualty in the recovery position.

Recovery Position

a. Turn casualty on side by kneeling and tucking near arm under body, palm upwards.

b. Cross ankle farthest away from you over one nearest to you.

c. Put other arm over chest.

d. Turn casualty towards you supporting head with your hand.

e. Place your other hand on casualty's hip farthest away, and roll him towards you.

f. Hold casualty's chin forward. This extends neck and stops tongue falling back into throat.

g. Bend casualty's knee to stop him rolling over to far.

h. Pull the other arm out behind the body so that the casualty is prevented from rolling back.

i. Pull up casualty's arm nearest to you so that point of elbow is in line with shoulder.

j. Don't leave casualty unattended.

2.b Various types of fire – oil, electrical and chemical

Fire in the workplace can be extremely dangerous. It can rapidly spread if it is not put out quickly. It is important that you use the right type of fire extinguisher to fight the sort of fire that you face. Below are listed various types of fire and the most appropriate type of fire extinguisher. Note that it is dangerous to use water on electrical fires since water is a good conductor of electricity.

Type of Fire	Extinguisher
Flammable liquids including petrol, oils and fats	*Foam*
Flammable liquids and fires in electrical equipment	*Carbon Dioxide* (Carbon dioxide displaces air and, therefore, should be used in a confined space for best effect.)
Flammable liquids and fires in electrical equipment	*Vaporising Liquid (BCF)* (This can be dangerous when used in a confined space.)

2.c Physical injury

Any injury, however minor, should receive immediate attention. It must be recorded in an accident book and drawn to the attention of management, so that a similar accidents can be prevented. While minor cuts and abrasions should be treated by a person trained in first-aid, a more serious injury requires medical help. If you suspect that a person has a fracture, do not move the patient without medical supervision, in case you cause additional injury. Try and call for help from a qualified person who can assess the injury and will, if necessary, apply splints to support the injury.

Serious burns require immediate attention from a doctor. Do not attempt to touch the burned area as this increases the risk of infection. Eye injuries are serious, and you should immediately take the injured person to a doctor. If liquid has splashed in the eye, apply sterile water in order to neutralise the liquid. If small particles of material have entered the eye, do not attempt to remove them, but immediately seek medical help.

3   Recognise the importance of safe electrical working in protecting life and property

- likely sources of electrical danger
- personal safety precautions regarding clothing, dampness, tools
- effect of shock and burns on the human body
- likely damage to property

3.a   *Likely sources of electrical danger*

Mains electricity is dangerous! Before starting work on electrical equipment, switch off the power and make sure that it cannot be switched on accidentally.

When a fuse blows, switch off the current, using the appropriate manual switch, before rectifying the fault which caused the fuse to blow. Then replace the fuse.

It is advisable to use a 110 volt operating voltage when using portable handtools. Fires may be started by cables, appliances or plugs which overheat as a result of their inadequate cable current-carrying capacities. Sparks from normal operating conditions, or from a circuit being broken, or from faulty connections and terminals are also potential sources of fire. You can minimise these dangers by: making sure that

- the capacity of the plugs you use is adequate,

- the insulation is not cut back further than necessary,

- connections are tight and secure, and, the continuity of earth wires is checked at regular intervals.

3.b   *Personal safety precautions regarding clothing, dampness, tools*

Possible injury to feet	Protective clothing
Falling objects or impact injuries	Shoes or boots with steel reinforced toe-caps of the appropriate strength
Oil or water penetration	Suitable resistant material for shoes or boots
Slipping	Slip resistant soles
Sharp objects through the soles	Steel mid sole
Burns	Heavy leather clothing (including gaiters where necessary.)

Types of protective clothing used for different environments

1.   Chemical-resistant clothing for various occupations

2.   Inclement weather clothing

3. High-visibility clothing

4. Cold temperature clothing

5. Hot temperature clothing

6. Aprons

Hand protection in a variety of materials, leather, fabric, PVC, rubber, etc.

Head protection in a variety of forms, including helmets (light-duty and heavy-duty), and hairnets

Personal safety precautions when using tools or machinery

No person should operate tools or machinery unless the following conditions have been met:

1. Sufficient information has been given to the operator.

2. Effective instruction has been given to the operator.

3. Effective training has been received by the operator.

4. Adequate supervision is being given to the operator.

3.c   *Effect of shock and burns on the human body*

As noted in 1.d, electric shock can be dangerous. It may cause muscular contractions, respiratory failure, verticular fibrillation of the heart, cardiac arrest or injury from internal burns: any of these could be fatal. The nature and severity of the injuries depends upon the magnitude, duration and path of the current through the body and, in the case of alternating current, the frequency.

Burns result in plasma (the clear liquid part of the blood) escaping. Plasma loss is the same as blood loss and must be taken seriously. Anyone with a burn covering more than 10% of the body can die without hospital treatment. Burn victims with a serious injury should be escorted to hospital as the shock associated with burns may not become apparent immediately or even for a considerable period of time after the injury.

3.d   *Likely damage to property*

Flammable materials are ignited easily by an electric spark and it is necessary to use flameproof equipment in areas where flammable gases and vapours are involved. Electrical accidents are not particularly common, but when they do occur they tend to be severe. In fact, electrical accidents are ten times more likely to cause a fatality than the average industrial accident.

4   Carry out simulation exercises successfully and outline procedures to be followed in cases of electric shock, respiratory or cardiac failure; outline likely effects, identifying symptoms. Explain procedure when a person is in contact with a live line

Safety should always be a major concern for you, not just throughout your course, but also all throughout your working life. The procedure for mouth to mouth resuscitation has already been described on page 4. However, if someone is electrocuted, there is a set procedure that should be followed.

Remember, when someone comes into contact with a live wire, that person also becomes part of the electric circuit, and has current flowing through his or her body. Follow this sequence carefully.

1.   Switch off the electrical supply, or remove the plug from the socket.

2.   Call, or send someone else, for assistance.

3.   Avoid direct contact with the victim; use a dry non-conductive material to drag the victim away from the electrical supply.

4.   Apply artificial respiration until the victim's breathing returns to normal.

B Hand and machine processes

5 **Perform marking out exercises on plane surfaces, select the relevant handtools for a task and use them. Explain the following:**

- the function of datum lines and centre lines
- which equipment is required for simple tasks to mark out profiles
- the relative merits of powered and non-powered tools, in terms of speed of production, cost, accuracy, human fatigue
- how to maintain handtools in good condition

5.a   *The function of datum lines and centre lines*

Marking out is a means of providing an outline on the surface of a material from which a component can be produced. The *scribed lines* are a guide for machining or fitting the component.

A *datum line* is a fixed starting line from which you make take all measurements. A *datum* may be an edge or the face of a component; it may be a point, or a combination of these. The datum line may also be a line running through the centre of a hole or through the centre of the component being worked on, in which case it is referred to as the *centre line*.

5.b   *The equipment required to mark out profiles for simple tasks*

You will need the following equipment to mark out profiles:

1. *Marking-out table or surface plate*
   You can use these as a datum for locating all equipment as they provide a flat horizontal surface.

2. *Marking-out fluid or ink*
   Before starting, you will need to highlight the lines to be marked by using marking-out blue.

3. *Scriber*
   This is made from hardened steel and is used to mark lines on the component.

4. *Centre punch*
   This is used to produce shallow conical indentations on the work surface.

5. *Engineer's rule*
   This is made from flexible steel usually at lengths of 150mm and 300mm.

6. *Engineer's square*
   You can use the blade of the square as a straight edge to scribe lines at right-angles to the datum.

7. *Dividers*
   These are used to mark out circles and arcs or for marking off lengths.

5.c   *The relative merits of powered and non-powered tools, in terms of speed of production, cost, accuracy, human fatigue*

Speed of production	You can maintain your output at a relatively high and consistent level if you use *powered* handtools rather than conventional handtools. Powered hand tools facilitate sawing, shearing, grinding, drilling, riveting and for adjusting screws, nuts and bolts.
Cost	Powered handtools are more expensive than conventional handtools, but the difference in cost should be recovered through increased output. In the last century, in the UK (and even now in many parts of the developing world), most engineering was still carried out by hand; since labour was cheap and access to power sources was scarce. Today, in the UK, the opposite is true; it is worth considering mechanising any process, provided that the investment is economically sound and will result in cost saving.
Accuracy	It is important that you are accurate and keep the components' dimensions to within given tolerances. The use of powered handtools facilitates the production of components to close tolerances with repeatability as a feature.
Human fatigue	As stated earlier, output can be maintained at a steady level if powered handtools are used. Fatigue is greatly reduced, since the operator has only to guide the tool, rather than having to power *and* guide the tool. Thus, powered tools can be used in confined or awkward situations where it would be difficult and tiring to use conventional handtools.

5.d   *How to maintain handtools in good condition*

You should find that power tools require very little maintenance, and what is required is confined mainly to the electric power tools. These if neglected, can cause problems. Dust may find its way into the motor and cause it to fail. Electric power tools used in dusty conditions need to be stripped and cleaned regularly. Pneumatic power tools are less likely to be affected by dust as air is exhausted from them, whereas air is drawn into an electric handtool to cool the motor. Since bearing failure is the most common fault in power tools, the bearings of both types of motors must be kept lubricated .

You should be careful not to overload electric power tools. Electric leads should be checked regularly and not subject to chafing. Dangers from electric shock are minimised by operating at 110 volts.

Always make sure that the correct fuse is fitted to power tools. Even though electric handtools normally are well insulated, make sure that they are properly earthed before you use them.

Because pneumatic power tools can be affected by moisture in the air-supply, always check the water traps to prevent water carry over to the power tool. It is important that you are aware of the dangers of compressed air; *never* allow compressed air to come into close contact with the skin as it can enter the bloodstream through the skin.

6   Use suitable equipment to measure components, explain the principles and identify limitations governed by accuracy , robustness etc. Examine equipment including micrometers; verniers; plunger dial gauges; level type test indicators

The *micrometer* is one of the most familiar measuring instruments used in engineering workshops. There are three basic types:

- the external micrometer
- the internal micrometer and
- the depth micrometer

The main features of the *external micrometer* are:

1. *The fixed anvil face*
   This is the datum from which measurements are made.

2. *The moving anvil face*
   This face on the spindle is parallel to the fixed anvil face, square to the spindle centre line, and is flat.

3. *The spindle*
   The spindle rotates and has a precision screw thread, which provides accurate longitudinal adjustment.

4. *The barrel*
   This has an internal screw thread, which acts as a nut on the threaded part of the spindle. It is graduated at 0.5 millimetre intervals.

5. *The thimble*
   The thimble, whose inside bore is slightly larger than the outside diameter of the barrel, has 50 equally spaced divisions, each division being 0.01mm.

6. *The ratchet*
   The ratchet is set in such a way that it rotates without turning the thimble, thereby providing a constant measuring pressure.

The bore of the barrel has a thread of 0.5mm pitch, and the spindle screws through the barrel. The spindle is attached to the thimble; one turn of the thimble causes the spindle to move a distance of 0.5mm.

The barrel is graduated in 1mm and 0.5mm divisions, so that a reading may be taken without noting the number of turns. In order to read fractions of a turn, the thimble is divided around its circumference into 50 equal divisions. A reading of one of these divisions represents a spindle movement of one fiftieth of the pitch i.e. 0.01mm.

To read the micrometer:

(a)   Read the number of whole turns uncovered by the barrel

(b)   Add the fraction of the turn shown on the thimble.

The spindle and anvil faces of an internal micrometer are radiused to ensure proper contact with the curvature of a bore. The internal micrometer measures in ranges of 12.5mm, the smallest size being 50mm. Interchangeable spindles are used to measure bores up to 300mm.

The scales on the barrel and thimble of a depth micrometer indicate the amount by which the spindle extends.

The *Vernier calliper* is an instrument which makes use of adjustable jaws. The distance between the jaws is read from a line scale.

The *Vernier Scale* was invented by a Frenchman, Pierre Vernier in 1631. It can be used to measure the width of a block or the internal diameter of a hole.

The principles of Vernier Scales are:

1.   There are two scales; one fixed, and the other slides relative to the first.

2.   Intervals between the graduations on the fixed scale are normally more widely spaced than those on the moving scale.

3.   The smallest reading, or accuracy of a vernier instrument, is the difference between the intervals of the fixed scale graduation and those of the moving scale graduation.

There are several types of Vernier scales. One has a fixed scale graduated at 1mm intervals with a moving scale of 50 divisions over a distance of 49mm. The interval between the moving scale graduations will be 49 / 50 = 0.98mm and the accuracy of the instrument reading will be:

$$1.00 - 0.98 = 0.02mm.$$

Vernier scales are also incorporated into depth gauges, and height gauges.

Angular measurement can be made using a protractor with a Vernier scale.

The fixed scale of a Vernier protractor is graduated at intervals of 1 degree and the moving scale has 12 divisions spaced into an angle of 23 degrees.

The interval between the moving scale divisions are:

23 degrees ÷ 12 = 1 degree 55 minutes.

The spacing of the moving scale is bigger than that of the fixed scale so the accuracy will be:

The spacing of two fixed scale divisions – the spacing of the moving scale divisions
2 degrees – 1 degree 55 minutes
= 5 minutes.

Every third divisions on the moving scale is numbered for direct reading.

The most common types of *Dial Test Indicators* are the *lever type* and the *plunger type*. In each design, small linear movements of the stylus or plunger are magnified and converted into rotary movements which are displayed on a graduated circular dial.

The usual accuracy of a dial test indicator is 0.01mm. The measuring range of the plunger type can be up to 20mm, however, the design of the lever type normally restricts its range to no more than 1mm. The main advantage of the lever type is the ease with which it can be used in restricted spaces.

You can use a dial test indicator for measuring the variation between components or to measure individual components by first setting it to a datum of known size. It can also be used to measure roundness or concentricity.

7   **Use machines and outline problems and limitations which could arise, also identify design and operational features and safety precautions. The following machines and processes should be included:**

- sensitive drilling machine, centre lathe
- twist drills, trepanning tools, reamers, cutting angles, holding and clamping methods
- grabbing, lobed holes
- clogging, overheating and toxic fumes when producing holes in plastic
- three methods of taper turning
- cutting speeds for common tool/workpiece material combinations
- machine spindle speeds for turning, boring and drilling

7.a *Sensitive drilling machine, centre lathe*

A *sensitive drilling machine* is a compact structure built around a sleeve, within which a spindle rotates.

Cutting drills are located and held in the machine spindle which can be rotated at speeds within range of the drilling machine. The feeding (or vertically downward movement) of the rotating drill is achieved by hand, permitting a sense of feel, which is particularly helpful when drilling small diameter holes. Speed ranges are normally provided by pulley clusters, and a back gear arrangement. When the back gear is disengaged, the belt can be positioned on the pulleys to give four possible speeds. When the back gear is engaged, a slower range of four gears can be selected.

A *centre lathe* is a machine tool designed to produce both external and internal cylindrical surfaces. The components of the centre lathe are:

1. *The cast iron base*
    This carries the headstock and drive systems, the carriage or saddle and the tailstock.

2. *The headstock*
    This contains all the principal gearing to operate the lathe. It has three output drives:

    (a)   The *spindle*, to which the work-holding device is attached, can be set to run at various speeds, using speed change levers.

    (b)   The *leadscrew* which drives the screw-cutting saddle.

    (c)   The *feedshaft* which drives the machining saddle.

3.   *The saddle*
     This is made up of four principal parts:

   (a)   *The apron,* where the gearing that picks up the drive from both the feedscrew and the leadscrew, is housed.

   (b)   *The cross slide,* which traverses the bed.

   (c)   *The compound slide,* which can be set to traverse the bed at an angle. (Has no power drive; must be hand-fed).

   (d)   *The tool post,* which carries the tooling and sits on the compound slide.

7.b   *Twist drills, trepanning tools, reamers, cutting angles, holding and clamping methods*

Any cutting tool point has a *rake angle* and a *clearance angle.*

The face of the tool doing the cutting is called the *rake face*; the angle it makes with a perpendicular from the surface being cut is called the *rake angle.*

The other face of the tool is called the *clearance face*; the angle it makes with the surface that is being cut is called the *clearance angle.*

The features of a *twist drill* are the right-handed spiral flutes that provide a cutting edge and a positive rake angle. They also allow for swarf removal and for the passage of cutting fluids to the cutting edge.

Trepanning is used when a large hole is needed in a component and where a drill would be too large for the drill capacity.

Drilling large holes in thin gauge material could be dangerous. You should initially drill a pilot hole, to locate the cutting tool and to provide support.

Reamers are available with straight or spiral flutes. *Reaming* is an operation that is carried out to increase the diameter of a drilled hole by about 0.5mm, in order to produce a good surface finish or to achieve an accurate fit.

Methods of work-holding for drilling operation are:

1.   *Vice*
     This is used for rectangular work.   15.8

2.   *Clamping direct to the drilling machine table*   15.4
     This is used for large components.

3.   *Clamping to the drilling machine table using vee blocks*   15.6
     This keeps the location of cylindrical components in a plane parallel to the machine table.

4.   *Chuck* 15.7 & 9
     This maintains the location of cylindrical components in a plane at right-angles to the machine table.

5. *Angle plate clamped to the machine table* 15.5
   This keeps the location of a flat face on the component at right-angles to the machine table and is used when large numbers of components are manufactured.

7.c Grabbing, lobed holes

It is possible, when drilling sheet metal, that a drill point will break through the material, before the outer corners of the drill bit begin to cut. The drill will tend to grab, as it has no support, and you will end up with an 'out of round' hole. The helix of the drill will behave like a screw, and thread itself into the sheet metal. You can prevent this by using a smaller drill, or by increasing the support for the sheet metal.

7.d Clogging, overheating and toxic fumes when producing holes in plastic

Plastic materials are mostly poor heat conductors, and the heat generated by cutting and drilling may cause serious problems. The plastic may weld itself to the drill, causing the drill to break; the same problem can be caused by the plastic shrinking when it is heated. Drills which have the following special features can be used to minimise such problems:

(a) Slow helix angle and a 90 degree point angle.

(b) Wide flutes and thin webs, to prevent clogging.

(c) Large clearance angles, to minimise the problem of shrinking.

You can help to to dissipate heat by frequently withdrawing the drill from the hole.

You should be careful not to inhale fumes when drilling plastics, since such fumes can be noxious.

7.e Three methods of taper turning

One specialist turning operation that is performed on a centre lathe is *taper turning*. For a taper to be generated on a lathe, the tool must move at an angle to the axis of the lathe.

1. The *compound slide method* of taper turning enables a taper of any angle to be generated, but the length of the taper is restricted to the length of the slide travel.

2. The *offset tailstock method* of taper turning requires work to be mounted between centres, so the tailstock can be moved over the base. Only external tapers can be turned and they are limited to small included angles.

3. An extra slideway at the rear of the lathe bed (known as a a taper turning attachment), can be inclined to the axis of the lathe. When operating, and the automatic traverse is engaged, the entire cross-slide mechanism is pulled over.

7.f Cutting speeds for common tool/workpiece material combinations

Machine tools (such as milling machines, lathes, slotting and planing machines) remove metal by a cutting tool in order to produce a desired shape and surface finish.

The speed of the cutting tool will depend on the material of which the tool is made, the material of the component and the depth of the cut. High carbon steel is used most often to make cutting tools as it retains its hardness up to temperatures of 400 degrees centigrade.

The cutting speeds in m/min for the most common materials, using high speed tools, are as follows:

Mild steel	20 to 30
High carbon steel	10 to 20
Cast Iron	20 to 25
Aluminium	up to 250
Brass	30 to 60
Bronze	15 to 20
Plastic	up to 200

7.g   *Machine spindle speeds for turning, boring and drilling*

The relationship between the surface cutting speed, the work or tool diameter (mm) and the speed in (revs/min) is given below. The cutting speed for the workpiece material must be converted into the machine spindle speed, which is in revs/ min.

$$\text{The lathe speed} = \frac{\text{Cutting speed}}{\text{circumference } (\pi d)}$$

$$N = \frac{1000 \times s}{\pi d}$$

Where N is the lathe speed in revs/minute
              s is the cutting speed m/minute
              d is the workpiece diameter in mm.

8   Select appropriate tools and cutting fluids for various machining operations and describe suitable tool maintenance

- identification of relevant angles on common cutting tools
- the advantages of using cutting fluids
- identification of drilling faults and reasons

8.a   *Identification of relevant angles on common cutting tools*

As noted in 7.b, every cutting tool point has a rake angle and a cutting angle. The *rake angle* is the angle of the tool face which the material chips slide over. The *clearance angle* is the angle at which the second tool face clears the work surface.

Front rake angle – the angle that falls back along the tool.

Side rake angle – the angle that falls across the tool.

Compound rake angle – combination of front and side rake.

The clearance angle can also be used on the front, the side or in combination.

The lathe tool may also have at its leading edge a *plane approach angle* and a *trail angle* behind the cutting edge.

Lathe tools may be either left-handed, if they point to the right, or right-handed, if they point to the left. (Refer to 7.b.)

8.b The advantages of using cutting fluids

Although the principal function of a cutting fluid is to remove heat and provide lubrication, it may also help to:

(a) reduce friction between the tool and the work piece

(b) conduct heat from the tool and the working surface

(c) improve the surface finish

(d) reduce the energy requirements

(e) extend the life of the cutting tool

(f) clear the swarf from the cutting surface.

The following cutting fluids are commonly used:

Soluble oils (Emulsion of oil and water)	The principal use for soluble oils is cooling and they are used in a wide range of materials and cutting operations.
Straight oils (Not mixed with water)	The principal use for straight oils is lubrication. Mineral oils are used for light cutting on brass and aluminium.
Water mixed with *anti-corrosive agent*	This is used principally for a range of precision grinding operations.

8.c Identification of drilling faults and reasons

The following faults are common in drilling:

1. Sharpening the drill
    The two cutting edges are ground at different angles to the axis of the drill.
    The two cutting edges are ground such that the drill point is off-centre.

2. Centre punching the hole inaccurately or too lightly.

3. Using too large a drill without drilling a smaller hole as a pilot hole.

4. Insufficient clamping of the workpiece.

5. Drilling thin sheet metal (see section 7.c).

C   Fastening and joining of materials

9   Carry out various joining methods for materials, identify their applications, advantages and disadvantages, and describe any process involved

- screws, bolts, nuts and washers commonly available and types of thread
- techniques employed in various locking devices, such as spring washers, self-locking nuts, castle nuts
- riveting methods, with particular emphasis on hollow rivets using a mandrel
- adhesives, resins and solvents, with particular attention to safety hazards
- silver soldering; gas and arc welding; brazing
- welding of thermoplastics

9.a   *Screws, bolts, nuts and washers commonly available and types of thread*

In all branches of engineering *bolts* are used as a means of *fastening*. A bolt is used with a washer and a nut. The bolt is passed through clearance holes in the components to be fastened, through the washer, and a nut is fitted to it. This means of fastening is used when components must be assembled and dismantled at regular intervals.

Unlike a bolt a *screw* is threaded along its whole length and when fastening components together, it avoids the need for long bolts when the components are very thick. However, it does require that the hole in one of the components is threaded. The most widely used temporary fastening is the screw thread, as found in bolts, screws and nuts.

The heads of screws vary in shape, depending upon their intended application. Their heads include slotted, hexagonal (standing proud or sunk into the surface), cheese head, countersunk head and round head. The types of washers most commonly used are: plain; bevelled; or tapered for use on sloping surfaces. Washers usually are inserted between the nut and the component.

A *screw thread* is formed by rolling, or cutting, a helical groove around a cylindrical surface. The thread form is the shape of the groove rolled or formed. The most common thread forms in use are divided into three distinct groups:

The *vee* form, which is found most often, is used in bolts, screws and in studs.

The *square* form is used because of its low friction properties, principally to transmit power.

The *acme* form is a combination of the vee and square forms. It is easier to manufacture than the square form. It is used for the lead screws on lathes and has slightly higher friction properties than the square thread.

9.b   *Techniques employed in various locking devices, such as spring washers, self-locking nuts, castle nuts*

Mechanical locking devices are used so that component parts of an assembly may be removed easily for repair or overhaul when required, a locking device can prevent a screwed fastening from slackening off as a result of vibration. This type of fastening is called a *friction locking device*, as it relies on the increased friction between the bolt and nut threads.

Examples of this type of device are a spring washer, a lock nut, a Simmonds' lock nut (which has a fibre inset ring), and the Wedgelock bolt, (which has a nylon inset).

Where mechanical failure might cause serious breakdown in machine tools, heavy industrial plant or in transport vehicles, *positive locking devices* are used for critical connections. Examples of this type of device are:

> standard hexagonal nuts cross-drilled and pinned, slotted nuts, castle nuts,
>
> hexagonal nuts with a locking plate, a tab washer, wired bolt heads.

9.c   *Riveting methods with particular emphasis on hollow riveting using a mandrel*

Riveting is a method of fastening together two pieces of plate. It consists of drilling or punching clearance holes in the plates being connected. The rivet is then passed through the hole and the end hammered over. This forms the rivet head, the rivet body swelling with the compression to fill the clearance hole. The correct clearance for the drilled hole is calculated as:

$$D + \frac{D}{16}$$

where D is the diameter of the rivet.

The correct length of the rivet can be calculated by taking the diameter of the rivet D, multiplying by 1.5 and adding that to the thicknesses of the plates being fastened together. The three principal methods used in producing a riveted joint are:

1.   where the rivet is supported by a dolly

2.   where a mandrel has to be used for tubular and cylindrical sections

3.   where for hollow box sections which have no support, hollow pop rivets have to be used.

9.d   *Adhesives, resins and solvents, with particular attention to safety hazards*

Most *synthetic adhesives*, that is solvents, hardeners and catalysts, are highly toxic and highly flammable. They must be stored in facilities which have good ventilation and fire protection alarms. Strict safety regulations should be enforced in workplaces where adhesives are used, and such workplaces should be declared non-smoking zones.

The precautions neeeded for safe working with adhesives are:

1.   ensuring adequate ventilation in the store and workplace.

2.   ensuring the adhesive is stored in sealed containers.

3.   always wearing the appropriate protective clothing, including rubber gloves, no matter how inconvenient such precautions may seem at the time.

4.   always using barrier cream to reduce the likelihood of dermatitis.

5.   always washing thoroughly with soap and water after use.

Adhesives are of three types:

1.   Natural glues made from animal products.

2.   Natural glues made from vegetable products.

3.   Synthetic, high-polymer adhesives, developed by the plastics industry.

The *synthetic adhesives* fall into two categories:

- thermo-plastic adhesives
- thermo-hardening adhesives.

The *thermo-plastic adhesives* fall into three categories:

- heat-activated adhesives — *soften with heat*
- solvent-activated adhesives — *soften with ~~heat~~ solvents*
- impact adhesives. — *soften with solvents (bonds on contact*

Heat-activated adhesives soften with heat. *Solvent-activated adhesives* soften with solvents. Impact adhesive also softens with solvents, but it bonds immediately on contact.

Thermo-hardening adhesives fall into two main categories:

- Phenolic and amino resins
- Polyester and epoxy resins.

These adhesives, unlike thermo-plastic adhesives, can not be softened after the curing process.

9.e   Silver-soldering; gas-and arc-welding; brazing

The *silver-soldering joining process* uses soldering alloys which are mostly silver and, consequently, are expensive. However, the joint made, however, is very strong and pliable. This type of soldering is used for precise work where a strong bond is required. The composition of silver-solders are :

BS184 Type	Silver % Min – Max	Copper % Min – Max	Zinc % Min – Max	Cadmium % Min – Max	Melting Range oC
3	49 – 51	14 – 16	15 – 17	18 – 20	620 – 640
4	60 – 62	27.5 – 29.5	9 – 11	–	690 – 735
5	42 – 44	36 – 38	18.5 – 20.5	–	700 – 775

The characteristics of the different types are:

Type 3   Suitable for joining metals with low melting point.
            Low melting range, very fluid.

Type 4   Suitable for electrical connections.
            Good electrical conductivity.

Type 5   Suitable for general purposes.
                 Stronger properties than 3 or 4.

All types use the standard, proprietary fluxes.

A heat source capable of producing very high temperatures is necessary to achieve fusion during the welding process. Principally there are two heat sources for welding:

- electric-arc

- gas (oxy-acetylene).

In *electric-arc welding*, the electrode provides the filler material and the heat source. A low voltage and high amperage current passes from the electrode to the material being joined, forming an arc. A pool of molten metal caused by the high temperature is formed in the vicinity of the arc.. Metal from the end of the electrode is driven across the arc to the pool. The electrode is slowly drawn along the joint; and the molten metal already laid down, solidifies.

In *oxy-acetylene welding*, the gas flame is applied to the joint, the edges of which melt to form a pool of molten metal. The flame, the pool and the filler rods are moved along the joint, and the molten metal already laid down, solidifies.

Brazing is a typical hard-soldering process which uses *spelters* (hard solders) made of copper-zinc alloys (up to 50% zinc). The surface of the parts to be brazed have to be perfectly clean before the brazing can be achieved. *Flux* is needed to preserve the cleaned surfaces, and to prevent the formation of a metal oxide on the metal surfaces when the heat is applied.

The joining surfaces, coated with flux, are heated using a gas flame, until the melting temperature of the hard solder (spelter) of $870\text{-}890^{\circ}$ C is reached. The spelter is applied to the joint and is allowed to melt and run between the surfaces being joined. *Borax* is used as the flux. The zinc in the spelter tends to burn off during the brazing operation, leaving the final joint alloy high in copper.

9.f   Welding of thermoplastics

Only methods producing a *continuous* joint can be applied to thermoplastic materials. Such methods involve softening the two components, either by the use of chemical solvents, or by heating, so that when the parts are pressed together they form a joint.

If you use solvents, they must be liquids, in which the plastic will dissolve quickly and which evaporate rapidly so that the joint is made fairly quickly. The following solvents are suitable with different thermoplastics:

Thermoplastic	*Solvents*
Acrylic materials	Trichlorethylene Chloroform Ethylene Dichloride Methylene Chloride
Rigid and Non-rigid P.V.C.	Cyclohexane

The thermoplastic parts should be clean and well fitting, and should be immersed in the solvent until they become tacky. Under slight pressure, bring the surfaces into contact until the joint is dry.

Three welding methods can be used, the only difference being the method of heating.

Heated tool welding	This method is usually applied to sheet or film plastic. The two parts to be welded are placed together, and a tool with a temperature high enough to raise to softening point the temperature of the parts, is run along the line of the weld. The tool pressure forms the joint.
Hot gas welding	This process is similar to the oxy-acetylene welding of steel, since a stream of gas, air or nitrogen, at a temperature of 200-500o° C, is played along the weld area until the two parts fuse together. A filler rod, made of the same plastic as the parts being welded, is used to fill the joint. You should prepare the joint by filing the edge of both parts to form a vee which has an included angle of 60 degrees.
Friction welding	The temperature necessary for welding is produced in this process by rubbing the two parts together, under pressure, until they have softened enough to weld together. Accurately locate the two parts together in a suitable machine, such as a lathe or a drilling machine. One part is rotated by the machine while the other part is held stationary. The two parts are pressed together so that the resulting friction causes heating, softening and fusion between them. When the materials are suitably soft, the stationary part is released, so that the two parts rotate together and the weld is formed. Suitable materials for this type of welding are PVC, nylon, acrylics, and ABS.

D Working in plastics

10 Use and describe the techniques available within conventional workshops to produce shapes in plastic materials and subsequently indicate applications, give details of techniques used, associated problems and safety measures

- problems associated with the machining of plastics and the speeds and feeds necessary
- the use of casting to form plastic materials with special reference to encapsulation techniques for electrical components

10.a   Problems associated with the machining of plastics and the speeds and feeds necessary

When machining plastics you should use high-speed steel tools with cutting speeds between 76 and 150 metres/min. Laminated plastics are best machined with no top rake, while top rakes of up to 7 degrees should be used for softer plastics. The use of soluble oil, or an air jet, for cooling is essential, and the use of a live centre when turning between centres will reduce friction.

During the machining of plastic, extreme stresses are set up due to the distortion of the material. The effect of these stresses may only be evident in the form of cracks, which appear some time after the machining operation. It is advisable to anneal thermoplastic materials, after machining, in a thermostatically controlled hot water bath at 70° centigrade, for approximately 45 minutes.

When you are drilling small holes, of up to 0.125ins diameter, conventional drills are adequate, but for larger holes you should use special drills. These drills have wide polished flutes, a long lead with the lip ground thin, with a minimum rake angle. You should use the maximum cutting speed possible, without over-heating. An air blast is an excellent coolant. If you release the drill frequently, this should prevent clogging and will help to release swarf.

10.b   The use of casting to form plastic materials with special reference to encapsulation techniques for electrical components

When you use electrical components, such as transformers, condensers, resistors and tape-heads they are subject to vibration, shock and moisture, each of which is a possible cause of damage. It is common practice to encapsulate components in a plastic material, such as epoxy resin, which will provide them with protection from moisture, heat and mechanical handling. The component to be encapsulated is set up in a brass fixture which has been coated with a silicon grease release agent. The resin with its hardener are mixed up in the correct proportions and then cast around the component in the fixture. The resin is then cured at room temperature, or may be heated to 100° centigrade for up to 30 minutes to reduce the curing time. Common resins used in the encapsulation process are Araldite and Spikote. Methylene chloride is an effective solvent for removing excess epoxy resins from components.

E Engineering drawing

11 Explain with the aid of drawings the meaning of orthographic projection

- principle planes of projection
- points
- lines
- areas
- simple 3-dimensional objects.

and produce neat and clear drawings including the use of hidden detail lines, using the following types of projection:

- first angle projection.
- third angle projection.

11.a Principle planes of projection

The figure below shows an L-shaped piece of thick paper or card. The dotted lines are intended to be fold lines. When the card is folded, three sides of a cube are formed. Using the shape formed, the three principle planes of projection are the *Plan* (P), the *Front Elevation* (FE) and the *End Elevation* (EE).

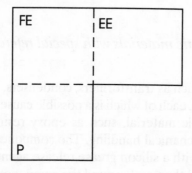

11.b Points

The projection of a point in space onto three planes is relatively easy to understand, but it is an important step in the development of spatial ability. The figure shows a single point in the space between the three planes. It does not matter where the point is in this space, its projection onto each of the three planes will always be a point.

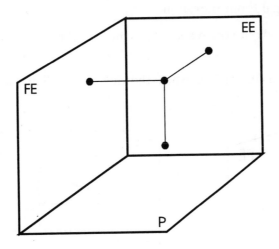

11.c   Lines

Consider a line in the space set between the principal planes:

1.   First, a line is drawn parallel to the Plan. In the diagram the line in space is a horizontal line in the Front Elevation, and a horizontal line in the Plan, but in the End Elevation it is a dot.

2.   Second, a line is inclined only in the Front Elevation.

In the diagram, points *A* and *B* are projected onto the three planes and each is joined with a line. In the diagram, the line in space is   – a horizontal line in the plan
                                          – a vertical line in the end elevation.

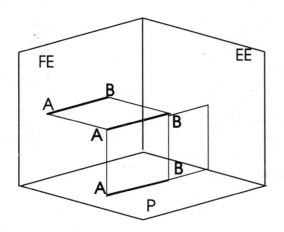

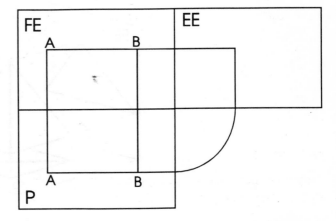

11.d   Areas

Consider an area in space set between the three planes and project it onto the principal planes of projection. The diagram shows a triangle as the area in the space. The triangle *ABC* is shown to be drawn with its plane parallel to the plane of the principal Front Elevation.

The points *A*, *B* and *C* are projected onto the respective planes, in a fashion similar to that carried out for the line in space.

The view on the End Elevation is a vertical line, whilst the view on the Plan is a horizontal line.

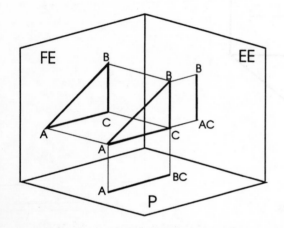
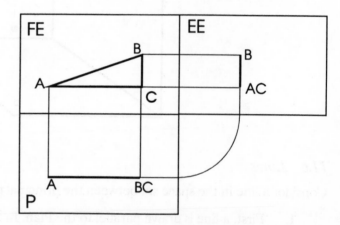

11.e   Simple 3-dimensional objects

Using your previous knowledge, consider a solid object in the space set between the three principal planes of projection and project it onto the planes. The object is a four-sided square based regular pyramid with its base in a plane parallel to the Plan principal plane. The projection onto the plane of the End Elevation and the plane of the Front Elevation is a triangle. The projection onto the plane of the Plan is a square.

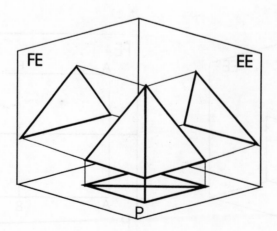

11.f   First angle projection

Consider again the L-shaped piece of thick paper or card. Fold it along the lines indicated in the diagram in order to produce the three surfaced shape shown.

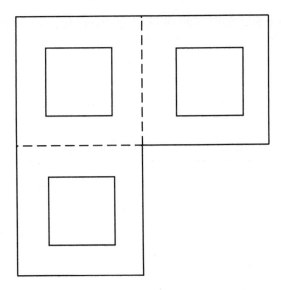

Consider a cube suspended in the space, enclosed by the three surfaces, and not in contact with surfaces. A bright light directed in turn at the sides of the cube will project shadows onto the three surfaces.

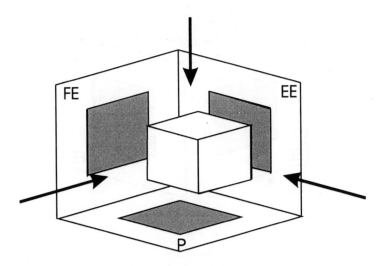

With one face of the cube selected as the front view, its projection is called the *Front Elevation* (FE). The projection of the end view is called the *End Elevation* (EE), and the projection of the view looking down on the cube is called the *Plan* (P). When the planes are unfolded into a single plane, the cube is represented on a drawing by the three views.

You should note that the British Standard symbol used to depict first angle projection, is taken from two views of a circular taper.

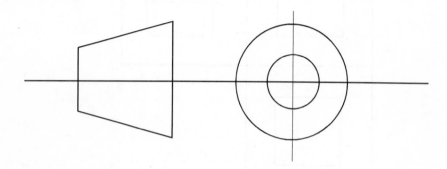

11.g   Third angle projection

Consider the situation where the same cube is viewed so that the shadows projected on the planes of projection are seen as through translucent surfaces. The cube is suspended in an upturned corner of the three surfaced shape, the light is shown on the cube, and the shape is projected back onto the three surfaces.

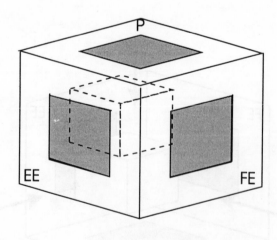

Having decided on the Front Elevation, the planes can be unfolded into one plane, as shown in the diagram below. In third angle projection, the End Elevation is on the left, and the Plan is above the Front Elevation.

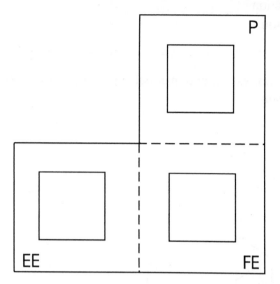

Note that the British Standard symbol used to depict third angle projection is, again, taken from two views of a circular taper.

To differentiate between the symbols used to depict first and third angle projection, note the following:

First angle projection – End Elevation appears to the right of the Front Elevation.
Third angle projection – End Elevation appears on the left of the Front Elevation.

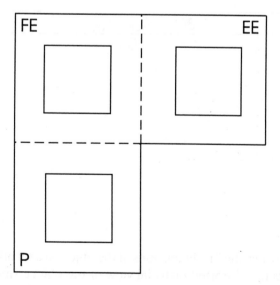

12   Produce neat and clear drawings using pictorial projection

- isometric projection
- oblique projection.

12.a   Isometric projection

Isometric projection is used to portray a 3-dimensional object by means of a single diagram. A 30° set-square is used, as shown in the diagram.

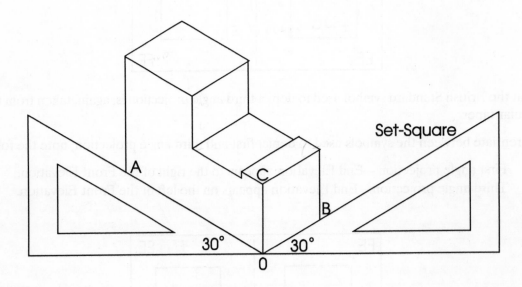

In conventional isometric drawing, the full dimensions of the object are set off in each of the three directions *OA*, *OB* and *OC*. This results in a distorted pictorial view of the object, since no account has been taken of the foreshortening of the sloping edges. The correction for this distortion is dealt with by using an isometric scale.

12.b   *Oblique projection*

Oblique projection is another method of making a pictorial drawing of an object. This type of projection is most useful for portraying an object which has curves and/or circles.

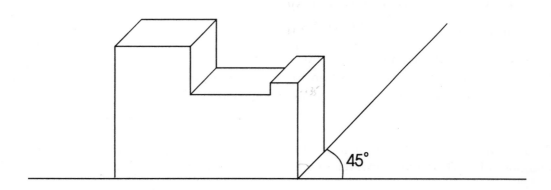

A front view, with any circles and curves, is drawn as in orthographic projection. Then the side edges are drawn, using parallel lines, thereby making an angle with the horizontal. If the same scale is used along the inclined parallel edges as for the front face, this is known as *cavalier projection*.

However, use of the same scale, on both the side and front face views, leads to a very distorted effect. To partially correct for this, the side edge measurements are drawn as a fraction of the front face scale.

Parallel side measurements 1/3, 1/2 or 2/3 of the front face measurements would use angles of 60, 45 or 30 degrees repectively. However, in general, however, an oblique drawing is made full-scale on the front face, and half-scale on the sides, at an angle of 45 degrees to the horizontal.

13   **Draw from given orthographic drawings**

- isometric views with no isometric scale
- oblique views to include rectilinear and curved objects

and draw orthographic views from the following given drawings

- isometric views
- oblique views

13.a   *Isometric views with no isometric scale*
13.b   *Oblique views to include rectilinear and curved objects*

13.c   *Isometric views*
13.d   *Oblique views*

These are covered in sections 12.a, 12.b and 11 respectively:

14   Use the conventions shown in the British Standards to produce sectioned and dimensioned working drawings for:

- components from electrical/mechanical devices
- assemblies (not more than 6 parts)

including:

- functional and non-functional dimensions
- fastenings, locking devices, threads, knurling, square on shaft, related holes, bearings, springs, gears, matching symbols, welding symbols.

Note:

BSI Education document PP 7308 aims to introduce students of technical drawing to the principles and conventions of BS 308. It is not, however, intended to be a replacement for the complete standard BS 308.

14.a   *Components from electrical/mechanical devices*

Generally, a section or cross section is a view or an outline taken at a cutting plane through an object which will be in particular either

a.   Section: an elemental slice, having no substance, taken through an object or part of an object revealing the outline shape solely at the selected cutting plane:

or

b.   Sectional view: the resultant view at the cutting plane revealing detail not otherwise readily visible, or an object or part of an object including other visible outlines situated beyond that selected cutting plane when seen in the direction of viewing (see BS 308 Part 1 Clause 9.1).

14.b   *Assemblies (not more than 6 parts)*

An assembly drawing shows two or more parts, or sub-assemblies, in their assembled form, including any dimensions and instructions necessary to effect assembly; an item list should be included or referred to. (see BS 308 Part 1 Clause 2.5)

14.c   *Functional and non-functional dimensions*

A functional dimension is a dimension that is essential to the function of an object or space. These dimensions should be expressed directly on the drawing.

A non-functional dimension is a dimension that is not essential to the function of an object or space. These dimesions may be chosen to aid production or inspection. (see BS 308 Part 2 Cluases 2.4 and 2.5)

14.d Fastenings, locking devices, threads, knurling, square on shaft, related holes, bearings, springs, gears, matching symbols, welding symbols

Item references are used on assembly drawings to identify the components (parts, items). All item references are shown in an item list giving the appropriate information on the items concerned.

Symbols and abbreviations are used on drawings to conserve space and time and yet to give precise and clear discription. Only commonly used and understood symbols and abbreviations should be used: others should be avoided and the intended meaning expressed in words. (see BS 308 Part 1 Clauses 10 and 11)

15 Use conventions shown in appropriate standards to interpret and draw electrical circuit diagrams

These conventions conform to British Standard 3939

15.a Power supplies – battery, earth, a.c. mains, d.c. mains

power supplies	02-02-13 02-02-14		+ Positive supply – Negative supply
batteries	06-15-01		Primary cell
			(the longer line represents the positive pole, the shorter line the negative pole)
earth	02-15-01		General symbol
a.c. mains	02-02-04		Alternating current
			(the numerical value of the frequency or the frequency range may be added to the right hand side of the symbol)
d.c. mains	02-02-01		Direct current
			(the voltage may be indicated at the right of the symbol and the type of the system at the left)

15.b   *Connections, junctions, cables(twin-core, 3-core, screened)*

junctions	03-02-04		
cables	03-01-08		Twin core (general symbol)
cable	03-01-09		3 – core
cable	03-01-07		Screened

15.c   *Lamps – filaments*

lamps	08-10-01		General symbol
filaments	11-15-04		Luminaire, fluorescent lamp (general symbol)

15.d   *Switches, etc. – single-pole, two-pole, relay and contacts*

single pole	11-14-01		Manually operated (general symbol)
two pole	11-14-04		
relay	07-15-02		Operating device (general symbol)
contacts	07-06-01		Make contact with spring return

15.e Circuit elements – resistor (fixed variable, potential divider), capacitor (fixed, variable), inductor (air-cooled, iron-cored), transformer (double-wound)

resistor	04-01-03		Fixed
			Variable
resistor	04-01-07		Potential divider

(Potentiometer with sliding contact)

capacitor	04-02-01		Fixed (general symbol)
capacitor	04-02-07		Variable
inductor	04-03-01		Air cooled (preferred form)
inductor	04-03-03		With magnetic core
transformer	06-09-02		With two windings

15.f Electronic devices – semiconductor diode, transistor, LEDs and Zener diode

semi conductor diode	05-03-01		General symbol
transistor	05-05-01		PNP tranistor
Leds and Zener diode	05-03-02		General symbol

F Electrical measuring instruments

16   Carry out tests/measurements for:

- insulation resistance, using IR tester (multi-meter)
- continuity, using a lamp and battery
- resistance (in the region 10 to 100 ohms) using a voltmeter and an ammeter
- resistance, voltage and current, for continuity using multi-range instrument

16.a   Insulation resistance using IR tester (multi-meter)

A *multi-range meter* combines the functions of a *milliammeter*, a *voltmeter* (a.c. and d.c.) and an *ohmmeter*. It is known as a *Universal meter* or as a *Multimeter* (volts-ohms-milliamp). Separate scales are provided for:

1. *Resistance*

2. *Voltage* and *current*.

To read the resistance scale, follow these guidelines:

When the meter is set to the resistance R range, read the scale directly.
When the meter is set to the resistance R/100 range, divide the scale reading by 100.
When the meter is set to the resistance 100R range, multiply the scale reading by 100.

16.b   Continuity using a lamp and battery

In a battery operated insulation test set, the battery supplies a variable low voltage to a transistorised inverter . The a.c. output voltage is increased by a transformer, and then rectified, to give the required final d.c. output. The indicator is a moving coil type, with its scale calibrated in megohms.

The voltage changes from the battery are corrected by adjusting the variable resistor. In this way, the indicator pointer is set in the correct position *before* the test is performed.

It is often necessary to determine whether an electrical circuit is live, without measuring the voltage present. Test lamps, or neon indicators, are used for this purpose. You must take care when interpreting results obtained with a neon test lamp.

16.c   Resistance (in the region 10 to 100 ohms) using a voltmeter and an ammeter

An *ammeter* is used to measure current, and a voltmeter is used to measure voltage. A *voltmeter* must be connected *in parallel* with a resistor, so that it forms a bridge across the resistor; it can then measure the potential difference between its ends. The ammeter measures the current flowing through the resistor, and it has to be connected *in series* with the resistor, in the line supplying the current.

Using *Ohm's law*, the value of the resistor can be found by measuring the potential difference, V, between its ends and the current, I, which flows through it.

$$V = IR$$
$$\text{and } R = \frac{V}{I}$$

16.d Resistance, voltage and current, for continuity using multi-range instruments

Normally, two linear scales are used on all voltage and current (a.c. and d.c.) ranges. Usually, one scale is calibrated 0 – 100, and the other 0 – 25 or 0 – 30.

Follow these guidelines when using the voltage scale:

When the meter is set to the 1,000 V (a.c. or d.c.) range:
use the 0 – 100 scale, multiply the reading by 10.

When the meter is set to the 2.5 V (a.c.or d.c.) range:
use the 0 – 25 scale, divide the reading by 10.

Some meters use a separate scale for a low voltage a.c. range.

Follow these guidelines when using the *current* scale:

When the meter is set to the 100mA (a.c. or d.c.) range:
use the 0 – 100 scale, and read the scale directly.

When the meter is set to the 1A range:
use the 0 – 100 scale, and divide the reading by 100.

When the meter is set to the 250mA range:
use the 0 – 25 scale, and multiply the reading by 10.

17 Use a cathode ray oscilloscope to measure the amplitude and frequency of sinusoidal signals and for a regular train of pulses, and demonstrate the purposes of the following controls:

- x and y gain
- time base
- focus
- brilliance
- trigger.

17.a x and y gain

The *cathode ray oscilloscope* consists of an evacuated tube with a fluorescent screen at one end and an electron gun at the other. The *electron beam*, sent from the electron gun to the screen, passes between two pairs of parallel metal plates. One pair is vertical, while the other pair is horizontal. If the electron beam potentials are adjusted, so that a small spot appears at the centre of the screen, and a potential difference is applied across the horizontal plates, the spot will move up or down, depending on the polarity of the potential difference. The horizontal plates are known as the Y plates. A potential difference applied to the vertical plates will cause the spot to move to the left or to the right. These plates are known as the X plates. The magnitude of the deflection of the spot is dependent on the voltage applied across the plates.

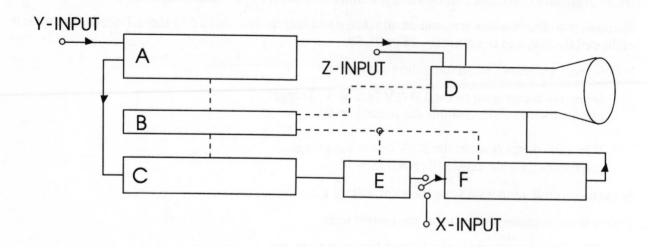

Key:

    A – *Y* amplifier, (a.c./d.c. selector, attenuator, Y-gain, Y-shift
    B – Power supply
    C – Trigger (trg level, auto)
    D – Cathode ray tube (brilliance and focus)
    E – Time base
    F – *X* amplifier (X-gain,X-shift)

17.b   Time base

The most common use of the cathode ray oscilliscope is as a graph plotter, with time measured on one axis (normally the *X* axis). This is achieved by applying to the *X* plates a voltage, which increases steadily with time up to a certain value, and then returns, almost instantaneously, to its initial value before repeating the cycle. This causes the spot to travel from left to right across the screen at constant speed, and then to go back to its starting point in a very short time. This arrangement is known as a *time base*.

17.c   Focus

An *electron lens* consisting of metal plates, or cylinders, kept at a high potential relative to the cathode. Changes in potential, vary the focal length of the lens, so that the electron beam can be focused onto the screen, and the high potentials of the metal plates (which are anodes), produce a fast-moving electron beam whose energy can be converted into light energy or fluorescence.

17.d   Brilliance

Brightness, or brilliance, can be increased by amplifying the intensity of the electronic beam. A plate with a central hole is set between the cathode and the electron lens is kept at negative potential, so that the number of electrons per second reaching the screen, or brightness of the image, can be controlled.

17.e   Trigger

One method of achieving synchronisation between the time base and the signal frequencies is to feed part of the Y-amplified output to a trigger circuit. This results in a pulse at a selected point on the Y-amplified output, as chosen by the trig level control which starts the sweep of the time base sawtooth. That is to say it triggers the time base. In many oscilliscsopes, automatic triggering takes place if the trig level control is set at 'auto'. When the mean d.c. level of the input is detected, the time base starts.

G Electrical connection and termination

18 Produce soldered joints and explain limitations and precautions (e.g. close clean surfaces; non-corrosive flux; correct heat from clean source; quality solder; surface flow for tinning)

To make a sound joint, the solder must flow evenly over and between the surfaces to be soldered. *Wetting* is a term used to describe the extent to which this occurs. To achieve a successful joint, you should ensure that:

1.   surfaces are clean

2.   enough flux of the correct type is used

3.   surfaces are hot enough

4.   the surface has been tinned.

The process of soldering does not melt and fuse together the two surfaces, but makes the solder flow between – and actually combine with – the surfaces of the metals to be joined. If you are soldering a wire to a terminal, the solder must solidify rapidly. This will reduce the risk of the components becoming displaced before the solder cools. The type of solder used for this work is known as *tinman's solder*. Solder used for electrical or electronic work is normally in a cored form: that is, it has a core of resin flux. Only *non-corrosive* flux may be used in electrical/electronic work. There are two types

- resin fluxes
- active fluxes.

Resin fluxes

These fluxes flow quickly over the joint, and speed up the transfer of heat to the workpiece. They also protect the metal from the atmosphere and thus prevent it from oxidising when it becomes heated.

Active fluxes

These fluxes have an additional purpose: they clean the metal surfaces by removing grease and oxidised film. Although active when hot, they are non-corrosive at room temperature. Most surfaces to be soldered will have been pre-tinned. Make sure that the surface is clean. Heat the surface with an iron, apply the solder to the surface, remove the solder and then remove the iron. Solder baths are used to put a very thin coat of solder on to a metal. This is appropriate when large surfaces are to be soldered.

19 Identify different types of connection method, recognise their characteristics, and select a method of connection for a given job, giving reasons for the choice. Types of connection method should include:

- pinched screws
- soldered lug
- crimped lug
- bolted connections
- mechanical clamping

19.a Pinched screws

Pinched screws are suitable for securing the ends of cables which have rubber or plastic insulation. Some types of single-strand conductor, particularly aluminium, tend to work loose in time, due to the conductor material becoming deformed . To prevent this happening, do not overtighten the pinched screw. Pinched screws are used in the terminals of switches, socket outlets etc.

19.b Soldered lug

Often, large cables are connected to switchgear or busbars by fixing *lugs* to the ends of the conductor. The traditional method is to sweat the lug solidly to the conductor, using tinman's solder and a non-corrosive flux.

19.c Crimped lug

A *crimped lug* is fixed to the cable by means of pressure and indentation. The conductor is inserted into the lug and an indentation is made, using either a handtool or hydraulic press. The pressure compacts the lug and the cable into a single solid mass, so that the joint is stronger than the cable. This type of termination is quicker and cheaper than soldering, and causes no damage to the insulation. The *compression lug* is used with copper and aluminium cables, which are difficult to solder, because of the rapid oxidation of their surfaces after cleaning.

19.d Bolted connections

In the *bolted connection method* metal strips, or bars of copper, flattened at their ends, are drilled and bolted together. Earthing conductors or busbar connections are first tinned, in order to maintain good electrical contact and prevent corrosion. They are then bolted together, using brass or galvanised bolts.

19.e Mechanical clamping

Other forms of mechanical clamping include the following:

1. Thimbles are made of porcelain and have a coarse internal thread. The cables to be joined are twisted together and the thimble is screwed tightly onto the join to form a connection.

2. Connectors made of brass are mounted in a moulded, insulated block, whose cables are clamped in place by grub screws. Some terminal blocks have clamp plates which press against the cable, thereby preventing damage to the cable by the screws.

3. Small cables may be formed into a loop using round-nosed pliers. The direction of the loop must such so that tightening of the nut does not cause the loop to open. A special claw washer may be used to achieve a better connection. The looped cable is laid into the pressing and a plain washer is placed on top of the loop, and the metal points are squeezed flat, using the appropriate tool.

20   Carry out an electrical jointing and connection assignment involving a number of techniques

Before working on electrical apparatus, switch off the power supply and make sure that it cannot be accidentally re-connected. If possible, disconnect it completely from the power supply.

H Lighting and power circuits

21   Demonstrate an understanding of the layout of lighting and power circuits by:

- defining a final sub-circuit as an assembly of conductors and accessories emanating from a final distribution board

- sketching the circuit diagrams for one-way and two-way lighting circuits

- studying and listing the IEE Regulations for the limitations of the number of lighting points and circuit ratings

- describing the following circuit arrangements
  - 15 amp radial circuit
  - 30 amp ring circuit supplying 13 amp socket outlets

21.a   Define a final sub-circuit as an assembly of conductors and accessories emanating from a final distribution board

A *final sub-circuit* is that part of an installation which is located between an item of current-consuming equipment and the fuse or circuit-breaker. In effect, it is the point where the load is applied to a system.

The design of a final sub-circuit is critical and you should take every precaution to make sure it does not constitute a hazard to a user. You should always consider design factors such as:

1.   the rating of the cables

2.   switches and protective devices

3.   size and form of earth continuity conductor

4.   protection, whether close or coarse

The following physical design factors are equally important:

1.   the distance from supply to the load. If this is too great it can produce voltage drop

2.   specialised hazards, such as fire and explosion, will affect the selection of switchgear, cables and other equipment

3.   the temperature and moisture levels in the environment surrounding the cables

4.   the proximity of the various cables, to each other.

21.b   Sketch the circuit diagrams for one-way and two-way lighting circuits

The single pole, one-way switch controls a point, or points, from one position only. When the switch is *closed* the lamp is *on*. When the switch is *open* the lamp is *off*.

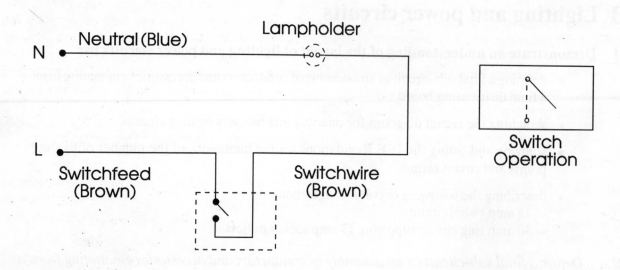

One-way lighting circuit

For ease of identification, cables are coloured-coded:

1. the cable feeding the switch, the *switchfeed*, is *brown*.

2. the cable from switch to lamp, the *switchwire*, is *brown*.

3. the cable from lamp to supply, the *neutral*, is *blue*.

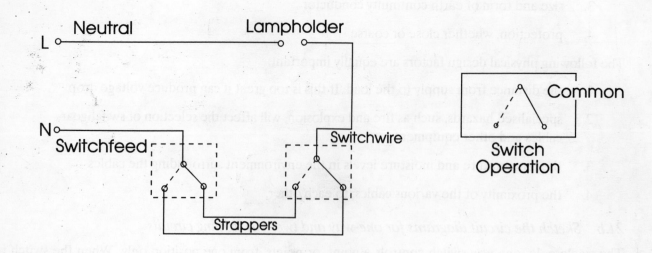

Two-way lighting Circuit

For independent control from two positions, *two-way switches* are required. The switches usualy have three terminals, one of which is called the *common*. In one position the common and another terminal are connected; in the other position the common and the third terminal are connected, as shown in the previous diagram. When used in pairs, these switches provide control from two positions, such as in rooms with two entrances, or on stairways. The common of one switch is connected to the *switchfeed* and the common of the other to the *switchwire*. The remaining four terminals (two per switch) are interconnected by two additional wires called *strappers*, which are coloured brown.

21.c *Study and list the IEE Regulations for the limitations of the number of lighting points and circuit ratings*

You should always make sure that you study the appropriate IEE Regulations in detail before starting an assignment or project work. The Regulations are comprehensive and are continually reviewed. When an installation is complete and ready for connection to the supply, it must be inspected and tested to see that it satisfies the IEE Regulations.

When carrying out the required tests you must be sure that you are not causing danger or damage to the equipment, even if the circuit being tested is faulty. The tester must have details of the installation in order to carry out the inspection tests. The Regulations require the electrical contractor to provide diagrams and charts showing the installation details.

Listed in the chart below are some common circuit types and their installation specifications.

A typical small installation chart				
Circuit Type	**Points Served**	**Phase Conductor (mm)**	**Earth (mm)**	**Protective and Switching Devices**
Cooker	Cooker	6.0	2.5	45A fuse, C.C.Unit
Ring main	13 amp Sockets	2.5	1.5	30A fuse, local switches
Heater	Immersion	2.5	1.5	15A fuse, local switches
Lighting Number 1	Downstairs	1.5	1.0	5A fuse, local switches
Lighting Number 2	Upstairs	1.5	1.0	5A fuse, local switches

21.d   Describe the following circuit arrangements
- *15 amp radial circuit*
- *30 amp ring circuit supplying 13 amp socket outlets*

Radial circuit

The *radial circuit* is similar to a lighting circuit. The cable is installed from the consumer unit to the first socket outlet, and then looped to each consecutive socket outlet in turn, in a radial manner.

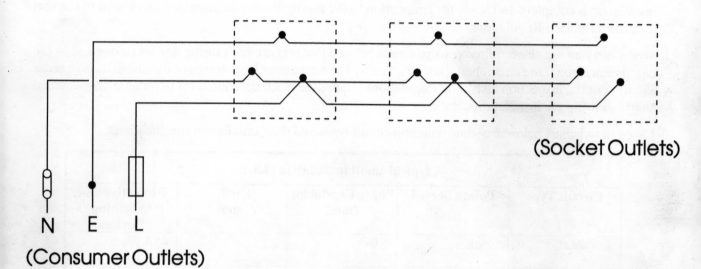

(Socket Outlets)

N   E   L

(Consumer Outlets)

Radial Circuit

Ring Circuit

The *ring circuit* is the final sub-circuit in which the pair of conductors form a loop, starting from, and returning to, the same terminals in the consumer unit. The *earth continuity conductor* must also be run in the form of a ring and both of its ends should finish at the same terminals in the consumer unit. The exception to this is when the earth conductor is either metal conduit or metal trunking.

The conductors should remain unbroken as they are looped into the socket outlets or joint boxes which form part of the ring. If the conductors have to be cut, the joints must be re-made, and must be checked to ensure they are electrically and mechanically sound.

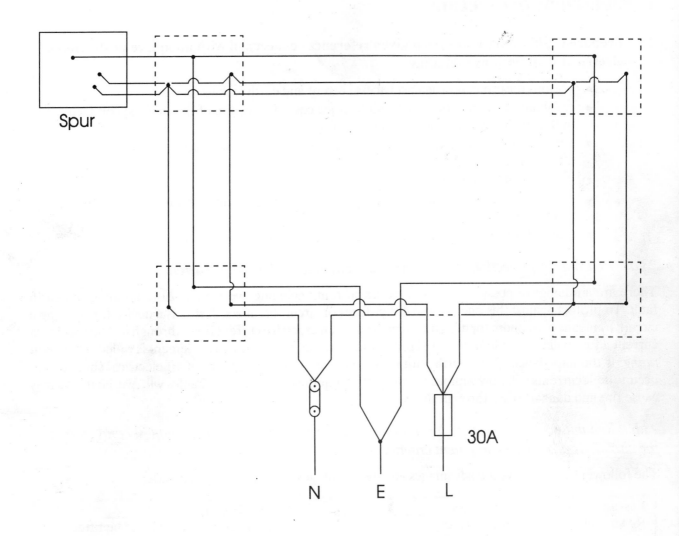

Ring Circuit

22   **Carry out an assignment involving the building and testing of a lighting circuit (for safety reasons the circuit MUST NOT be connected to the mains supply)**

This objective is covered under section 21.

I Electrical protection

23 Prepare explanatory notes from given references concerned with adequate protection of electrical installations including:

- reasons for protection against excess current and earth leakage current
- reliability, discrimination, low maintenance costs, protection of the smallest conductor in the circuit, as protection equipment criteria
- construction advantages and disadvantages of rewireable fuses and cartridge fuse elements
- inherent time lag in fuses
- minimising danger from shock and fire by isolating circuits through earth leakage protection
- reason for non-current carrying metal being earthed.

23.a *Reasons for protection against excess current and earth leakage current*

There are a number of possible causes of excess current, including overload, a short circuit, or an earth fault. To protect against this one can use either fuses or circuit-breakers. A *fuse* is a device for opening a circuit, by means of a conductor designed to melt when an excessive current flows through it. The maximum current a fuse will carry indefinitely, without undue deterioration of the fuse element is called the *current rating*. If the impedance of the earth path of an installation is too high, when an electrical short-circuit occurs, fault currents will flow without the protection equipment operating. Cables will overheat, and may cause fire and danger to life through shock.

23.b *Reliability, discrimination, low maintenance costs, protection of the smallest conductor in the circuit, as protection equipment criteria*

The following chart shows the advantages and disadvantages of different types of fuse.

Fuses	Advantages	Disadvantages
Rewireable	Initial cost low Repair cost low	Wrong size fuse wire can be fitted Age deterioration Damage due to severe short circuit
Cartridge	Accurate current rating Not liable to deterioration.	Expensive to replace Not suitable for extremely high fault current
HBC	Consistent, reliable Discriminating Fusing factor as low as 1.2.	Expensive
Earth electrodes		
Earth plates		Cost of installation is high
Earth rods	Highly effective	Possible damage to other services during installation
Inspection	Additional protection covers for electrode connection	

23.c *Construction advantages and disadvantages of rewireable fuses and cartridge fuse elements*

This is covered in section 23.b

23.d *Inherent time lag in fuses*

The *current rating* of a fuse is the current it will carry continuously without deterioration. The minimum fusing current is the current which will cause the fuse to operate under given conditions in a given time. In BS 88 the given operating time is four hours.

$$\text{Fusing Factor} = \frac{\text{Rated minimum fusing current}}{\text{Current rating}}$$

It follows that the *fusing factor* must exceed 1; the closer it is to 1 the less likely it is that the fault current will fail to operate the fuse. The lower the fusing factor, the better the fuse. A fuse providing close excess current protection is one with a fusing factor of 1.5 or less. If the fusing factor exceeds this figure, only coarse excess current protection is provided.

23.e *Minimising danger from shock and fire by isolating circuits through earth leakage protection.*

You need to make sure that the following are not potential faults in the circuit:

1. A low-resistance fault between live and earthed metal will result in a fault current, and could result in a fire. This is called an *earth fault loop*.

2. A failure of the protective device to open the circuit. This could also result in a fire risk.

3. Since the fuse or circuit breaker is current operated, a sufficiently large current must flow to operate it with a low resistance in the current path. If this situation is not maintained, overheating of the earth continuity conductor can result.

4. Shock from live conductor to earth can be caused when replacing a lamp with the supply to the lampholder still switched on.

One method commonly used to reduce the severity of shock is to employ a transformer with its secondary-winding centre tapped to earth. The voltage to earth from either conductor is only half that of the transformer's secondary voltage.

23.f *Reasons for non-current carrying metal being earthed*

An appliance may be disconnected from earth by a break in an earth continuity conductor. This fault is unlikely to be noticed until a second fault occurs from the live conductor to the case, which will become live relative to the earth. Owing to the normal time delay of fuses and circuit breakers, no protection from shock is offered. Your only protection is to make sure that the circuit conductors are efficiently insulated and that there is continuity of the earthing system.

J Electronic systems

24   Demonstrate and compare different types of input and output waveforms and frequencies on examples of each of the following systems

- d.c. supply operating from an a.c. mains (the term *ripple* should be introduced)
- oscillators giving sinusoidal, square and sawtooth outputs
- amplifiers, voltage amplifiers, current amplifiers, power amplifiers, d.c. and a.c. amplifiers
- using, for example, a CRO and in addition measure the gain of a simple a.c.amplifier.

24.a   d.c. supply operating from an a.c. mains

The voltage for circuits containing semiconductor devices seldom exceeds 30 V and may be as low as 1.5 V. Current demands vary from microamps to amps in large systems. In most power supply units a transformer steps down the a.c. mains from 240 V to the required low voltage. This is then converted to d.c., using one or more junction diodes in a rectifier circuit.

In a simple *half-wave rectifier* circuit where the load is represented by R (piece of electronic equipment), a pulse of current is created by the positive half-cycles of the alternating input voltage forward biassing diode D. This produces a voltage across R of almost the same value as the input voltage, provided that the forward resistance of D is small compared to the value of R. For the negative half-cycles reverse bias D –, there is little or no current in the circuit, and the voltage across R is zero. The current pulses are unidirectional, and so the voltage across R is direct: it never changes direction.

In *centre-tap full-wave rectification*, both halves of every cycle of input voltage produce current pulses.

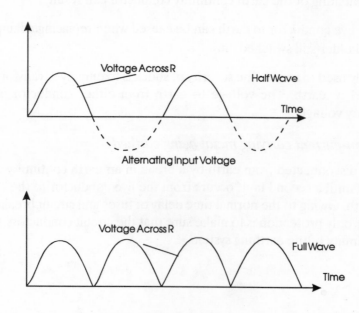

Alternating input voltage

24.b   Oscillators giving sinusoidal, square and sawtooth outputs

Oscillators, both at audio fequencies (a.f.) and radio frequencies (r.f.), are generators of alternating voltage and current. Basically, they are amplifiers, which supply their own input, using positive feedback. Oscillators are used in radios and televisions, in high-voltage supplies, and in test instruments, such as signal generators.

Oscillators convert d.c. from the power supply into undamped a.c., having a sine, square or other waveform, depending on which of the many possible circuits is used.

Most oscillators are *amplifiers* which ensure the following feedback characteristics, in phase with the input, and energy losses made good in the oscillatory circuit.

Sine wave oscillators, such as LC oscillators, do not require a sine wave input. The Hartley and Colpitts oscillator has a feedback circuit similar to the LC oscillator. *Crystal oscillators* use a piezoelectric crystal to provide a fixed and very stable frequency. A *relaxation oscillator* depends on the charging of a capacitor, followed by a period of relaxation, when the capacitor discharges through a resistor. Its output voltage is not a sine wave. In two important cases it is respectively, a sawtooth wave, and a square wave. A *sawtooth oscillator* is required in television receivers and cathode ray oscilloscopes.

Square wave oscillators are used to produce electronic music, (since square waves contain many frequencies), and in digital systems, such as computers. *Waveform generators* produce square, triangular, sine, sawtooth and pulse waveforms of great accuracy.

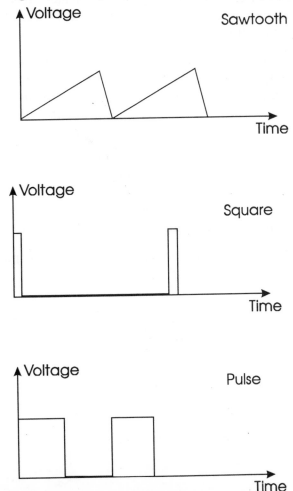

24.c   Amplifiers, voltage amplifiers, current amplifiers, power amplifiers, d.c. and a.c. amplifiers

Amplifier circuits handle analog signals that are the electrical equivalents of physical quantities which vary continuously with time and take on all values between a specified maximum and minimum. The information carried by such signals is represented by the shape and amplitude of the waveform.

The function of an amplifier is *to produce an output which is an enlargement of the input.*

Amplifiers are classified according to their function. In a voltage amplifier, the output voltage is greater than the input voltage. A *junction transistor*, in the common-emitter mode, is a current amplifier, but it can also act as a voltage amplifier, if a suitable resitor is connected in the collector circuit.

A *power amplifier* is designed to supply power to an output transducer. It converts d.c. power from supply into a.c. in the load. It is, in fact, a sturdy voltage amplifier, which uses a power transistor capable of supplying large output currents.

Operational amplifiers were originally designed to solve mathematical equations in an analogue computer. They were originally assembled from discrete components. However, presently they are produced in IC form. One of their many uses is as high-gain d.c. and a.c. voltage amplifiers.

24.d   Use a CRO and measure the gain of a simple a.c. amplifier.

When designing a *voltage amplifier*, the objectives are: to achieve a certain voltage gain, to minimise distortion of the output and, therefore, produce a good replica of the input, and to ensure that it operates within the limits of the transistor for current, voltage and power.

The choice of the *quiescent* (no input) d.c. operating point (values of Ic and Vce) for the transistor, determines whether these requirements will be met. This choice is made by constructing a *load line*. This load line is regarded as the output characteristic of the *transistor and load* for particular values of the power supply voltage and load resistor. The choice of load line and d.c. operating point affects the shape and size of the output waveform.

$$\text{Voltage Gain} \quad = \quad \frac{output\ voltage}{input\ voltage}$$

$$= \quad \frac{Change\ in\ Vce}{Change\ in\ Vbe}$$

Where *Vbe* is the base-emitter voltage and *Vce* is the collector – emitter voltage

Note that too large an input can cause distortion, even if the operating point has been chosen correctly.

K   Materials

25   Use laboratory tests and given reference sources to indicate the general composition, properties and application of the following engineering materials

- Low, medium and high carbon steel and cast iron
- Aluminium alloys
- Magnesium alloys
- Copper
- Copper alloys
- Tin/lead soldering alloys

25.a   Low, medium and high carbon steel and cast iron

Steel is an alloy of iron and carbon and can contains up to 2.0% carbon. By varying the content of carbon, and heat treating the resulting alloy, a greater range of mechanical properties can be obtained. These properties can be extended further by the addition of other alloying elements, such as chromium, molybdenum and nickel.

Cast iron is re-melted pig iron, the composition of which has been adjusted during the melting process. Cast iron is the cheapest metallurgical material available to the engineer.

The table below show a range of steels, their carbon content and their applications.

Class	Carbon Content %	Application
Dead mild steel	0.10-0.15	Sheet for pressed out components for body panels
Mild steel	0.15-0.30	Rods
Medium-carbon steel	0.30-0.50 0.50-0.70	Forgings
High-carbon steel	0.80-0.10 1.00-1.20 1.20-1.40	Coil springs Drills
Cast iron	2.30-2.40	Engine blocks

25.b   Aluminium alloys

These can be conveniently classified into the following groups:

1. *Wrought alloys*   which do *not* respond to heat treatment

2. *Cast alloys*   which do *not* respond to heat treatment

3. *Wrought alloys*   which *do* respond to heat treatment

4. *Cast alloys*   which *do* respond to heat treatment.

These alloys are best identified using the British Standards Institute specification which indicates the nomenclature to be used.

Wrought alloys

BS 1470	Plate, sheet and strip
BS 1471	Drawn tube
BS 1472	Forgings and forging stocks
BS 1473	Rivets, bolts and screws
BS 1474	Extruded round tubes and sections, bars
BS 1475	Wire

Casting alloys

BS 1490	The casting alloys are conveniently divided into two groups, the *general-purpose alloys* and the *special-purpose alloys*

25.c   Magnesium Alloys

The chief attribute of these alloys is their very low relative density (1.7), which makes them useful in the aircraft and space industries. Magnesium has a low tensile strength, but magnesium alloys, containing suitable amounts of aluminium, zinc or thorium, can be strengthened by heat treatment. These alloys are used in the aircraft industry for castings and forgings and are used in landing wheels, crank cases, petrol tanks and engine parts in all types of engines. These alloys, too, are best identified using the specifications, which indicate the nomenclature to be used.

Casting alloys – General purpose

BS 2970	MAG1	Automobile road wheels
	MAG3	Engine manifold covers
	MAG4	Structural elements
	MAG7	General purpose work

Special purpose

BS2970	MAG2	Instrument casings
	MAG5	Pressure tight alloy (high-strength)
	MAG6	Pressure tight alloy (high-temperature)
	MAG8	Creep resistant up to 350 C
	MAG9	High-duty structures

There is an additional aerospace 'L' series.

Wrought alloys

Type BS 3370, BS 3372, BS3373

MAG-E-101	Extrusion
MAG-S-111	Sheet
MAG-F-121	Forging
MAG-S-131	Sheet
MAG-E-161	Extrusion

There is an additional aerospace 'L' series.

25.d Copper

Copper is used extensively in the electrical industry, due to its high electrical conductivity, which is second only to silver. Its main competitor is pure aluminium, which has only half the specific conductivity of copper, but is also much less expensive.

Good thermal conductivity and corrosion resistance make copper highly suitable for hot-water systems.

Properties of Copper:

Tensile strength and hardness	low
Ductility	high
Ultimate strength	150 N/mm2
Cold-worked increases to	400 N/mm2
Hardness	45 Brinell hardness
Cold-worked increases to	90 Brinell hardness
Coefficient of thermal expansion	1.5 times that for steel
Relative density	8.9

There are four principal commercial grades of copper:

1. *Electolytically refined copper* — This is *cathode* copper and is the purest form of copper (97.5%). It has a high degree of electrical conductivity.

2. *Tough-pitch copper* — This is produced by fire-refining, and contains small amounts of impurities in the form of copper oxide. This has a significant effect on thermal conductivity.

3. *Phosphorous-deoxidised copper* — This is *tough-pitch* copper treated with a small amount of phosphorous just before casting. This reduces the electrical conductivity by up to 25%, and is useful when welding or brazing is required.

4. *Arsenical copper* — When small amounts of arsenic are added to the copper it goes into solid solution. This increases its corrosion resistance and strength. It is suitable for boiler tubes, although welding is not recommended.

25.e Copper Alloys

Copper readily forms alloys with a number of elements to give a wide range of properties. The four most important copper alloys are:

1. *Brasses* (copper-zinc alloys)

2. *Bronzes* (copper-tin alloys)

3. *Aluminium Bronzes* (copper-aluminium alloys)

4. *Cupro-nickels* (copper-nickel alloys)

Use the following BSI number and term when referring to these alloys:

Extrusion

| BS 2870 | *Tin bronze* | PB101 Cold-worked phosphor |
| BS 2874 | | PB102 bronze springs |

Forging

| BS2872 | *Aluminium bronze* | CA103 Hot-worked can be heat treated by |
| | | CA104 quenching & tempering |

Casting

BS 1400A	*Tin bronze*	LG2 Leaded gun metal
BS 1400B		CT1 Special purpose alloy
		LB5 Special purpose leaded alloy

| BS 1400C | *Aluminium bronze* | G1 Gun metal for pump valves |
| BS 1400b | | AB1 Most widely used aluminium bronze |

25.f   *Tin/lead soldering alloys*

The lead/tin alloys are the basis of many commercial soft solders, the two most significant being:

1. *Electrician's solder*

    This ideally should comprise 62% tin and 38% lead, so that it solidifies sharply at 183° C, and reduces to a minimum both the time required to produce a joint and also the time that the workpiece is exposed. As tin is expensive relative to lead, the lead content of commercial solders often exceeds 50%.

2. *Plumber's solder*

    This should solidify over a range of temperature to enable the plumber to *wipe* the joint in the damaged pipe. Plumber's solder contains approximately 67% lead and 33% tin and solidifies between 183° C and 265° C.

26   Carry out examples of heat treatment and record the individual stages of annealing; hardening and tempering as applied to commonly used metals and alloys; identify their effects on the properties

The properties of many metallic materials can be modified by a sequence of heating and cooling. The four most important processes are:

- annealing
- normalising
- hardening
- tempering.

Hardening

Hardening temperatures of steel vary according to the carbon content.

The temperature ranges from which the steels are quenched (see Heat Treament temperature range Equilibrium Diagram) are as follows:

0.3% carbon in steel	$910^{\circ}/880^{\circ}$ C
0.85% carbon in steel	$780^{\circ}/750^{\circ}$ C

The steel to be hardend is first heated to the appropriate temperature, as indicated by its carbon content, on the Equilibrium Diagram. To harden the steel, it is then cooled rapidly (quenched) from the temperature shown on the diagram.

The degree of hardness achieved will depend on:

1. the rate of cooling

2. the carbon content of the steel.

Steel Type	Carbon %	Quench Effect	Quench Media	Treatment Required
Medium carbon	0.3 – 0.5		oil	Toughing
	0.5 – 0.9		oil	
	0.5 – 0.9		water	Hardening
High carbon	0.9 – 1.3	Very hard	oil	

Note: below 0.5% carbon, steels are not hardened as cutting tools
above 0.9% carbon, water hardening the steels causes cracking.

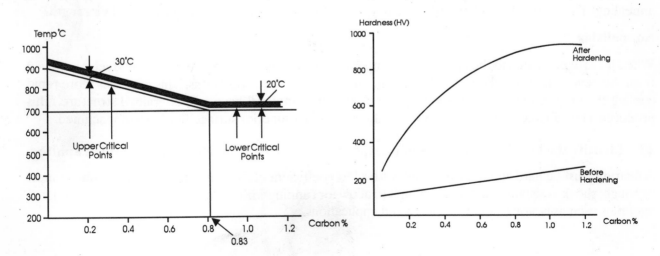

Hardening temperatures   **Carbon content of steel and hardness**

Tempering

To increase its toughness, the hardened steel is tempered by reheating it and quenching it in oil or water.

Typical tempering temperatures, for a range of applications are given below. The temperature is judged by the colour of the film of metal oxide on the surface of the metal.

Temperature in Centigrade	Temper Colour	Component
220	Pale straw	Edge tools
230	Medium straw	Turning tools
240	Dark straw	Twist drills
250	Brown	Taps
260	Brownish-purple	Press tools
280	Purple	Cold chisels
300	Blue	Springs
450-600	Dark blue	Toughened steels (medium carbon)

Annealing

Annealing is used to give already hardened steel soft, ductile properties, thus allowing further cold-working operations to be conducted. The type of process used depends on how the steel was originally hardened.

Full anealing is used to soften quench-hardened steel. The metal is heated to the same temperature range used in hardening, and allowed to 'soak' to achieve uniform temperature throughout, then allowed to cool very slowly.

Process annealing is used to soften plain carbon steels, which have been work-hardened by exessive cold working. The required temperature is between 350° C and 500° C, irrespective of the carbon content. This lies below the lower critical temperature for plain carbon steels. The workpiece is cooled slowly as for full annealing. This type of annealing restores a degree of ductility while maintaining the metal's strength.

Normalising

When it has been heated to the appropriate temperature for the given carbon content, the steel is removed from the heat source and allowed to cool in air, under draught-free conditions. This produces more rapid cooling than permitted in the annealing process, and the metal will have a finer grained structure. This produces a less ductile, but stonger, metal. It also results in a superior surface finish when machined.

27   Identify the bearing properties of phosphor bronze, cast iron, PTFE, nylon and graphite

A bearing must be hard and wear-resistant, with a low coefficient of friction, but, at the same time, it must be tough, shock-resistant and ductile enough to allow for running-in. The following table shows a range of materials used as bearings, their proprties and applications.

Materials	Properties	Applications
Phosphor-bronze	Low coefficient of friction Improved plasticity with lead	Medium duty, when lubricant is intermittent
Cast iron	Self lubricating with internal flakes of graphite	Heavy duty, low speed
PTFE	Heat-resistant and solvent Lowest known coefficient of friction	Light duty bearing bushes
Nylon	Relatively expensive Strong	Tough
Graphite	Solid lubricant used where a normal oil cannot be maintained	Heavy duty

28   Carry out simple tests to discover the differences between thermoplastics amd thermo-setting plastics; use reference sources to list engineering applications and properties of these materials

Thermoplastic polymers can be softened and remoulded repeatedly by the application of heat. At room temperature they are tough and sometimes rigid. They exhibit plastic properties only when heated.

Thermo-setting polymers are plastics in the primary stages of manufacture and, once moulded into shape, they 'set' and cannot subsequently be softened and remoulded by the application of heat. They are moulded in heated dies under high pressure. Thermo-setting plastics are generally more rigid than thermoplastics

Materials	Properties	Applications
Thermoplastic		
Acrylics	Excellent optical properties, tough, easily shaped	High-frequency electrical insulators
Teflon	Lowest known coefficient of friction	Very heat resistant
Nylon	Tough with low coefficient of friction	Used as a fibre or as a moulding material
Thermo-setting plastics		
Polyester resin	With added styrene becomes a thermo-set. Curing takes place by heat resulting from chemical reaction	Used as bond in glass fibre moulding
Epoxy resins	Strongest plastic materials, used as adhesive	Encapsulation of electrical parts, and as electrical insulators

Although the properties of plastic materials can vary greatly, they all have the following properties in common:

1.   excellent strength to weight ratio

2.   excellent corrosion resistance

3.   good electrical resistance

29   Use given reference sources to list the engineering application of:

- Rubber
- Ceramics

29.a   Rubber

Elastomers, as the name suggests, are elastic materials, which distort extensively when stressed, but return to their original shape immediately the applied stress is removed. Natural rubber is the best known example, but synthetic rubbers are now used much more extensively. The following table shows a range of natural and synthetic rubbers, their properties and applications.

Materials	Properties	Applications
Natural rubber		
Polyisoprene	High-tensile strength Low hysteresis, low resistance, ozone solvents, mineral oils	Shock absorber seals electrical insulation
Synthetic rubber		
Styrene-butadiene (SBR)	Resistant to skids and to attacks by, chemicals and weather	Tyres, floor tiles, hoses
Butyl	High resistance to ozone, ultra-violet light, gases and weather	Vapour barriers, tubeless tyres
Nitrile	Good adhesion properties Resistant to refrigeration gases	O-rings, fuel tank linings
Neoprene	Resistant to weather, oils and solvents; flame resistant	Safety clothes, engine mounts
Acrylic	Resistance to ozone, ultra-violet, oils, and oxygen	Latex paints, roofing membrane
Pliofilm	Tear resistant, high-tensile strength	Transparent film packaging
Silicon	Excellent temperature operating range	Low-temperature seals, high-temperature grease
Polyurethane	High tensile strength and elongation	Oil seals, heels, anti-vibration mountings

29.b *Ceramics*

The term *ceramics* is applied to a wide range of inorganic materials. These materials have been treated at high temperature during manufacture.

Ceramics can be classified into four main groups in terms of composition and structure.

Material	Properties	Applications
Amorphous (Soda-glass Lead glass Borosilicate glass)	High refractive index Resistant to heat, chemical attack	General purpose Optical lenses Pyrex
Crystaline	Very hard	Abrasives and cutting tools
Bonded	Very hard	Electrical insulator Furnace linings Domestic application
Cements	Very hard	Investment casting moulds

30 Discuss the safety hazards in the use of asbestos

Asbestos is the name given to a family of fibrous minerals. Sheets may be produced by bonding the fibres with a cement. Asbestos can also be woven into fabrics. It has the following properties and applications.

Material	Properties	Applications
Asbestos	Fire proof Chemically inert Thermal and electrical insulator Resistant to decay	Clutch and brake linings

In the regulations it is defined as any of the following materials:

- crocidolite
- amosite
- chrysotile
- fibrous anthopylite
- tremolite
- any mixture containing any of these materials.

There are three sets of regulations, specific to asbestos, currently in force:

- Asbestos (Licensing) Regulations 1983
- Asbestos (Prohibition) Regulations 1985
- Control of Asbestos at Work Regulations 1983

The use of asbestos has declined sharpley due to its association with respiratory diseases.

31   Distinguish between the electrical properties of conductors and insulators and give examples of each class of material

In the table below are the properties and applications of a range of insulators and conductors.

Material	Properties	Applications
Insulators		
Ceramics	Weather-resistant Heat-resistant	High-voltage High-frequency isolators Transistors Micro-chips
Mica	Heat-resistant	Dielectric for capacitors
Rubber	Flexible	Coverings, sleeves
Poplythene	Easily mouldable	Moulds, coverings
PVC	Tough, pliable, cheap	Flexible cables
Conductors		
Silver	Highest electrical conductivity	Heavy-duty electrical work
Copper	Second only to silver in electric conductivity	Electrical wire
Aluminium	Cheaper and lighter than copper	Drawn wire

32   Discover the reason for and methods of protecting materials from atmospheric attack

- the need for the protection of metallic materials from atmospheric corrosion
- surface attack

32.a   *The need for the protection of metallic materials from atmospheric corrosion*

Corrosion is the slow eating away of the metallic surfaces of a component, under the action of one or more of three factors:

1. the environment

2. the surface treatment

3. the metal used.

When metals are exposed to normal atmospheric conditions, a combination of atmospheric oxygen and moisture corrodes metal surfaces. The most common example of corrosion is the rusting of ferrous metals. This appears as 'red' iron oxide, when the ferrous metal is exposed to the weather conditions. Rusting is self generating: even after the environmental causes are removed, the rusting will continue. It is, therefore, essential to remove all rust before painting the affected surfaces. Dissolved chemicals in the atmosphere intensify the rusting process. Sulphur dioxide is the most damaging product of the burnt fossil fuels.

32.b   Surface Protection

Ferrous metals and alloys have attracted the greatest investment in the process of preventing and retarding corrosion. The following are some of the methods employed.

Galvanising	This is the coating of steel surfaces with zinc.
Electro-plating	This is the coating of a metal surface with another metal. Metals which are most commonly plated on to a base metal are: copper chromium nickel silver zinc
Anodising	This is an electrolytic process, similar to plating, and is used on aluminium and aluminium products.
Chromating	A hard oxide surface is produced by dipping the component into a hot potassium dichromate solution.
Painting	A wide range of paints are available.
Spraying	The surfaces to be protected are sprayed with molten metal.

Mathematics

A Arithmetic

1   Evaluate expressions involving integer indices and use standard form:

- base, index, power. reciprocal in terms of a^n

- $a^m a^n = a^{m+n}, \quad \dfrac{a^m}{a^n} = a^{(m-n)}, \quad (a^m)^n = a^{mn}, \quad a^0 = 1, \quad a^{-n} = \dfrac{1}{a^n}$

- standard form e.g. 1.234×10^5

- four basic operations using standard form

1.a Base, index, power, reciprocal in terms of a^n

Indices

If a number is multiplied by itself a certain number of times, it is said to be raised to a certain power. The index of a number is a way of illustrating how many times a number (the base) has been multiplied by itself.

$$a \times a \times a \times a \ldots = a^n$$
$$5 \times 5 \times 5 \times 5 = 5^4 \text{ where 5 is the } base \text{ and 4 is the } index$$

Power

A number a raised to a power n is given as a^n

A number raised to a *power* 1 is that number e.g. $8^1 = 8$

Reciprocal

A number raised to a negative power is the *reciprocal* of that number raised to the same positive power.

$$a^{-n} = \frac{1}{a^{+n}} \quad \text{or} \quad \frac{1}{a^n}$$

$$4^{-3} = \frac{1}{4^{+3}} \quad \text{or} \quad \frac{1}{4^3}$$

1.b $a^m a^n = a^{m+n}, \quad \dfrac{a^m}{a^n} = a^{(m-n)}, \quad (a^m)^n = a^{mn}, \quad a^0 = 1, \quad a^{-n} = \dfrac{1}{a^n}$

When a number raised to a power is multiplied by the *same number* raised to a power, *add* the powers.
$$4^3 \times 4^2 = 4^5$$

When a number raised to a power is divided by the *same number* raised to a power, *subtract* the powers.
$$4^5 \div 4^3 = 4^2$$

When a number raised to a power is its raised to a further power, *multiply* the powers.
$$(3^2)^4 = 3^8$$

When a number is raised to the power 0, it is equal to 1.

$$5^0 \quad = \quad 1$$

When a number is raised to a negative power it is equal to the reciprocal of the same number raised to the same positive power.

$$6^{-3} \quad = \quad \frac{1}{6^3}$$

1.c Standard form e.g. 1.234×10^5

It is sometimes convenient to write very large and very small numbers in standard form.

$$a \times 10^n$$

where a lies between 1 and 10 and n is a power (or an integer).

For large numbers n is positive and for small numbers n is negative.

$$
\begin{aligned}
18{,}300{,}000 \quad &= \quad 1.83 \times 10{,}000{,}000 \\
&= \quad 1.83 \times 10^7 \\
0.0000335 \quad &= \quad 3.35 \div 100{,}000 \\
&= \quad 3.35 \times 10^{-5}
\end{aligned}
$$

Problems can be simplified when standard form is used. It also has an advantage when using logarithms.

1.d Four basic operations using standard form

Addition

$$
\begin{aligned}
1.875 \times 10^{-2} &+ & 2.110 \times 10^{-3} \\
1.875 \times 10^{-2} &+ & 0.2110 \times 10^{-2} \\
(1.875 + 0.2110) &\times & 10^{-2} \\
2.086 &\times & 10^{-2}
\end{aligned}
$$

Subtraction

$$
\begin{aligned}
3.576 \times 10^{-4} &- & 4.211 \times 10^4 \\
(3.576 - 4.211) &\times & 10^4 \\
(-0.635) &\times & 10^4 \\
-6.35 &\times & 10^3
\end{aligned}
$$

Multiplication

$$
\begin{aligned}
(15.00 \times 10^2) &\times & (6.442 \times 10^3) \\
(15.00 \times 6.442) &\times & 10^{(2+3)} \\
96.63 \times 10^5 &= & 9.663 \times 10^6
\end{aligned}
$$

Division

$$
\begin{aligned}
(755 \times 10^4) &\div & (32.33 \times 10^{-2}) \\
(755 / 32.33) &\times & 10^{[4 - (-2)]} \\
23.353 &\times & 10^{(4+2)} \\
&= & 23.353 \times 10^6
\end{aligned}
$$

2   Evaluate expressions involving negative and fractional indices and relate indices and logarithms:

- index rules for negative and fractional indices
- combination of positive, negative and fractional indices
- inverse of $a^x = y$ as $x = \log_a y$
- logarithms of numbers

2.a   *Index rules for negative and fractional indices*

Negative indices

A number raised to a negative power is the reciprocal of the number raised to a positive power.

$$a^{-n} = \frac{1}{a^n}$$

Example 1

$$5^2 \times 3^{-2} = 5^2 \times \frac{1}{3^2} = \frac{25}{9}$$

Example 2

$$50n^{-2}m^{-5} = \frac{50}{n^2 m^5}$$

Fractional indices

Fractional indices are used to indicate the *roots* of numbers.

$$\text{e.g.} \quad 4^{½} = \text{the square root of 4}$$
$$\text{That is } (\sqrt{4}) = 2$$
$$\text{and} \quad 27^{⅓} = \text{the cube root of 27}$$
$$\text{That is } (\sqrt[3]{27}) = 3$$

Fractional indices also obey the rules of indices.

Example 3

$$[2^{½}]^6 = 2^3$$

Example 4

$$2^{½} \times 2^{½} \times 2^2 = 2^3$$

2.b   *Combination of positive, negative and fractional indices*

Example 1

$$a^2 \times a^{-3} \times a^{½} = a^{(2-3+½)}$$
$$= a^{-½}$$

Example 2

$$5^{-3} \times 5^4 \times 5^{1/3} = 5^{(4-3+1/3)}$$
$$= 5^{4/3}$$

2c. *Inverse of $a^x = y$ as $x = \log_a y$*

A *logarithm* or *log* of a number is the power that the base has to be raised to in order to give the number.

Example 1

$$1000 = 10^3$$
(where the number is 1000 and the base is 10)

10 is raised to the power 3 to give the number 1000. Therefore $\log_{10} 1000 = 3$ and log to the base 10 of 1000 is 3.

This is normally written as $\log_a y = x$ when $a^x = y$.

Example 2

Express the following index statement as a logarithmic statement.
$$8^3 = 512$$

3 is the index, 8 is the base which is raised to the power 3.
$$\log_8 512 = 3$$

Example 3

Express the following logarithmic statements as index statements:
$$\log_6 36 = 2$$
$$6^2 = 36$$

Where 6 is the base, 3 is the index (power) and 36 is the number:

2.d *Logarithms of numbers*

The first law of logarithms: when two numbers are multiplied, the log of the product is the sum of the logs of the two numbers, when the bases are the same.

$$a^m \times a^n = a^{m+n}$$
$$\text{let } x = a^m \quad \text{and} \quad y = a^n$$
$$\text{Then } \log_a x = m \quad \text{and} \quad \log_a y = n$$
$$\text{but} \quad xy = a^{(m+n)}$$

Converting this to a log statement.
$$\log_a(xy) = m + n$$
$$= \log_a x + \log_a y$$

The second law of logarithms: when one number is divided by another, the log of the answer is equal to the difference of the logs of the numbers, when the bases are the same.

$$\frac{a^m}{a^n} = a^{m-n}$$

$$\text{let} \quad x = a^m$$
$$\text{and} \quad y = a^n$$
$$\text{Then} \quad \log_a x = m$$
$$\text{and} \quad \log_a y = n$$
$$\text{But} \quad \frac{x}{y} = a^{m-n}$$

Converting to a log statement

$$\log_a\left(\frac{x}{y}\right) = m - n$$
$$= \log_a x - \log_a y$$

The third law of logarithms: the logarithm of a number raised to a power is equal to the power multiplied by the logarithm of the number.

$$\text{Let} \quad x = a^m \quad (1)$$
$$\text{Then} \quad \log_a x = m \quad (2)$$

Raise both sides of (1) to the power n

$$x^n = (a^m)^n$$
$$= a^{mn}$$

Converting this to a log statement

$$\log_a(x^n) = mn \quad (3)$$

Combining (2) and (3)

$$\log_a(x^n) = n\log_a x$$

3   Ensure the answers to numerical problems are reasonable:

- significant figures, validity and feasibility of solutions, approximations, checking results

3.a   *Significant figures, validity and feasibility of solutions, approximations, checking results*

Calculations involving measured quantities.

There is a limit to the accuracy to which a measurement can be made. When a calculation involving measured quantities is made, the answer should not normally be given to a greater accuracy than one significant figure more than the least accurate quantity. For example, if a calculation involves the multiplication of four measured quantities which have 2, 3, 4, 5, significant figures respectively, the answer should not have more than 3 significant figures.

Example

Express the following numbers correct to three significant figures (a) 6.0851 (b) 8304

(a) The first three significant figures give 6.08 but since 6.0851 is nearer to 6.09 than 6.08

Then 6.0851 = 6.09 to three significant figures

(b) As 8304 is nearer to 8300 than 8310

Then 8304 = 8300 correct to three significant figures

Calculations may be quite lengthy, especially if they involve numbers having several significant figures. The approximate answer may be found by rounding each number up or down so that it has one (or maybe two) significant figures and then completing the calculation. This is useful if a check is required on the accuracy of an answer. An approximate answer must be of the same order as the accurate answer. If for example a calculation gives the answer 654·8 and the approximation gives the answer 600, then it is reasonable to assume that the answer is correct.

4   Understand and use, tables and charts:

- logarithms, squares, cubes, square roots, cube roots, sine, cosine, tangent, reciprocal.
- conversion tables
- applications to practical problems

4.a   Logarithms, squares, cubes, square roots, cube roots, sine, cosine, tangent, reciprocal

A *Logarithm* is made up of two parts, the *mantissa*, the decimal fraction part, which is obtained from tables, and the *characteristic*, the whole number part. To find the log of a number, first change it to standard form; the mantissa is found in the table. This becomes the mantissa of the log and the exponent of the number becomes the characteristic of the log. The mantissa is always positive but the characteristic may be positive or negative.

Example

$$Log_{10}\, 3 \quad = \quad Log_{10}(3 \times 10^0)$$
$$= \quad 0.4771.$$
$$Log_{10}\, 300 \quad = \quad Log_{10}(3 \times 10^2)$$
$$= \quad 2.4771.$$
$$Log_{10}\, 0.03 \quad = \quad Log_{10}(3 \times 10^{-2})$$
$$= \quad \bar{2}.4771$$

The *square's* tables can be used to find the square of any number up to 4 significant figures. The number to be squared has first to be converted into standard form.

The first two significant figures are found on the left-hand side of the table. The third significant figure is found at the top of the table, and the fourth significant figure in the mean difference column. This is the square of the mantissa. Now square the exponent and multiply the two.

Example 1

Find the square of the number 413

$$413^2 = (4.13 \times 10^2)^2$$
$$= 4.13^2 \times (10^2)^2$$

4.13^2 can be found from a table of squares

$$4.13^2 = 20.32$$

$(10^2)^2$ using the 'Power Rule' for indices

$$(10^2)^2 = 10^2 \times 10^2 = 10^4$$

therefore $413^2 = 20.32 \times 10^4 \quad 203.200$

Note: There are usually two tables of squares, 1 to 9.999 and 10 to 99.99.

A number whose *square root* is required has to be converted into one of the above ranges. This is achieved by moving the point left or right two places at a time. The answer will be in standard form. Find the square of the exponent and multiply.

Example 2

Find the square root of 135

135 written in standard form is 1.35×10^2

So $\sqrt{135} = \sqrt{1.35} \times \sqrt{10^2}$
$$= \sqrt{1.35} \times \sqrt{10^2}$$

Now $\sqrt{1.35}$ is found from the tables of square roots

and $\sqrt{10^2}$ is evaluated using the 'Power Rule' for indices

$$\sqrt{135} = 1.162$$

and $\sqrt{135} = (10^2)^{\frac{1}{2}} = 10$

therefore $\sqrt{135} = 1.162 \times 10 = 11.62$

A number whose *reciprocal* is required has to converted into standard form and reconverted later. The mean difference has to be subtracted from the figures obtained from the table.

The *cube* and *cube root* of a number can be found from tables in a manner similar to that employed in finding the square and the square root of a number.

In the *sine* tables the angles are given in the left-hand column. The main columns sub-divide the degrees into 6 minute or 0.1 degree intervals. The mean difference column on the right of the table gives the correction for the angles between the 6 minute intervals and is added for an increase in the angle. The value of the sine is from zero (at an angle of zero) to 1 (at an angle of 90 degrees).

In the *cosine* tables the layout is similar to that of the sine tables but with an important difference. The value of the cosine goes from 1 (at an angle of zero) to zero (at an angle of 90 degrees). The figure in the mean difference column must be subtracted for an increase in angle.

In the *tangent* table the layout and use is the same as for the sine tables. The value of the tangent extends from zero (at an angle of zero) to infinity (at an angle of 90 degrees). This means that as the angle approaches 90 degrees the mean difference becomes insignificant.

In the *tangent* table the layout and use is the same as for the sine tables. The value of the tangent extends from zero (at an angle of zero) to infinity (at an angle of 90 degrees). This means that as the angle approaches 90 degrees the mean difference becomes insignificant.

In the *reciprocals* tables the numbers whose reciprocal is required has to be changed to the standard form and changed back later. The mean difference has to be subtracted from the figures obtained from the table.

4.b   Conversion tables

In the trigonometry tables the angles in radians is given in the left-hand column while the main columns of the page are set out to give the following conversions:

Radians / Degrees / sin
Radians / Degrees /tan
Radians / Degrees /cos
Radians / Degrees /Log sin
Radians / Degrees /Log tan
Radians / Degrees /Log cos

4.c   Applications to practical problems

Example 1

Find the value of Log 271.8
Since 271.8   = 2.718×10^2 the characteristic is 2.
From the table the mantissa of 2718 is 4343
Log 271.8   =   2.4343

Example 2

Determine the value of the quantity 67.42^2
Since 67.42^2 = $(6.742 \times 10)^2$
                = 45.46×10^2
67.42^2 =   4546

Example 3

Determine the value of the square root of 7291
Since   7291   = 72.91×10^2
square root of 7291   = $\sqrt{72.91} \times 10$
                = $\pm 8.539 \times 10$
                = ± 85.39

5   Perform basic arithmetic operations on a calculator:

- four basic operations
- numbers to a power
- reciprocals

- checking of calculations
- checking of results

5.a Four basic operations

Calculators can perform all the functions provided by tables quicker and more accurately. There are many makes of calculator and each has detailed instructions for its use provided with it. N.B.(CL) means 'clear' the calculator of any value stored in the accumulator. Usually the is marked 'AC' or Accumulator Clear.

Addition

Consider the sum of 9 and 8

	9	+	8	=	?
[CL]	9	[+]	8	[=]	

Calculator display

[0]	9	[9]	8	17

The result is displayed when [=] key is pressed

Subtraction

Consider the difference of 9 and 8

	9	–	8	=	?
[CL]	9	[–]	8	[=]	

Calculator display

[0]	9	9	8	1

Multiplication

Consider the product of 9 and 8

	9	×	8	=	?
[CL]	9	[×]	8	[=]	

Calculator display

[0]	9	9	8	72

Division

Consider the quotient of 9 and 8

	9	÷	8	=	?
[CL]	9	[÷]	8	[=]	

Calculator display

[0]	9	9	8	1.125

5.b Numbers to a power (Just use 'x^y' key)

Having covered the four basic operations, other procedures are best covered by using the particular instruction manual provided with each calculator.

5.c Reciprocals (Use '1/x' key)

Reciprocals may be treated as a straight division as in (5.a) or as a special case of (5.b), where the number is raised to the power of (–1).

5.d Checking of calculations

Example

The area A of a triangle is given by the equation

$$A = \frac{bh}{2}$$

The base b is 2.75cm and the perpendicular height h is 8.75cm.
Find the area of the triangle.
Making a rough estimate

$$\text{Area } A = \frac{3 \times 9}{2}$$

$$= 13.5\text{cm}^2$$

Actual calculation

$$\text{Area } A = \frac{2.75 \times 8.75}{2}$$

$$= 12.03\text{cm}^2$$

There are no obvious mistakes or order of magnitude errors.

The practice of rough checking is important when using a calculator in order to ensure that incorrect answers become obvious.

5.e Checking of results

The purpose of carrying out a rough check is to identify the size of an answer to a calculation. Repeat the calculation if the results do not agree with an approximation.

6 Use basic notation and rules of algebra:

- numbers and letters
- four basic operations, commutative, associative and distributive, precedence laws
- simplification of expressions

6.a Numbers and letters

Algebra is a system of using letters, symbols and numbers to make generalised arithmetic expressions, which will be true for all values.

Any number of terms, single separate quantities, can be multiplied together.

Example

1. ac , ef, u, wz

Example

2. $4a$, $2m$, $3abc$. A number such as '4' or '2' in this example is called the *coefficient* of the term

Example

3. Like terms $3y$, $5y$, $\frac{y}{2}$, $20y$

Like terms, that is terms which have the same letters or symbols raised to the same power, can be added or subtracted.

A *symbol* can be used to represent a number. The Greek letter π (pi) is used to represent a constant whose exact value is not known and is approximately 3.1416.

An *expression* is a collection of terms normally connected by a plus or minus sign.

1. $4x + 3y + 20$

2. $9a + 2b - c$

3. $q - p + 3p$

Fractional algebraic expressions can be simplified by cancelling.

An *equation* is a statement which includes an equals sign.

1. $5 + 4 = 6 + 3$

2. $8a + 6a = 12a + 5$

An *equation* is an expression in balance. The expression on one side of the equals sign balances the expression on the other side of the equals sign. The equation can be thought of as a set of scales.

6.b *Four basic operations, commutative, associative and distributive, precedence laws*

The *Commutative Law* has two applications, one for addition and one for multiplication.

Addition law:

$$2 + 4 = 6$$
$$4 + 2 = 6$$

The result is the same, no matter what the order of addition.
In general:

$$a + b = b + a$$

The *Commutative Law of addition* states that the order of addition of two terms does not affect the result.

Multiplication law:

$$4 \times 5 = 20$$
$$5 \times 4 = 20$$

The result is the same, no matter what the order of muliplication.
In general

$$a \times b = ab$$
$$b \times a = ba$$
$$ab = ba$$

The *Commutative Law of multiplication* states that the order of multiplication of two terms does not affect the result.

The *Associative Law* has two applications; as with the commutative law they relate to addition and multiplication.

> *Addition Law*:
> $$(2 + 3) + 6 = \quad 11$$
> $$2 + (3 + 6) = \quad 11$$
> The result is the same, the position of the bracket makes no difference.
> In general
> $$(a + b) + c = \quad a + (b + c)$$

The *Associative Law of addition* states that the order of addition of three terms is unaffected by the position of brackets.

> *Multiplication Law*:
> $$(5 \times 4) \times 3 \quad = \quad 60$$
> $$5 (4 \times 3) \quad = \quad 60$$
> The result is the same: the bracket position does not affect the result.
> In general
> $$(a \times b) \times c \quad = \quad a \times (b \times c)$$

The *Associative Law of Multiplication* states that the order of multiplication of three terms is unaffected by the position of the bracket.

The *Distributive Law* of algebra states that:

$$a (b + c) \quad = \quad ab + ac$$

The *Distributive Law* means that multiplication is carried out before addition:

$$5x (2y + z) \quad = \quad 10xy + 5xz$$
and
$$3a (b - 2c) \quad = \quad 3ab - 6ac$$

6.c   Simplification of expressions

Brackets

When an expression in a bracket is preceded only by a plus sign, the bracket may be removed without any change in the expression. When the bracket is preceded by a minus sign, each plus sign changes to a minus sign and each minus sign changes to a plus sign, when the bracket is removed. When one set of brackets is contained within further brackets, the simplification must begin with the inner brackets. It is important that expressions containing two or more of the signs and brackets, should be simplifed in the correct order. This can be remembered using the mnemonic BODMAS.

1. *Brackets*   Simplify and remove brackets

2. *Of*   Applies only to arithmetic fractions

3.   *Division*   Simplify all pairs of terms joined by a division sign

4.   *Multiplication*   Simplify all pairs of terms joined by a multiplication sign

5.   *Addition*   Add together all the positive terms and add together all the negative terms

6.   *Subtraction*   Subtract the positive term from the negative term.

7   Multiply and factorise algebraic expressions involving brackets

- multiplying expressions inside brackets by numbers, symbols or expressions within brackets
  e.g. $3a\,(2 + b) = 6a + 3ab$,
  $(a + b)(2 + c) = 2a + ac + 2b + bc$
- factorising as the reverse of expanding an expression
- grouping for factorisation

7.a *Multiplying expressions inside brackets by numbers, symbols or expressions within brackets*
e.g. $3a(2 + b) = 6a + 3ab$, $(a + b)(2 + c) = 2a + ac + 2b + bc$

An expression containing two terms is called a *binomial* expression. The rules for multiplication for positive and negative numbers are:

$$
\begin{aligned}
+ \text{ times } + &= \text{the result is a plus } + \text{ e.g. } 2 \times 3 &= 6 \\
- \text{ times } - &= \text{the result is a plus } + \text{ e.g. } 2 \times -3 &= 6 \\
+ \text{ times } - &= \text{the result is a minus } - \text{ e.g. } 2 \times -3 &= 6
\end{aligned}
$$

Routine for multiplying two binomial expressions

$$(W + X)\,(Y + Z)$$

(a)   Multiply together the first term in each bracket: $+WY$

(b)   Multiply together the first term in first bracket
      and the second term in the second bracket: $+WZ$

(c)   Multiply together the second term in first bracket
      and the first term in the second bracket: $+XY$

(d)   Multiply together the second term in first bracket
      and second term in the second bracket: $+XZ$

$$(W + X)\,(Y + Z) = WY + WZ + XY + XZ$$

Example

Multiply the following brackets
$$(2a - b)\,(a - 2b)$$

(a) $2a \times a \quad = \quad 2a^2$

(b) $2a \times -2b$ $=$ $-4ab$

(c) $-b \times a$ $=$ $-ab$

(d) $-b \times -2b$ $=$ $2b^2$

$(2a - b)\ (a - 2b)$ $=$ $2a^2 - 4ab - ab + 2b^2$

$=$ $2a^2 - 5ab + 2b^2$

(by collecting 'like' terms)

An expression such as $(X + Y)^2$ requires that the whole bracket is multiplied by itself e.g. $(X + Y)^2 = (X + Y)(X + Y)$

7.b Factorising as the reverse of expanding an expression

Factorising an expression with brackets is the reverse process of expanding a bracket.

The *common factor* of a given number of terms is the numbers or letters that will divide exactly into each term. Each number has at least a factor of 1.

The *highest common factor* (HCF) of a given number of terms is the highest number or largest group of letters which will divide exactly into each term.

The factors of the expression $5(a + 3)$ are 5 and $(a + 3)$.

Example 1

Find the factors of the expression $10x$ $+$ 5

    (a) The highest common factor of $10x$ and 5 is equal to 5

    (b) Divide each term of the expression by the HCF

$$\frac{10x + 5}{5} = (2x + 1)$$

    (c) The factors of the expression $10x + 5$ are 5 and $(2x + 1)$

$$10x + 5 = 5(2x + 1)$$

Example 2

Factorise the expression $ax + ay - az$

    (a) Find the highest common factor: a

    (b) Divide each term by the HCF and place in a bracket

$$\frac{ax + ay - az}{a} = (x + y - z)$$

    (c) The factors for the expression are: a and $(x + y - z)$

Factorisation of an expression is the process of extracting the highest common factor from a given number of terms.

7.c Grouping for factorisation

An expression does not have to have a common factor; the terms may be collected together into groups in such a way that it is possible to find a common factor for each group.

Consider the following expression:

$$ac + cb + db + da$$

There are no common factors for the whole expression.

By collecting the terms into two groups, a common factor for each group is found.

$$ac + da \text{ and } cb + db$$
$$a(c + d) \text{ and } b(c + d)$$

A common factor is $(c + d)$.

Divide each term by $(c + d)$

$$(c + d)(a + b)$$

The factors for the expression $ac + cb + db + da$ are

$$(c + d) \text{ and } (a + b)$$

Factorisation can be checked by simply expanding the bracket.

8 Solve, algebraically, simple equations and linear simultaneous equations:

- maintenance of equality
- linear equations with one unknown
- construction of equations from derived data
- simultaneous equations with two unknowns

8.a Maintenance of equality

A simple equation is an equation with one unknown value. It is true for only one value. It is important to remember that, when manipulating an equation, a state of balance must be maintained.

Whatever is done to one side of an equation must be done equally to the other. Provided each side is treated equally, it is possible to add to, subtract from, multiply or divide any equation.

Example

Solve the equation $4y - 6 \quad = \quad 2$

Re-arrange the equation in order that the unknown (y) is on one side of the equation by itself.

1. Add 6 to each side of the equation

$$4y - 6 + 6 = 2 + 6$$
$$4y = 8$$

2. Divide both sides of the equation by the coefficient of y

$$\frac{4y}{4} = \frac{8}{4}$$
$$y = 2$$

There are quicker ways to solve an equation, but it is better to follow the logic presented; that is to say, maintain the balance of the equation.

8.b Linear equations with one unknown

A simple equation is sometimes referred to as a *linear equation;* that is, an equation of one dimension, an equation with one unknown.

Example 1

Solve the equation $\quad 3x + 4 - 6x \quad = \quad 12 - 4x$

Re-arrange the equation in order that the unknown (x) is on one side of the equation by itself.

1. In order to have only the unknown on the left side of the equation subtract 4 from both sides.

$$3x + 4 - 6x = 12 - 4x$$
$$3x - 4 + 4 - 6x = 12 - 4 - 4x$$
$$3x - 6x = 8 - 4x$$

2. In order to have all terms containing the unknown on one side of the equation, add the term 4x to both sides.

$$3x - 6x + 4x = 8 - 4x + 4x$$
$$x = 8$$

Example 2

Solve the linear equation

$$3(2x - 7) - 4(3x - 10) = x + 12$$

Re-arrange the equation in order that the unknown (x) is on one side of the equation by itself.

$$3(2x - 7) - 4(3x - 10) = x + 12$$

1. Remove the brackets by expansion

$$6x - 21 - 12x + 40 = x + 12$$

2. Add 21 and subtract 40 from both sides of the equation in order to have the unknown by itself on the left-hand side of the equation

$$6x - 21 + 21 - 12x + 40 - 40 = x + 12 + 21 - 40$$
$$6x - 12x = x - 7$$

3. Subtract x from both sides of the equation

$$6x - 12x - x = x - x - 7$$
$$-7x = -7$$

4. Divide both sides of the equation by -7

$$\frac{-7x}{-7} = \frac{-7}{-7}$$

$$x \quad = \quad \frac{7}{7}$$
$$x \quad = \quad 1$$

8.c Construction of equations from derived data

In order to construct solve simple equations complete the following stages:

1. For the unknown quantity, select a letter.

2. Each written statement in the question must be changed into an algebraic statement involving the selected letter.

3. Form an equation by joining the statements, while maintaining the same units throughout.

Example

The cost of wiring a house is estimated to be £500. The cost of each lighting point is £25 and that of each power point is £35. The total number of points provided is 18. Calculate the number of lighting points to be installed.

1. Let L be the number of lighting points.

2. The number of power points must equal $(18 - L)$.

3. The cost of L lighting points at £25 per point is £25L and the cost of $(18 - L)$ power points at £35 per point is £35 $(18 - L)$.

4. Link both statements in 3.

5. The same units have been maintained throughout:
$$25L + 35(18 - L) \quad = \quad 500$$
$$25L + 630 - 35L \quad = \quad 500$$
Subtract 630 from both sides of equation
$$-10L \quad = \quad -130$$
Divide both sides of the equation by -10
$$L \quad = \quad 13$$
The number of lighting points to be installed is 13.

8.d Simultaneous equations with two unknowns

Simultaneous equations, as the term suggests, are equations which are considered together; each equation contains two unknown variables. The values held by the two variables satisfy both equations simultaneously.

Simultaneous equations can be solved by two methods: the elimination of terms methods and the substitution of terms method.

Elimination method

Take two equations:
$$x + 3y = 9 \text{ and } x + 2y = 7$$

$$\text{Let } x + 3y = 9 \quad (1)$$
$$\text{Let } x + 2y = 7 \quad (2)$$

Subtract equation (1) from equation (2)

$$0 + y = 2$$
$$y = 2 \quad (3)$$

The result is the x terms are eliminated and the y terms reduced to y. The first stage of solving simultaneous equations is to eliminate one of the unknowns.

Substitute equation (3) into equation (1):

$$x + 3 \times 2 = 9$$
$$x + 6 = 9$$

Subtract 6 from both sides of the equation:

$$x + 6 - 6 = 9 - 6$$
$$x = 3$$

Check by substituting the values of x and y in either equation (1) or (2)

Substitution method

Take two equations

$$7a - 4b = 37 \text{ and } 6a + 3b = 51$$

$$7a - 4b = 37 \quad (1)$$
$$6a + 3b = 51 \quad (2)$$

The first stage is to multiply one or both of the equations by a number such that one of the variable terms in each of the equations is the same.

Consider the variable a

Multiply equation (1) by 6 and equation (2) by 7:

$$42a - 24b = 222 \quad (3)$$
$$42a + 21b = 357 \quad (4)$$

Subtract equation (4) from equation (3):

$$0 - 45b = -135$$

Multiply each side of the equation by –1:

$$45b = 135$$

Divide each side of the equation by 45:

$$b = 3$$

The solution is completed by substituting for b in one of the equations to find a.

Substitute in equation (2):

$$6a + 3 \times 3 = 51 \quad (5)$$

Subtract 9 from both sides of the equation (5):

$$6a = 42$$
$$a = 7$$

Substitute for a b in equation (1)

$$6a + 3b = 51$$
$$6 \times 7 + 3 \times 3 = 51$$
$$42 + 9 = 51$$
$$\text{Left-hand side} = \text{Right-hand side}$$

If one or both of the equations contains a fraction, the fraction should be eliminated, first by multiplying each term in the equation by the lowest common denominator (L.C.M.) for that equation.

9   Evaluate and transform formulae:

- substitution of given data
- transformation to change subject of formula
- algebraic expressions involving whole number indices, negative indices, fractional and decimal indices

9.a Substitution of given data

Evaluating a formula means finding the value of it according to the data supplied. It involves substituting the values of the known quantities for their symbols and completing the arithmetic calculations to obtain the value of the unknown quantity.

When evaluating any formula the following rules of precedence must be adhered to:

- brackets
- exponents (powers)
- division
- multiplication
- addition
- subtraction

Example 1

The power P watts of an electric circuit is given by the equation
$$P = V^2/R$$

Find P when
$$V = 14.8 \text{ volts and}$$
$$R = 19.5 \text{ ohms.}$$

Substitute the given values into the power equation
$$P = (14.8)^2/19.5$$
$$= 219/19.5$$
$$= 11.23 \text{ watts}$$

Example 2

Calculate the value of I in the formula $I = \dfrac{nE}{R + nr}$ correct to 3 decimal places, given that
$$n = 65$$
$$E = 4$$

$$
\begin{aligned}
R &= 3.0 \text{ and} \\
r &= 0.9 \\
I &= \frac{65 \times 4}{3.0 + (65 \times 0.9)} \\
&= \frac{260}{3 + 58.5} \\
&= \frac{260}{61.5} \\
&= 4.228 \\
I &= 4.228 \text{ correct to 3 decimal places}
\end{aligned}
$$

9.b Transformation to change subject of formula

A formula can be re-organised to make any variable in it the subject of that formula. This process of re-organisation is known as *transposition*.

A general guideline for moving the variable in a formula are:

1.   numbers

2.   constant value symbols

3.   letters in alphabetical order.

Example 1

In the formula $\frac{M}{I} = \frac{E}{R}$ make I the subject

Multiply both sides of the equation by I

$$
\frac{M}{I} \times I = \frac{E}{R} \times I
$$

Cancel I on left-hand side of equation

$$
M = \frac{E \times I}{R}
$$

Multiply both sides of the equation by $\frac{R}{E}$

$$
\frac{R}{E} \times M = \frac{R}{E} \times \frac{E}{R} \times I
$$

Cancel E and R on the left-hand side of equation

$$
\frac{R \times M}{E} = I \qquad \therefore I = \frac{RM}{E}
$$

Example 2

In the formula $I = \frac{E - e}{R + r}$ make r the subject.

Multiply both sides of the equation by $(R + r)$:

$$
I(R + r) = \frac{E - e}{(R + r)} \times (R + r)
$$

Cancel $(R + r)$ on the righ-hand side of the equation:

$$I(R + r) \quad = \quad E - e$$
$$IR + Ir \quad = \quad E - e$$

Subtract IR from both sides of the equation:

$$Ir \quad = \quad E - e - IR$$

Divide both sides of the equation by I:

$$r \quad = \quad \frac{E - e - IR}{I}$$

9.c Algebraic expressions involving whole number indices, negative indices, fractional and decimal indices

Example 1

Transpose the formula $I = \dfrac{2M}{d^3}$ and make d the subject.

Multiply both sides of the equation by d^3:

$$d^3 \times I = \quad 2M$$

Divide both sides of the equation by I

$$d^3 \quad = \quad \frac{2M}{I}$$

Take the cube-root of both sides of the equation:

$$d \quad = \quad 3\sqrt{\frac{2M}{I}}$$

Note: For example, the cube-root of 27 is 3.

Example 2

Transpose the formula $E = M / 2V^{-2}$ to make V the subject.
Multiply the right-hand side by V^2 / V^2
The V^{-2} and the V^2 in the right-hand side denominator cancel out:

$$E \quad = \quad \frac{M \times V^2}{2}$$

Multiply both sides of the equation by $\dfrac{2}{M}$:

$$\frac{2 \times E}{M} \quad = \quad \frac{M}{2} \times \frac{2}{M} \times V^2$$
$$= \quad V^2$$

Take the square-root of each side of the equation:

$$V \quad = \quad + \frac{\sqrt{2 \times E}}{M}$$

Note: For example, the square-root of 9 is 3.

Example 3

Transpose the formula $M = L\dfrac{(CL-1)\sqrt{X}}{27}$ and make X the subject.

Note: $\quad\quad\quad\quad\quad \sqrt{X} = X^{1_2} = X^{0.5}$

Maintain this term until the end of the transposition.

Multiply both sides of the equation by 27:

$$27 \times M = \frac{27 \times L(CL-1)\sqrt{X}}{27}$$

$$27M = L(CL-1)\sqrt{X}$$

Divide both sides of the equation by $L(CL-1)$:

$$\frac{27M}{L(CL-1)} = \frac{L(CL-1)}{L(CL-1)} \times \sqrt{X}$$

$$\frac{27M}{L(CL-1)} = \sqrt{X}$$

$$X = \left[\frac{27M}{[L(CL-1)]}\right]^2$$

10   Illustrate direct and inverse proportionality:

- dependent and independent variables
- coefficient of proportionality from given data
- applications of Boyle's Law, Charles' Law, Hooke's Law, Ohm's Law

10.a Dependent and independent variables

Consider the algebraic equation $Y = 3X + 1$. This is an equation in which two variables, Y and X, are related. The values 3 and 1 are constants.

A *variable in an equation* is a letter used to represent a quantity.

A number which has a fixed value is called a *constant*.

When working with equations of this form, it is usual to give a value to X and to calculate the corresponding value of Y.

The *Dependent Variable* in the given equation is Y, since it depends upon what value is given to X.

The *Independent Variable* in the given equation is X, its value is randomly chosen.

10.b Coefficient of proportionality from given data

Two quantities are *directly proportional* to each other when one quantity varies *directly* with the other; also, when corresponding pairs of the quantities are in the same ratio.

The ratio linking two such quantities is called the *constant* or *coefficient of proportionality*, represented by the symbol k. From a statement such as $P \propto Q$ that is P is proportional to Q,

an equation can be formed: $P = kQ$ where k is the coefficient of proportionality.

When two quantities are inversely proportional to each other, the product of any two pairs is a constant.

If a variable quantity P is inversely proportional to another variable quantity Q, then Q is inversely proportional to P.

$$P \propto \frac{1}{Q} \text{ or } P = \frac{k}{Q} \text{ where } k \text{ is the constant of proportionality.}$$

10.c Applications of Boyle's Law, Charles' Law, Hooke's Law, Ohm's Law

Boyle's Law states that for a given mass of gas at constant temperature, the pressure (p) is inversely proportional to the volume (v).

$$P \quad = \quad K.\frac{1}{V} \text{ or}$$

$$P.V \quad = \quad K \quad (\textbf{K} \text{ is a constant})$$

or

$$P_1 V_1 \quad = \quad P_2 V_2$$

where V_1 and V_2 are the volume of a certain mass of gas at pressures P_1 and P_2 respectively, at constant temperature.

Charles' Law states that for a fixed mass of gas, at constant pressure, the volume (v) is proportional to the temperature (t).

$$V \quad = \quad \text{a constant} \times T$$

or

$$\frac{V}{T} \quad = \quad \text{constant}$$

or $\qquad \dfrac{V_1}{T_1} \quad = \quad \dfrac{V_2}{T_2}$

Hooke's Law states that within the limit of elasticity the deformation of a material (e) is directly proportional to the force (L) producing it.

$$e \quad = \quad \text{a constant} \times L$$

or

$$\frac{e}{L} \quad = \quad \text{a constant.}$$

Ohm's Law states that the current (amps) passing through a wire is directly proportional to the potential difference (volts) between its ends.

$$I \quad = \quad \text{a constant} \times V$$

or

$$\frac{I}{V} \quad = \quad \text{a constant.}$$

11   Determine the equation of a straight-line graph:

- three or more points from co-ordinates of equation of form $y = mx + c$
- intercept with the y axis
- gradient of the straight-line graph

- positive, negative and zero gradients

11.a Three or more points from co-ordinates of equation of form y = mx + c

Consider the algebraic equation $Y = 3X + 1$. This is an equation in which there is a relationship between two variables Y and X.

Three simple values for X are taken and put in a table of values 1; 2; and 3, knowing that the value of Y is three times the value of X plus 1.

In the table, under each of the three values of X, *the value of 3X* is placed, and under each value of X the constant 1 is placed.

X	1	2	3
3X	3	6	9
1	1	1	1
Y	4	7	10

The value of Y for each value of X is the sum of the values of $3X$ and 1.

When a graph of an algebraic equation is to be drawn, the *dependent variable* (Y) is always plotted on the vertical axis and the *independent variable* (X) on the horizontal axis.

The graph can be plotted using the corresponding values of Y and X.

1. First, scales have to be chosen for the Y axis and the X axis.

2. Plot the three co-ordinates (1,4), (2,7), and (3,10).

3. Draw a straight line through the three points.

11.b Intercept with the y axis

The selected X and corresponding Y values in 11.a are given in a table:

X	1	2	3
Y	4	7	10

The graph which would result from plotting the table of values in 11.a can be related to its linear law in that the point where the graph intersects the Y axis is $X = 0$, corresponding to c in the generalised equation, $Y = mX + c$.

11.c Gradient of the straight line

The slope of the resulting graph in 11.a can be calculated using the formula

$$\text{Gradient} = \frac{Y_2 - Y_1}{X_2 - X_1}$$
$$= \frac{7 - 4}{2 - 1}$$
$$= 3$$

The gradient value of 3 corresponds with the m value in the general straight line law.

In the general straight line law $Y = mX + c$, m represents the gradient and c represents the Y intercept.

Example:
Find the slope and the intercept on the Y axis of the equation $2Y = 4X + 5$.
Convert the given equation to the general linear law form by dividing through by 2, the coefficient of Y.

$$Y = 2X + 2.5$$

The correct value for m, the slope, is 2, and for c, the intercept on the Y axis, is 2.5.

11.d Positive, negative and zero gradients

When a graph of an algebraic equation is to be plotted, the following conventions are used:

- Negative values of X are plotted to the left of the origin, and positive values are plotted to its right.
- Negative values of Y are plotted below the origin, and positive values are plotted above the origin.
- In a straight-line graph $Y = mX + c$ in which the coefficient of the independent variable m is positive, the slope of the graph is upwards from left to right. That is, by convention, it is a graph with a positive gradient.
- In a straight-line graph $Y = -mX + c$ in which the coefficient of the independent variable $-m$ is negative, the slope of the graph is downward from left to right. That is, by convention, it is a graph with a negative gradient.
- Consider the equation $Y=5$. Whatever the value of X, the value of Y is 5.
  The graph $Y=5$ is parallel to the X axis. It does not slope in any direction; it is called a graph of zero gradient.

C   Geometry and trigonometry

12   Calculate areas and volumes of plane figures and common solids using given formulae:

- area of triangle, square, rectangle, parallelogram, circle, semi-circle

12.a – Area of triangle, square, rectangle, parallelogram, circle, semi-circle

Area formulae

Triangle	=	$\frac{1}{2}$ × base × height
	=	$\frac{1}{2}$ × b × h
	=	$\frac{bh}{2}$
Square	=	length × breadth
	=	a × a
	=	a^2
Rectangle	=	length × breadth
	=	a × b
	=	ab
Parallelogram	=	length × perpendicular distance (c) between the parallel sides
	=	a × c
	=	ac
Circle	=	π × the square of the radius
	=	$\pi \times r^2 = \frac{\pi d^2}{4}$ where $r = \frac{diameter(d)}{2}$
Semi-circle	=	$\frac{1}{2}$ × area of a circle
	=	$\frac{1}{2}\pi\ r^2 = \frac{1}{2}\pi\frac{d^2}{4}$

Where π is the Greek leter (pi) which is approximately 3.142.

12.b – Volume of cubes, prisms, cylinders

Volume of cube

A cube is a three-dimensional object having sides of equal length.

Volume of a 1cm cube = 1cm × 1cm × 1cm   = 1cm^3

Volume of a prism

A prism is a three-dimensional object having a fixed cross-sectional area along its length.

Volume   =   cross-sectional area × length

Example

The volume of a block of wood length 12cm, width 10cm and thickness 5cm

= (10cm × 5cm) × 12cm
= 600cm^3

Volume of a cylinder

A cylinder is another form of prism where the cross-sectional area is a circle.

Volume   =   cross-sectional area × length

Example

The volume of a liquid container 12cm high and 7cm diameter:

$$= \left[3.1242 \times \frac{(7)^2}{4}\right] \times 12cm$$
$$= 462cm^3$$

12.c   *Surface areas of cubes, prisms, cylinders*

Surface area of a cube

A cube has six surfaces of equal area:

Surface area   =   6 × area of one face
                   =   6 × a^2 (where the length of one side is *a*)

Surface of a prism

A prism has a surface area made up of two surfaces of equal area, plus the area of the remaining surfaces.

The prism shown in the figure has a length of 12cm, a width of 10cm and a thickness of 5cm.

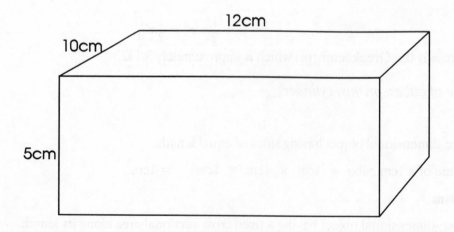

$$
\begin{aligned}
\text{Surface area} \quad &= \quad 2 \times \text{area of cross-section} + \text{area of other surfaces} \\
&= \quad (2 \times \text{surfaces of equal area}) + \text{other four surfaces} \\
&= \quad (2 \times \text{width} \times \text{thickness}) + \text{other four surfaces} \\
&= \quad (2 \times 10\text{cm} \times 5\text{cm}) + (2 \times 12\text{cm} \times 10\text{cm}) + (2 \times 12\text{cm} \times 5\text{cm}) \\
&= \quad 100 + 240 + 120 \\
&= \quad 460\text{cm}^2
\end{aligned}
$$

Surface area of a cylinder

A cylinder, as a type of prism, has a surface area made up of two surfaces of equal area plus the area of the remaining surface.

$$
\begin{aligned}
\text{Surface area} \quad &= \quad 2 \times \text{cross-sectional area} + \text{area of other surface} \\
&= \quad 2 \times \text{area of a circle} + (2\pi r)\ \text{circumference} \times \text{height} \\
&= \quad 2 \times 3.142 \times \text{radius}^2 + 3.142 \times (2 \times \text{radius}) \times \text{height}
\end{aligned}
$$

The cylinder considered above has a radius of 3.5cm and a height of 12cm. The surface area is:

$$
\begin{aligned}
&= \quad 2 \times 3.142 \times 3.5^2 \quad + 3.142 \times (2 \times 3.5) \times 12 \\
&= \quad \qquad 77 \qquad\qquad + \qquad 263 \\
&= \quad 340\text{cm}^2
\end{aligned}
$$

12.d   Proportionality

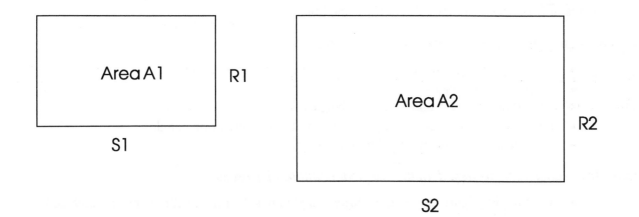

For similar figures:

$$\frac{S1}{R1} = \frac{S2}{R2}$$

Therefore $S1 \quad = \quad \frac{S2 \times R1}{R2}$ 1

Area $A1 \qquad = \qquad S1 \ \times \ R1$ and

Area $A2 \qquad = \qquad S2 \ \times \ R2$

Therefore $\frac{A1}{A2} \qquad = \qquad \frac{S1 \times R1}{S2 \times R2}$ 2

Substitute $S1$ from equation 1 into equation 2

$$\frac{A1}{A2} \quad = \quad \frac{S2 \times R1}{R2} \ \times \ \frac{R1}{S2 \times R2}$$

$$\frac{A1}{A2} \quad = \quad \frac{R1^2}{R2^2}$$

In the two figures the ratio of the areas is equal to the ratio of the square of their corresponding sides.

In similar fashion, it can be proved that the ratio of the volume of any two similar three-dimensional objects are equal to the ratio of the cube of their corresponding sides.

$$\frac{V1}{V2} \quad = \quad \frac{S1^3}{S2^3}$$

Where $V1$ and $V2$ are the volumes of the two similar objects concerned, and S1 and S2 are the lengths of two corresponding sides of the same object.

13   Recognise the types and properties of triangles:

- acute-angled, right-angled, obtuse-angled, equilateral, isosceles
- complementary angles
- Pythagoras – 3, 4, 5 and 5, 12, 13 triangles
- similarity or congruency – applications to find one side or one angle
- construction of triangle given limited information

13.a *Acute-angled, right-angled, obtuse-angled, equilateral, isosceles*

- A *triangle* is a figure enclosed by three straight lines. It contains three angles which add up to 180 degrees.
- An *acute-angled* triangle is one in which all angles are less than 90 degrees.
- A *right-angled* triangle is one in which one angle is equal to 90 degrees and the other two angles are less than 90 degrees.
- An *obtuse-angled* triangle is one in which one angle is greater than 90 degrees and the other two angles are less than 90 degrees.
- An *equilateral* triangle is one in which all angles are equal (e.g. all are equal to 60 degrees) and all sides are equal.
- An *isosceles* triangle is one in which two angles are equal and two sides are equal.

13.b Complementary angles

Any two angles whose *sum* is 90 degrees are *complementary angles*. Each angle is the complement of the other. In any right-angled triangle the two acute angles are complementary.

In a right-angled triangle, an acute angle of 25 degrees is complemented by an angle of 65 degrees.

13.c Pythagoras - 3, 4, 5 and 5, 12, 13 triangles

The Theorem of Pythagoras states that:

> *"In any right-angled triangle the square on the hypotenuse is equal to the sum of the squares on the other two sides."*

(The *hypotenuse* is the name given to the side of the right-triangle opposite to the 90 degrees, e.g. the longest side.)

In a triangle ABC, with sides AB, BC and CA, side BC is the hypotenuse, the side opposite the 90 degree angle. Let the length of the sides be $BC = a$, $CA = b$ and $AB = c$.

$$a^2 = b^2 + c^2$$

Example

Find the value of the hypotenuse of a triangle given that the other two sides have values of 3 and 4.

Using Pythagoras's Theorem:

$$
\begin{aligned}
a^2 &= b^2 + c^2 \\
&= (3)^2 + (4)^2 \\
&= 9 + 16 \\
&= 25
\end{aligned}
$$

Take the square-root of both sides of the equation

$$a = 5$$

Example

Find the value of the hypotenuse of a triangle given that the value of the other two sides are 5 and 12.

Using Pythagoras's Theorem:

$$
\begin{aligned}
a^2 &= b^2 + c^2 \\
&= (5)^2 + (12)^2 \\
&= 25 + 144 \\
&= 169
\end{aligned}
$$

Take the square-root of both sides of the equation

$$a = 13$$

13.d Similarity or congruency – applications to find one side or one angle

- Two triangles are *similar* if the angles of one are equal to the angles of the other. The corresponding sides of similar triangles are not equal, but they are all in the same proportion.

- Two triangles are *congruent* if they are identical in all respects, that is to say, the three angles and the three sides of one triangle are equal to the three angles and the three sides of the other triangle.

Similar Triangles

If two triangles *ABC* and *DEF* are similar, then the angle *A* must equal the angle *D*, angle B must equal angle *E* and angle *C* must equal angle *F*.

If *a*, *b*, *c*, *d*, *e*, and *f* are the sides of the triangles opposite the angles *A*, *B*, *C*, *D*, *E* and *F*

$$\frac{a}{d} = \frac{b}{e} = \frac{c}{f}$$

It is possible to find the lengths of unknown sides of similar triangles, if the lengths of some sides are known, also the ratio of the lengths of corresponding sides of the two triangles are known.

Example

If the sides of a triangle are in the ratio $1 : \sqrt{3} : 2$.
Find the length of the perimeter of the triangle, when the shortest side is 80 mm.
The sides of the triangle are in the ratio $1 : \sqrt{3} : 2$.

The smallest side is	=	80mm
The second shortest side	=	$80 \times \sqrt{3}$
	=	80×1.732
	=	138.6mm
The longest side	=	80×2
	=	160mm
The perimeter of the triangle is	=	80 + 138.6 + 160
	=	378.6mm

Congruent Triangles

To prove that triangles are congruent, it is necessary to prove that three angles or three sides are equal, but the three facts must be in one of the following.

1. Three sides of one must be equal to three sides of the other (SSS).

2. Two sides and the included angle of one must be the same as two sides and the included angle of the other (SAS).

3. Two angles of one are equal to two angles of the other, and one side of one is equal to the corresponding side of the other (ASA).

4. Two right-angled triangles are congruent if their hypotenuses are equal, and if one side of one is equal to the corresponding side of the other (RHS).

These are the only proofs of congruency.

13.e Construction of triangle given limited information

Triangles of any shape or size can be constructed accurately if the following data is known:

1. Three sides

2. Two sides and the included angle

3. One side and two angles

4. A right-angle, a hypotenuse and one other side.

14   Identify the geometric properties of a circle:

- radius, diameter, circumference, chord, tangent, secant, sector, segment, arc
- applications relating radius, circumference and diameter
- relationship of angles

14.a *Radius, diameter, circumference, chord, tangent, secant, sector, segment, arc*

1. A *circle* is a plane figure enclosed by a curved line; every point on the line is equidistant from a point called the *centre*.

2. The curved line which is the circle boundary is called the *circumference*.

3. The *radius* of a circle is any straight line joining the centre of the circle to any point on the circumference.

4. The *diameter* of a circle is any straight line passing through the centre of the circle joining any two points on the circumference.

5. A *chord* is a straight line joining two points on the circumference of a circle dividing it into two parts.

6. A *tangent* is a straight line which touches the circumference of a circle, in one place only.

7. A *secant* is a straight line which is drawn from a point outside a circle and cuts it in two places.

8. A *sector* is part of a circle bounded by two radii and the arc joining them. The larger sector is the *major* sector, the smaller sector is the *minor* sector.

9. The two parts into which a circle is divided by a chord are called *segments*. The larger segment is the *major* segment, the smaller segment is the *minor* segment.

10. An *arc* is part of the circumference of a circle.

14.b *Applications relating radius, circumference and diameter*

Diameter $= 2 \times$ *radius*

The ratio of a circle's circumference to its diameter, no matter its size, is equal to a constant value. The value of the constant is approximately 3.142. This constant has been given the symbol π to represent it. This is a Greek letter and is pronounced *pi*.

Where C is the circumference of a circle, and D is the diameter of the circle, the relationship between them is:

$$C = \pi D$$

or

$$= 2\pi R$$

That is, the circumference of a circle is equal to the product of π and the diameter of the circle.

The area of a circle of diameter D and radius R is given by the equation:

$$\text{Area } A = \pi \frac{D^2}{4}$$

or

$$= \pi R^2$$

The area of a circle is equal to the product of π and the diameter squared divided by 4, or the product of π and the radius squared.

14.c Relationship of angles

The following are goemetric theorems that identify the relationship of angles within the geometric properties of circles.

1.   The angle, which an arc of a circle subtends at the centre of a circle, is twice the angle which the same arc subtends at the circumference.

2.   Angles at the circumference of a circle and in the same segment are equal.

3.   The angle in a semi-circle is always a right-angle.

4.   The opposite angles of a cyclic quadrilateral are supplementary (they add up to 180 degrees).

5.   The external angle of a cyclic quadrilateral is equal to the interior opposite angle.

6.   A straight line drawn from the centre of a circle at right-angles to any chord, bisects it.

7.   The angle between a tangent and a chord drawn from the point of tangency is equal to the angle in the alternate segment.

1
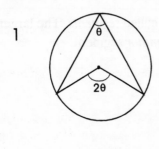

2
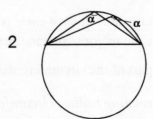

3
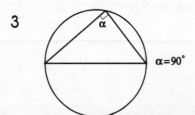

4
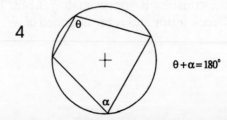

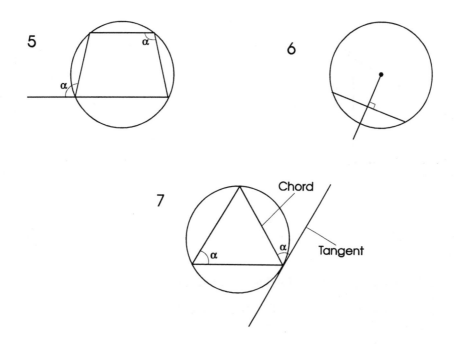

15   Solve right-angled triangles for angles and length of sides using sine, cosine and tangent functions:

- construction of right-angled triangles
- trigonometric functions
- use of tables or calculators
- standard triangles (60° 30° 90° and 45° 45° 90° trigonometric properties)
- trigonometric relationships [$\cos A = \sin (90 - A)$, $\sin A = \cos (90 - A)$]
- applications to technical problems

15a. Construction of right-angled triangles

Trigonometry is the branch of mathematics which deals with the relationship between the angles and sides of a triangle.

The triangles being considered are right-angled triangles and it is important to recognise that the techniques used apply only to right-angled triangles.

In a right-angled triangle, if the length of the lines are either increased or decreased but the angles are kept the same, the relationship between any two sides remains the same. Let triangle ABC be a right-angled triangle with the right-angle at B, angle A and angle C are both acute angles. The side AC, the side opposite the right-angle, is called the *hypotenuse*. The remaining sides are called the *opposite side* (the side opposite the angle being considered) and the *adjacent side* (the side adjacent or next to the angle being considered): which is which depends on the angle being considered.

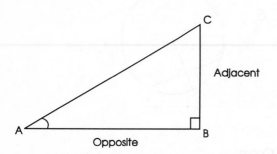

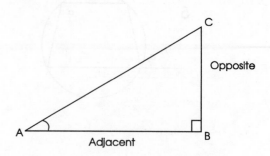

In the case of angle A, BC is the opposite and AB is the adjacent.

In the case of angle C, AB is the opposite and BC is the adjacent.

15.b Trigonometric functions

Consider the triangle ABC in (15.a).

1. The *sine* of an angle, in a right-angled triangle, is defined as the ratio of the opposite side divided by the hypotenuse.

$$\text{sine } A \quad = \quad \frac{Opposite}{Hypotenuse} \qquad \text{[SOH]}$$
$$= \quad \frac{BC}{AC}$$

2. The *cosine* of an angle, in a right-angled triangle, is defined as the ratio of the adjacent side divided by the hypotenuse.

$$\text{cosine } A \quad = \quad \frac{Adjacent}{Hypotenuse} \qquad \text{[CAH]}$$
$$= \quad \frac{AB}{AC}$$

3. The *tangent* of an angle, in the right-angled triangle, is defined as the ratio of the opposite side devided by the adjacent side.

$$\text{Tangent } A \quad = \quad \frac{Opposite}{Adjacent} \qquad \text{[TOA]}$$
$$= \quad \frac{BC}{AB}$$

(A mnemonic that will help you remember this is SOHCAHTOA).

15.c Use of tables or calculators

Any sine, cosine or tan value of an angle may be obtained from an appropriate calculator. For the detailed operation of a particular calculator, refer to its instruction leaflet.

In general:

1. Select mode DEG from choice of DEG, RAD and GRAD; that is use the angles measured in degrees.

2. Enter the angle value.

3. Press the appropriate SIN, COS or TAN key.

4. The calculator can be used to evaluate angle A by keying in the value of the gradient [Example 0.35] and then pressing either [INV][TAN] or [ARC][TAN]. Ensure that the calculator is in the degree mode. The answer is 19.28.

Tables of *natural tangents* may also be used to evaluate the angle A (gradient [0.35]). Three simple steps are involved in their usage.

Consider the table of natural tangents.

1. Find the nearest number below 0.35 in the main section of the table. This is 0.3482 in the third column.

2. Find in the same row the number in the mean difference columns which, when added to 0.3482, gives the nearest value to 0.35.

3. The answer is obtained from the row and column headings which coincide with these two figures.
   The answer is 19 degrees 12 minutes + 5 minutes
   $$= \quad 19 \text{ degrees } 17 \text{ minutes}$$
   $$= \quad 19.2833 \text{ degrees.}$$

This is similar to the answer obtained from the calculator. To evaluate sine and cosine ratios, a similar method is employed, but by using the appropriate natural sine and natural cosine tables. There is one important difference: when using the cosine tables, the mean difference must be *subtracted*.

15d. Standard triangles (60 30 90 and 45 45 90 trigonometric properties)

Consider an *equilateral triangle*, that is a triangle where each angle is 60 degrees and each side is 2 units long. The perpendicular height, that is, the length of the perpendicular line drawn from the peak of the triangle to its base,can be found, using the Theorem of Pythagoras.

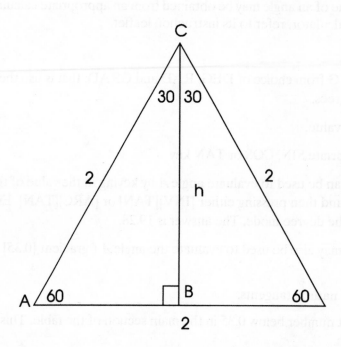

The perpendicular divides the equilateral triangle into two right-angled triangles.

Let the height of the triangle be h.

From Pythagoras, the square on the hypotenuse of a right-angled triangle is equal to the sum of the squares on the other two sides.

$$
\begin{aligned}
AC^2 &= AB^2 + BC^2 \\
2^2 &= 1^2 + BC^2 \\
4 &= 1 + BC^2 \\
BC &= \text{Square Root of 3} \\
&= \sqrt{3}
\end{aligned}
$$

In a 60 degree, 30 degree, 90 degree triangle, the length of the sides are in the ratio 2, 1, and $\sqrt{3}$.

From the diagram:

$$\sin 30 = \frac{opposite}{hypotenuse}$$

$$= \frac{AB}{AC}$$

$$= \frac{1}{2}$$

$$\sin 60 = \frac{opposite}{hypotenuse}$$

$$= \frac{BC}{AC}$$

$$= \frac{\sqrt{3}}{2}$$

$$\cos 30 = \frac{adjacent}{hypotenuse}$$

$$= \frac{BC}{AC}$$

$$= \frac{\sqrt{3}}{2}$$

$$\cos 60 = \frac{adjacent}{hypotenuse}$$

$$= \frac{AB}{AC}$$

$$= \frac{1}{2}$$

$$\tan 30 = \frac{opposite}{adjacent}$$

$$= \frac{AB}{BC}$$

$$= \frac{1}{\sqrt{3}}$$

$$\tan 60 = \frac{opposite}{adjacent}$$

$$= \frac{AB}{BC}$$

$$= \frac{\sqrt{3}}{1}$$

Consider an *isosceles right-angled triangle*. That is, a triangle where two angles are 45 degrees, and two sides are of equal length. Let the two equal sides be of one unit length.

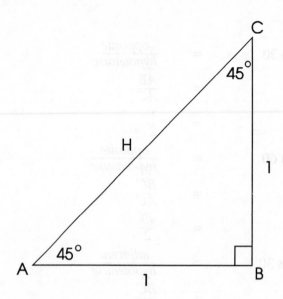

With the length of the two equal sides being one unit, the length of the hypotenuse can be calculated using the Theorem of Pythagoras.

$$
\begin{aligned}
H^2 &= 1^2 + 1^2 \\
&= 1 + 1 \\
&= 2 \\
H &= \sqrt{2}.
\end{aligned}
$$

That is, the length of the hypotenuse is the square-root of 2. In a 45 degree, 45 degree, 90 degree triangle the length of the sides are in the ratio 1, 1 and $\sqrt{2}$.

From the diagram:

$$
\begin{aligned}
\sin 45 &= \frac{opposite}{hypotenuse} \\
&= \frac{AB}{AC} \\
&= \frac{1}{\sqrt{2}}
\end{aligned}
$$

$$
\begin{aligned}
\cos 45 &= \frac{adjacent}{hypotenuse} \\
&= \frac{BC}{AC} \\
&= \frac{1}{\sqrt{2}}
\end{aligned}
$$

$$\tan 45 \quad = \quad \frac{opposite}{adjacent}$$

$$= \quad \frac{AB}{BC} \quad = 1$$

15.e Trigonometric relationships [cos A = sin(90-A), sin A = cos(90-A)]

Complementary Relationships

In any triangle the sum of the three angles is 180 degrees; in a right-angled triangle the sum of the other two angles is 90 degrees.

In 15.d, the ratio of sides for the 30, 60, and 90 degree triangles are stated.

On examination:

$$\sin 30 \quad = \quad \cos 60$$
and
$$\sin 60 \quad = \quad \cos 30$$

In any right-angled triangle:

$$\text{angle } A + \text{angle } B \quad = \quad 90 \text{ degrees}$$
$$\sin 30 \quad = \quad 0.5$$
and
$$\sin 60 \quad = \quad 0.8660$$
$$\cos 60 \quad = \quad 0.5$$
and
$$\cos 30 \quad = \quad 0.8660.$$

The sin of any angle is equal to the cosine of its complement.

$$\sin A \quad = \quad \cos (90 - A).$$

The cosine of any angle is equal to the sin of its complement.

$$\cos A \quad = \quad \sin (90 - A).$$

15.f Applications to technical problems

From the top of a cliff 140 m high, the angle of depression of the top and bottom of a lighthouse which is at sea level are observed to be 30 degrees and 36 degrees. Find the height of the lighthouse.

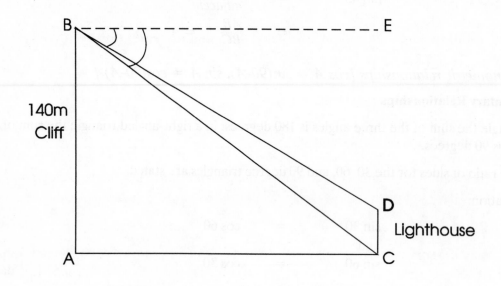

$$\tan 36 \quad = \quad \frac{CE}{BE}$$

Make *BE* the subject of the equation.
Multiply both sides of the equation by *BE*:

$$BE \times \tan 36 \quad = \quad \frac{CE}{BE} \times BE$$

$$BE \times \tan 36 \quad = \quad CE.$$

Divide both sides of the equation by tan 36:

$$BE \quad = \quad \frac{CE}{\tan 36} \qquad (1)$$

$$\text{Also} \quad \tan 30 \quad = \quad \frac{DE}{BE}$$

$$DE \quad = \quad BE \tan 30 \qquad (2)$$

The height of the lighthouse	=	DC
	=	CE − DE
	=	140 − DE (3)

Substitute equations (1) and (2) into (3):

Height of the light house	=	140 − DE
	=	140 − BE tan 30
	=	$140 - \left[\dfrac{CE \tan 30}{\tan 36}\right]$
	=	$140 - \left[\dfrac{140 \times 0.5774}{0.7265}\right]$
	=	140 − 111
Height of the light house	=	29m.

D Statistics

16 Collect, tabulate and summarise statistical data and interpret it descriptively:

- data collection
- discrete and continuous data
- sample and population
- range and density
- frequency and relative frequency
- tally counts
- pictorial presentation – bar charts, component bar charts, pie charts, pictograms
- histogram, frequency polygon, ogive-interpretation

16.a Data collection

Statistics is a scientific approach to the collecting, tabulation and summarising of data in order that it might be analysed so that an overall picture can be seen. The statistical analyses of numerical data enable conclusions to be drawn, from which reasonable decisions and predictions may be made.

Any numerical quantity which can be counted or measured is referred to as *data*.

- Counting
- Measuring
- Experimental results.

Example

In the construction of a vehicle with 20 component parts, the numbers of steel washers for each component part were as follows.
Raw data: 5, 4, 4, 7, 3, 5, 2, 2, 8, 5, 2, 6, 6, 1, 5, 6, 5, 3, 6, 5
This data can be re-arranged using a *tally chart*.

Washers	Tally	Frequency
1	/	1
2	///	3
3	//	2
4	//	2
5	//// /	6
6	////	4
7	/	1
8	/	1
Total		20

The left-hand column shows all the possible 'numbers of washers' recorded.
The middle column is the *tally column* which is ticked each time a 'number of washers' occurs.
The right-hand column is the *frequency column*; it shows the total number of times each

'number of washers' occurs.

The *total* is a check to show that every number of washers has been recorded.

16.b Discrete and continuous data

Discrete data is data where each separate quantity has an exact value.

In the example, the 'number of washers' was given as a whole number. No 'part-washers' were included. This is *discrete* data.

Continuous data is data which can be at any point within a range of values:
Data can be collected by measuring any value within a given range of values.
e.g. Accuracy of value depends on the measuring instrument.

Suppose the 20 steel washers were subjected to a dimensional check. Each washer would have its own dimensions recorded. If they were measured to the nearest thousandth of a metre, it is possible they would have sizes ranging between say 19.96 mm and 20.04 mm.

16.c Sample and population

When data is collected for analyses, the results will be correct only if information is collected from every person or situation which could possibly be included. Statistically this is called the *population*.

Where the total population can not be considered, information is collected from some of the people or situations.

A statistical *sample* is a selection of the total population which could possibly be included in a survey.

16.d Range and density

The following data was collected for an analysis; the total population of the survey was 150 people. They are grouped according to age.

Group Age Range in Years	Tally	Frequency
16/20	//// //// //// ///	15
21/25	//// ///	7
26/30	//// //// //// ///	15
31/35	//// //// ///	11
36/40	//// //// //// //// //// //// ////	28
41/45	//// //// //// //// //	18
46/50	//// //// //// ////	16
51/55	//// //// //// //// //// ////	24
56/50	//// //// //	10
61/65	//// //	6
Total		150

From the data, the lowest age is 16 years and the highest is 65 years. The *range* of values is 50 from 65 to 16 since the ages of 65 and 16 must both be included.

The range of values in each range group is known as the *class width* or *class interval*.

The *density* of the data is a measure of the *concentration* of the data.

16.e Frequency and relative frequency

Frequency is the number of times each value occurs and it is obtained from the tally chart.

The *relative frequency* is the relationship between the number of observations of data within a class compared to the total number of observations.

$$\text{Relative Frequency} \quad = \quad \frac{Class\ Frequency}{Total\ Frequency}$$

16.f Tally counts

A tally chart, often known as a *frequency distribution chart,* is one which records all the given data in a logical order, making it more meaningful. A mark is placed against each value every time it occurs (see 16.a).

16.g Pictorial presentation – bar charts, component bar charts, pie charts, pictograms

Bar charts, both horizontal and vertical, represent data by bars or strips; the length or height of the bars are proportional to the class frequencies.

*Pie chart*s or bar diagrams represent data by a circle. The circle is drawn and divided into slices Each slice represents and is proportional to the relative frequency percentage of one of the classes.

Component bar charts are similar to pie charts in that the total length of the bar represents the total number of observations. It is divided up such that each section represents the relative frequency of a class.

Pictograms are when small pictures of an object related to the data are shown in a line or a block. If one small picture represents a certain number of items, the group of pictures represent the total number.

16.h Histogram, frequency polygon, ogive-interpretation

Histograms consist of rectangles drawn vertically with their height representing class frequency and their width representing class intervals. The area of a rectangle is proportional to the number of observations within the class concerned. For equal class intervals the heights of the bars represent the different frequencies. The histogram represents a single variable and shows the general shape of the distribution.

Frequency polygons demonstrate the general shape of the frequency distribution. Frequencies are plotted vertically against their respective mid-point values. The points are then joined by straight lines to form a polygon. The area enclosed by the polygon is equal to the total frequency.

Ogive curves or *cumulative curves* show the cumulative frequencies (or percentage cumulative frequencies), of sets of data. Cumulative frequencies are plotted vertically against upper class boundary conditions.

Science

A Oxidation

1   **Establish through experiments, the basic chemical processes involved in burning and rusting as examples of chemical reactions (interactions between substances which result in a rearrangement of their atoms) and apply this knowledge to a variety of practical situations. Cover the following:**

- composition of air
- mass gain of metals such as copper, brass, iron and steel
- analysis of oxides
- effects of oxygen and water
- examples of damage caused by rusting
- preventative treatments.

1.a   Composition of air

Air is a mixture of gases. Its main constituents are nitrogen and oxygen in the ratio of 4 to 1. Together they make up 98% of air.

Because it contains oxygen, air can support combustion. Air exerts pressure on everything it comes into contact with (high pressure in a coal mine, low pressure in the mountains). Air, like all other gases, has weight.

1.b   Mass gain of metals such as copper, brass, iron and steel

Atoms are the smallest units of matter that can take part in a chemical reaction and which have all the properties of the element.

Molecules are the smallest parts of elements which can exist separately.

Molecules of an element are formed by the joining together of the element's atoms.

A *compound* is a substance in which the materials from which it is made are changed completely. It is the chemical combination of two or more elements.

A *mixture* is the result of two or more elements or compounds being mixed together. When elements such as copper, brass, iron and steel burn in air, they combine with its oxygen to form a new substance that is a *compound*.

The mass of the *compound* is greater than the mass of the element before heating occurred.

1.c   Analysis of oxides

An *oxide* is produced when an element forms a compound with oxygen. The process is called oxidation.

Not all oxides are the result of the burning process. For example, a scale is formed on iron when it is left out in the atmosphere; the scale is known as *rust*.

The chemical equation for this reaction is:

$$4Fe + 3O_2 > 2Fe_2O_3$$
4 iron atoms + 3 oxygen molecules > 2 molecules iron oxide
where *Fe* is the symbol for iron.

Steel is essentially an alloy of iron and carbon, containing approximately 2.0% carbon. The addition of elements, such as nickel and chromium, extends the steel's properties, including its resistance to corrosion.

1.d   Effects of oxygen and water

The action of air (oxygen) and water together on iron causes rust. Where there is rust there is *corrosion,* and the iron is slowly eaten away.

Rusting is an oxidation process where oxygen from the atmosphere combines with iron to form the compound iron oxide (red rust).

Other metals corrode and produce their own oxides:

Aluminium	forms a white powder.
Copper	forms a green rust called *verdigris.*
Zinc	forms a grey powder.

Metals which do not rust significantly under normal conditions include: silver, gold, platinum and nickel.

The corrosion process for some metals is speeded up when certain atmospheric conditions prevail.

1.e   Examples of damage caused by rusting

The cost to the nation of metal corrosion is enormous, adding up to thousands of millions of pounds annually. The rusting of iron and steel frameworks is a major problem. Structures, such as reinforced concrete buildings and bridges which can be weakened seriously by the eating away of the metal. In the case of reinforced concrete structures, the increase in volume caused by the rusting metal can cause structural failure.

Since the process of rusting is slow, silent and often invisible it is only when something happens that the hidden damage becomes apparent.

Examples of iron rusting can be seen on a wide range of objects, including car bodies, nails, bridges and ships.

1.f   Preventative treatments

Whatever the method of preventative treatment chosen, the purpose is the same: to stop the exposed surface of a metal being attacked by the combination of oxygen and moisture.

The most common preventative methods are: oil and grease; painting; plating; coating with metal or plastic; alloying with chromium.

Oil and *grease* protect machinery as well as preventing corrosion.

Painting reduces the effects of rust; the film of paint protecting the iron from air and water. Special paints, such as red lead and zinc chromate, are particularly useful. Large steel structures, such as the Firth of Forth railway bridge, are protected by continuous painting.

Coating with metal is practised extensively in the production of metal containers, where tin-plated steel is used.

Aluminium is *anodised;* that is, an aluminium oxide film is added to the skin of the metal surface.

Zinc plating *(galvanising)* is used as a protective surface on iron and steel.

Plastic is used as a coating to protect metal from corrosion. It is used on crates, refrigeration shelves, etc.

B Statics

2 Produce graphs from results obtained experimentally to determine the relationship between force and extension for different given materials and subsequently verify Hooke's Law relating to elasticity by solving practical problems

Elasticity is the ability of a material to return to its original shape and size, after the removal of an external force which had caused it to deform.

The *Elastic Range* for a material is the force range from zero to maximum, that can be applied to a material before it becomes overstretched; that is, before it exceeds its *elastic limit*

Hooke's Law states that: provided a material remains elastic, the extension produced in it is directly proportional to the applied load.

Example

What amount of extension will be produced in a steel wire subjected to a load of 1.25 kN, if the same wire stretches 0.5 mm when subjected to a load 250 N? Assume that it stays within the elastic range.

Extension, according to Hooke's Law, is proportional to the applied load.

Load W is proportional to extension X

Therefore $\qquad\qquad W = kX$

where k is a constant for a particular material

$$W = kX$$
$$250 = k \times 0.5$$
$$k = 500$$

When $\qquad W = 1.25\text{kN}$
$$= 1250\text{N}$$

and $\quad k = 500$
$$W = 500 \times X$$
$$X = \frac{1250}{500}$$
$$= 2.5 \text{ mm}$$

3 Establish the effect of a force rotating about a point and solve simple problems related to static equilibrium. Cover the following:

- co-planar forces

- scalar and vector quantities

- principle of moments

- centre of gravity

- use of calculation, practical and vector diagram techniques.

3.a   Co-planar forces

Co-planar forces are forces which are restricted to the same plane and can be represented by a two-dimensional drawing on a sheet of paper.

Consider a situation where a number of forces are acting at a point; they must act in the same plane if they are to be described as co-planar.

3.b   Scalar and Vector quantities

Scalar quantities can be described purely by a number; they are completely described when their *size* or *magnitude* is known.

Examples of *scalar* quantities are:

- area
- volume
- time

Vector quantities are only completely described when both their *magnitude* and *direction* are known.

Examples of *vector* quantities include:

- velocity
- force

Force as a vector quantity can be represented by a line drawn to scale, in a stated direction, with an arrow indicating the direction of the force.

Example

Two co-planar forces, *F* and *P* are acting at an angle to each other at a point *O*.

Let	F	=	40N
and	P	=	60N

What will be the total effect (the resultant force)?

	F	=	40N
	P	=	60N Scale: 1 mm to 1 N.

Starting at a point *O*, draw a line *Oa*, parallel to *P* and of the correct length (to scale).

Continuing from *a*, the end of the first vector, draw a line *ab* parallel to *F* and at the correct length (to scale).

Draw a line from *O* to *b*.

The line *Ob* represents the *resultant* force whose magnitude and direction can be found from the vector diagram.

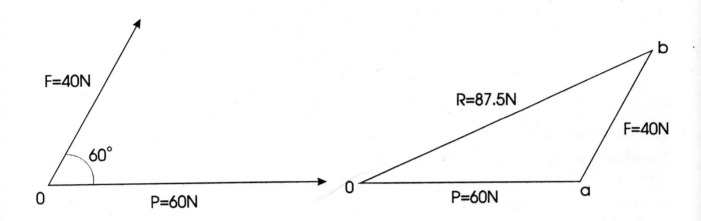

3.c Principle of Moments

The turning effect of a force is called its *moment.*

The moment of a force about a point is equal to the product of the force and the perpendicular distance from the point to the line of action of the force.

Examples are: opening a door; using a pair of pliers; adjusting a nut.

$$\text{Turning Moment} = \text{Force} \times \text{perpendicular distance}$$
$$= F \times d$$

The *Principle of Moments* states that, if an object is in equilibrium under the action of a number of forces, then the sum of the clockwise moments about any point must equal the sum of the counter clockwise moments about the same point.

Example

Calculate the force which has to be exerted at the end of a see-saw in order that a state of equilibrium can be maintained when a load of 70N is placed at the other end.
The length of the see-saw is 4.25m and the fulcrum is 2.5m from the 70N load.
For a state of equilibrium to exist, the clockwise moments about the fulcrum, O, must equal the counter clockwise moments about O.
Take moments about O:

$$\text{Clockwise moments} = \text{Force} \times \text{distance}$$
$$= 70n \times 2.5m$$
$$= 175Nm$$
$$\text{Counter clockwise moments} = \text{Force} \times \text{distance}$$
$$= F \times 1.75m$$
$$= 1.75 \times Fm$$

For equilibrium:

Clockwise moments	=	Counter clockwise moments
175Nm	=	1.75*Fm*
F	=	$\dfrac{175Nm}{1.75m}$
	=	100N

Thus, a force of 100N is required to maintain equilibrium.

3.d   Centre of Gravity

The *centre of gravity* of an object is that point at which the total mass or weight appears to act. It is the object's *point of balance*.

Some examples of the position of centre of gravity are:

Disc	Ring	Rectangular Sheet	Triangular Sheet
centre	centre	intersection of diagonals	intersection of median lines

If an object is suspended from a point in line with its centre of gravity, its weight will be supported in perfect balance.

3.e   Use of calculation, practical and vector diagram techniques

Example

A sheet of metal is cut into a shape equivalent to a combined rectangle and triangle. (see diagram below)
Using moments calculate the position of its centre of gravity .
The centre of gravity of rectangle *abcd* is at a distance of 50mm from the line *bc*; that is, it is at the mid-point of the rectangle.
The centre of gravity of the triangle is two-thirds from apex e along the meridian

	=	2/3 × 120
	=	80mm
Area of rectangle *abcd*	=	60 × 100
	=	6000mm^2
Area of triangle *bce*	=	1/2 × 60 × 120
	=	3600mm^2

If the weight of 1mm^2 of the sheet metal is *w*:

The weight of the rectangle *abcd*	=	6000*w*
The weight of the triangle *bce*	=	3600*w*

Let the distance of the centre of gravity for the whole sheet G be at a distance, X, from the centre of gravity of the rectangular section.

The distance from the centre of gravity of the rectangle to the centre of gravity of the triangle is

$$= \quad 50 + 40$$
$$= \quad 90\text{mm}$$

Take moments about G:

$$6000\text{w} \times X = 3600\text{w} \times (90 - X)$$
$$9600\text{w} \times X = 90 \times 3600\text{w}$$
$$X = 33.75\text{mm}$$

The centre of gravity is 33.75 mm from $G1$ along the line $G1.G2$.

Where G, is the centre of gravity of the rectangle, and G2 is the centre of gravity of the triangle.

4   Establish by experiments that fluid pressure at any level is equal in all directions, is normal to its containing surface, and is dependent on density and head of liquid

- definition of pressure
- absolute and gauge pressure
- measurement of pressure
- application to simple problems (including gas pressure)

4.a   Definition of pressure

Pressure is the effect of a force acting on an area.

$$\textit{Pressure} \quad = \quad \frac{\textit{Applied Force}}{\textit{Area}}$$

An applied force acting on a series of different areas, will produce a series of difference pressures.

The units of pressure are Newtons/m/m. (N/m^2)

A pressure of 1 N/m/m is a Pascal (Pa)
$$1 \text{ kilopascal} = 1000 \text{ Pa}$$
$$1 \text{ megapascal} = 1{,}000{,}000 \text{ Pa}$$

4.b   Absolute and gauge pressure

Gauge pressures are measured, as the name indicates, by a pressure gauge. These gauges are normally calibrated to indicate pressure above or below atmospheric pressure. Normal atmospheric pressure is 101325 N/m/m or Pascals above zero. When a pressure gauge reads zero, the actual or absolute pressure is 101325N/m/m, This is usually written as:

101·325 kN/m/m or 1·01325 bar.

Absolute pressure   =   Gauge pressure + 101·325 kN/m/m.

4.c   *Measurement of pressure*

The pressure beneath a column of fluid depends on the following parameters.

the *height* of the fluid column, referred to as the *head of liquid*
the *density* of the fluid (the greater the density, the greater the pressure)
the *pressure* acting at a point in a fluid is given by:

$$P \quad = \quad p \times g \times h$$

Where P	=	pressure in the fluid column	N/m/m or Pa
p	=	density of the fluid	kg/m/m/m
g	=	acceleration due to gravity	m/s/s
h	=	height of fluid column	m

Therefore, the pressure acting at any point in a fluid is proportional to the depth of the fluid at that point.

4.d   *Application to simple problems (including gas pressure)*

A *mercury barometer* records the height of a column of mercury in millimeters (mm), supported by atmospheric pressure.

A simple *manometer*, which is a U-tube device, records the gauge pressure of a gas by comparing it with the atmospheric pressure. This is done by comparing the levels of fluid in the two legs of the U-tube. The vertical difference in height between the levels of the fluid gives a measure of the difference in pressure. The manometer may also be used to measure negative pressure, or a partial vacuum, which may have been caused by the withdrawal of gas from a closed vessel.

C Motion and energy

5 Determine experimentally distance/time data (including average speed), plot distance/time graphs, determine gradients of such graphs and interpret the slopes as speeds, explaining why speed is a scalar quantity and velocity is a vector quantity.

Example

A train took 30 seconds to travel 900 metres. This can be shown on a distance/time graph by points marked with crosses.

Assuming that the train was travelling at constant speed, between two points, the points can be connected by a straight line to give a graph of distance against time. The graph shows the total distance travelled and the total time taken.

Two points A and B are chosen. Their coordinates are 30;500 and 10;250 respectively. From the triangle *ABC*, where the angle *C* is 90 degrees:

The speed (m/s) at which the train travelled between A and B $\quad = \quad \dfrac{distance\ (metres)}{time\ (seconds)}$

$$= \quad \frac{AC}{BC}$$

$$= \quad \frac{600}{20}$$

$$= \quad 30\text{m/s}$$

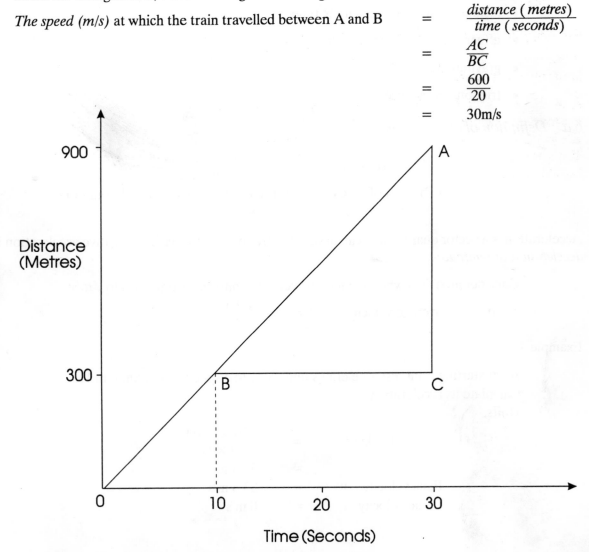

The *gradient* or *slope* of a distance time graph represents the speed or velocity of the object.

$$\text{Gradient} = \frac{vertical\ measurement}{horizontal\ measurement}$$

$$= \frac{distance\ (metres)}{time\ (seconds)}$$

$$= speed \text{ or } velocity$$

Speed – rate of change of distance; magnitude only is a *scalar* quantity.
Velocity – rate of change of distance; travelled in a *given direction* is a *vector* qunatity.

6   Construct velocity/time graphs from given data, calculate the gradient, interpret the slope as acceleration and solve simple problems using graphical and calculation techniques

- definition of acceleration
- distance = average velocity × time
- effect of force on acceleration
- gravitational force
- frictional resistance

6.a   Definition of acceleration

$$\text{Acceleration} = \frac{Change\ of\ velocity}{time\ taken}$$

(The unit of acceleration is the metre/second squared or m/s/s)

$$a = ms^{-2}$$

Acceleration is a vector quantity and can have a positive or negative value. Negative acceleration is called *deceleration* or *retardation*.

Consider an object which changes its velocity uniformly from u m/s to v m/s:

Then   average velocity $= \dfrac{u + v}{2}$

Example 1

A car starting from rest accelerates uniformly to a speed of 120 km/h in 15s.
Calculate its acceleration.
Units:

$$120 \text{ km/h} = \frac{120 \times 1000}{60 \times 60}$$

$$= 33.3 \text{ m/s}$$

Final velocity v $=$ 33.3 m/s
Initial velocity u $=$ 0 m/s

Time taken	t	$=$	15.0 s
Acceleration	a	$=$	$\dfrac{\textit{Final velocity} - \textit{initial velocity}}{\textit{Time}}$
		$=$	$\dfrac{v-u}{t}$
		$=$	$\dfrac{33.3-0}{15}$
		$=$	2.22m/s/s

Example 2

A vehicle increases its velocity from 5 m/s to 15 m/s uniformly, in 25 seconds.
Find (a) the distance it travelled and (b) its acceleration.

Distance travelled	$=$	average velocity $\times$ time (m/s $\times$ s)
	$=$	$\dfrac{(u+v)}{2} \times t$
	$=$	$\dfrac{(5+15)}{2} \times 25$
	$=$	250m
Acceleration	$=$	$\dfrac{(v-u)}{t}$
	$=$	$\dfrac{(15-5)}{25}$
	$=$	$\dfrac{10}{25}$
	$=$	0.4 m/s/s

6.b *Distance = average velocity × time*

Velocity time graphs

A velocity-time graph shows the relationship between Velocity and Time and can be used to solve problems involving moving objects.

Note:

(a)   Velocity time diagrams always have velocity plotted vertically

(b)   Select suitable scalesfor the axes.

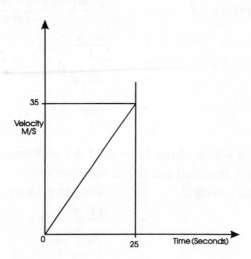

Example

A cyclist is freewheeling down a slope from rest and reaches a speed of 35 m/s after 25 s. If the acceleration is uniform, draw a velocity time graph to illustrate this motion, and find the distance travelled after 25 s.

Units:

$$
\begin{aligned}
v &= 35 \text{ m/s} \\
u &= 0 \text{ m/s} \\
t &= 25s \\
a &= ?\text{m/s/s}
\end{aligned}
$$

Scales:

Horizontal	Time	from 0 to 25
Vertical	Velocity	from 0 to 35

$$
\begin{aligned}
\text{Distance travelled, } s &= \text{average velocity} \times \text{time} \\
&= \frac{(0 + 35)}{2} \times 25 \\
&= 437.5\text{m}
\end{aligned}
$$

Constant Velocity, v

This graph is of constant velocity, v over time period, t.
The gradient is zero flat), since acceleration is nil.
Acceleration = zero
Distance travelled is given by area under graph
so $s = v \times t$

Uniform Acceleration From Rest

This graph shows uniform acceleration from rest to velocity, v over time period, t.
The gradient is constant; that is, the acceleration is uniform.
Distance travelled is equal to area under graph
so $s = 1/2\, vt$

Uniform Retardation to Rest	*Uniform Acceleration from Velocity u to Velocity, v,*
This is a graph of uniform retardation from velocity, v, to rest. The gradient is constant and negative; Distance travelled is found from area under the graph $$s = 1/2vt$$	This is a graph of uniformly accelerated motion. For initial velocity, u, and final velocity, v, with uniform acceleration, a, the gradient is constant and positive. Distance travelled is given by area under the graph $$s = ut + 1/2at^2$$

6.c   *Effect of force on acceleration*

Newton's Laws of Motion

1. An object will continue in its state of rest or uniform motion in a straight line unless acted upon by an external force.

2. The rate of change of momentum of an object is directly proportional to the applied external force and is in the same direction as the force (momentum = mass × velocity)

3. To every action there is an equal and opposite reaction.

Notes:

1. The first law says that under the action of a force, the object will tend to accelerate or decelerate.

2. The second law says that there is a relationship between the change of momentum of an object and the applied force.

   Change of momentum = final momentum − initial momentum

   Let m = object mass m (kg)

   Let v = final velocity (m/s)

   Let u = initial velocity (m/s)

   Let t = time (sec)

   Let F = force (N)

   Change of momentum = $mv - mu$

   Rate of change of momentum = $\dfrac{Change\ of\ velocity}{time\ taken}$

   $= \dfrac{mv - mu}{t}$

   $= \dfrac{m(v - u)}{t}$

   But acceleration a = $\dfrac{change\ of\ velocity}{time\ taken\ for\ change}$

   Rate of change of momentum = $m \times a$

According to the second law, force is directly proportional to the rate of change of momentum.

$$F \text{ is proportional to } m \times a;$$

therefore,
$$F = ma \times \text{constant}$$

The constant equals '1' if a force of 1 unit acts on a mass of 1 unit to produce an acceleration of 1 unit.

The SI unit of force is the *Newton*, which is the force necessary to give a mass of 1 kilogram an acceleration of 1 metre per second squared.

Example

An object of mass 350 kg is accelerated at 15 m/s/s.
What is the force being applied to the object?

Force	=	mass × acceleration
	=	350kg × 15 m/s/s
	=	5250 kgm/s/s
1 Newton	=	1 kg m /s/s
Force	=	5250N
	=	5.250 kN

6.d   Gravitational force

At any point on the earth's surface, the acceleration in free fall is a constant. It is denoted by the symbol, g, and it has the value of 9.81 m/s/s.

The force which causes this acceleration always acts toward the centre of the earth, and is called the *weight*.

Weight is the gravitational force exerted by every object which has mass.

Weight =		mass × gravitational acceleration
Gravity Force =		mass × acceleration due to gravity
where m	=	mass in kg
where g	=	9.81 m/s/s

Example

An object is dropped down a pot-hole. If it takes 4.0 seconds. for the object to hit water, calculate in metres the depth of the hole to the water level, and the velocity of the object on impact.

v	=	$u + gt$
u	=	0m/s
g	=	9.81 m/s/s
t	=	4.0s
v	=	0 + (9.81 x 4.0)
	=	39.24 m/s
Distance travelled, s	=	average velocity × time

$$= \frac{(u + v)}{2} \times 4.0$$

$$s \qquad = \frac{(0 + 39.24)}{2} \times 4.0$$

The depth of the pot-hole is 78.48 metres and the velocity of the object on impact is 39.24 metres per second.

6.e *Frictional resistance*

When the surfaces of two objects are brought into contact and one of the objects is made to slide over the other, a resistance to movement is experienced. This resistance to motion is known as *friction* and the force necessary to overcome the resistance is called the *frictional force*.

The larger the mass of the object, the greater the force necessary to overcome the friction of the object and the resting surface.

Therefore, there is a relationship between the frictional force and the weight of the object. Let N be the normal upward reaction force applied by the resting surface, N, it is equal and opposite to the weight, W.

The frictional force is directly proportional to the normal reaction.

F is proportional to N

| The Frictional force | F | = | Normal reaction $\times$ constant |
| | F | = | $N \times$ a constant |

The constant is called the *coefficient of friction,* and is given the symbol μ,(pronounced *mu).*

$$F \qquad = \qquad N \times \mu$$

Example

What would be the force required to overcome friction for a 32 kg object, if the coefficient of friction between the object and the resting surface is 0.3?

N the normal reaction	=	$m \times g$
	=	32×9.81
	=	$313.9N$
μ the coefficient of friction	=	0.3
Friction force	=	$\mu \times N$
	=	0.3×313.9
	=	$94.18N$

Here, the force required is 94.18 N

7 Describe wave motion and solve problems involving wave velocity

- wavelength
- frequency
- $v = f\lambda$

7.a   Wavelength

Waves are the result of some form of disturbance or vibration. They contain energy which they transfer from one location to another.

Wave motion enables energy to be transferred through a medium, without the medium being transferred.

Wave Forms

There are two types of waves:

- transverse waves
- longitudinal waves.

Transverse waves are created by a displacement or vibration at 'right angles' to the direction in which the wave is travelling.

An example of transverse waves is when a length of rope, lying on a flat surface, is given a quick upward motion at one end. A wave is created along its length. The rope itself does not move forward. It is the wave which moves.

Longitudinal waves are waves which are formed in the same direction as the vibration.

An example of longitudal waves is when a spring is stretched along its length and then released. The spring will vibrate longitudinally, since its energy passes in the direction in which the force is applied.

Waveform Characteristics

1. The top of the wave form is the *peak*.

2. The bottom of the waveform is the *trough*.

3. The *amplitude* (symbol a) of the waveform is the vertical distance between the crest/the trough and the mean line.

4. The *wave length* (symbol λ)of the wave form is the distance between two similar points on adjacent waves of the waveform.

5. One complete waveform is called a *cycle* (*peak-peak*).

6. One complete vibration is called an *oscillation* (*peak- trough*).

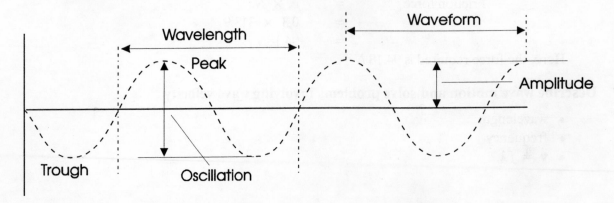

1ST DIP (B). 30/3/95.

7.b   Frequency

The number of complete vibrations or oscillations made per second is called the *frequency* (symbol f).

Example

If 8 waves pass a point in one second, what is the frequency of the wave?
The frequency is 8 waves per second   =   8/sec
The SI unit of frequency is the hertz, (Hz). One hertz is equal to one cycle, or oscillation, per second.

$$\text{Frequency} \quad = \quad 1\text{ Hz}$$
$$= \quad 1\text{ cycle per second}$$
$$= \quad 1/\text{sec}$$

A wave with a frequency of three Hz means that 3 complete waveforms are generated in one second.

$$1 \text{ kilohertz (kHz)} \quad = \quad 10^3 \text{ Hz}$$
$$1 \text{ megahertz (MHz)} \quad = \quad 10^6 \text{ Hz}$$

(Radio frequencies are measured in kHz or MHz.)

Low frequency vibrations produce low-pitched sounds.

High frequency vibrations produce high-pitched sounds.

This is demonstrated best by the range of sounds in musical instruments, each of which is designed to produce its own particular sound.

7.c $v = f\lambda$

The velocity of a wave is dependent on:

- the *distance* the wave travels
- the *time taken* to cover that distance.

The *frequency* is the number of times the wave is repeated per second. If f waves pass any point in one second, then the frequency is f waves per second.

If the wavelength is λm and the frequency of the wave is f waves per second, then the wave has a velocity of $f\lambda$ m/s.

Therefore v = $f\lambda$ m/s

Units: Velocity (m/s) =   frequency (Hz) × wavelength (metres)

Example 1

A sound wave has a frequency of 100 Hz and a wavelength of 3.125 m. What is the speed of the sound in air?

$$f \quad = \quad 100 \text{ Hz}$$
$$\lambda \quad = \quad 3.125\text{m}$$

$$v \quad = \quad f \times \lambda$$
$$= \quad 100 \times 3.125 \text{m/s}$$
$$= \quad 312.5 \text{ m/s}$$

The time taken for one complete cycle is called the Periodic Time of the waveform.

Note:

Periodic Time, *T*, of a waveform is the reciprocal of Frequency.

$$\text{Periodic Time} \quad = \quad \frac{1}{\text{frequency}}$$
$$T \quad = \quad \frac{1}{f}$$

Example 2

A wave completes 50 cycles in 0.5 s. Determin the frequency and periodic time.

(a) f $= \quad$ 50 cycles ÷ 0.5 sec.
$$= \quad 100 \text{ cycles/sec}$$
$$= \quad 100 \text{Hz}$$

(b) T $= \quad \frac{1}{f}$
$$= \quad \frac{1}{100}$$
$$= \quad 0.01 \text{s}$$

8   Carry out tests and solve problems associated with energy

Cover the following:

- work in terms of force applied and distance moved
- graphs
- identification of forms of energy
- efficiency in terms of energy input and output
- power

8.a   *Work in terms of force applied and distance moved*

Calculating Work Done

Work is done when force is applied to an object, causing it to move through a distance.

The amount of work done depends on two things:

1.   the *size of the force* being applied

2.   the *distance* the object moves

To calculate the amount of work done, multiply the value of the applied force by the distance travelled.

The applied force is in newtons N
The distance is in metres m
Work done on an object   =   force applied x distance moved

Example 1

A force of 25N is required to move an object through a distance of 20 m. What is the work done?

Force   = $25N$
Distance moved   =   20m
Work done   =   force applied ö distance moved
   =   25 × 20
   =   500Nm

The units for work done are Newton metres (Nm). In the SI system of units the name given for a Newton metre is the *Joule* which has the symbol, J.

1 Newton metre is equal to 1 joule
1Nm   =   1J
1000Nm   =   1KJ (kilojoule)
1,000,000Nm   =   1MJ (megajoule)

Example 2

How much work is done if a mass of 18 kg is lifted through a vertical height of 10 m?
Solution:

Work done   =   applied force × distance moved
Work done   = $F × d$

Note: First you must calculate the value of F, the Force required to lift the 18 kg mass.

Force   =   mass × acceleration
Gravitational Force   =   mass × acceleration due to gravity
Therefore F =   mass × 9.81
F =   18 × 9.81
   =   176.6N

Now consider the work done, WD, in vertically lifting the 18kg mass through a height of 10 m;

If F =   176.6N
and   ds   =   10m
WD   =   176.6 × 10
   =   1766Nm
   =   1766 joules

8.b   Graphs

Work diagrams

You can represent work done on an object by a diagram, once you know the applied force and the distance moved in the direction of the force.

Example 1

Draw a work diagram for a constant force of 33N applied to an object and moving through a distance of 30m.

Note: It is normal in all work diagrams to plot the applied force vertically and the distance moved horizontally.

$$
\begin{aligned}
\text{Work done} &= \text{force} \times \text{distance} \\
\text{Work done} &= F \times d \\
&= 33 \times 30 \text{Nm} \\
&= 990 \text{Nm}
\end{aligned}
$$

The diagram is a rectangle, representing 33N force by 30m moved, with an area of 33N × 30m   =   990Nm

This is the same result as achieved by using the formula:

$$
\text{Work done} = F \times d
$$

Therefore, the area under a force distance graph represents the work done by the force.

Example 2

A shaping machine has a stroke of 750 mm. At the beginning of the stroke the resistance to cutting is 450N, and this rises uniformly to 1.0kN when the cutting tool has moved a distance of 600 mm. The resistance remains at 1.0kN for the remainder of the stroke. Draw the force distance diagram, and from it find the total work done during one stroke.

Scale: The units for work done are Newton metres or joules.

Note: (The mm in the example must be converted to metres).

Divide the area under the graph into three areas A,B,C,

To find the work done determine the area under the graph.

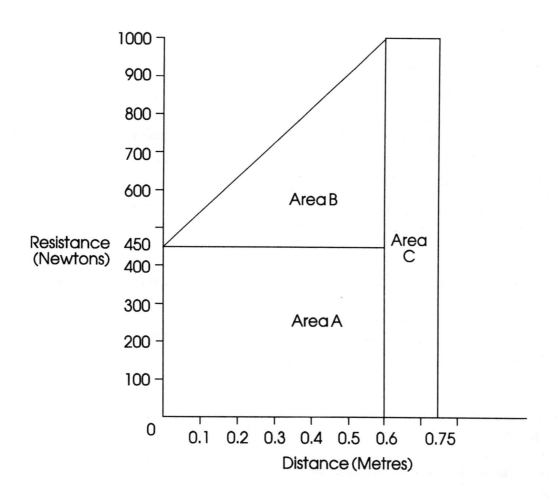

Work done	=	Area *A* + Area *B* + Area *C*	
	=	Rectangle + triangle + rectangle	
Area *A*	=	Base × Height	(rectangle)
	=	0.6m × 450N	
	=	270Nm	
Area *B*	=	½ Base × Height	(triangle)
	=	½ x 0.6 × (1000 − 450)	
	=	0.3 × 550	
	=	165Nm	
Area *C*	=	Base × Height	(rectangle)
	=	(0.75 − 0.60) × 1000	
	=	0.15 × 1000	
	=	150 Nm	
Total Area	=	Total Work Done	
	=	Area *A* + Area *B* + Area *C*	

$$= \quad 270 + 165 + 150$$
$$= \quad 585 \text{ Nm}$$
$$= \quad 585 \text{ J}$$

The total work done $= \quad 585$ joules

8.c   Identification of forms of energy

Energy is the capacity to do work; its unit of measurement is the *joule*, J.
Potential energy is energy which is potentially available, stored up and awaiting release. The abbreviation is PE

Kinetic energy is the energy due to motion; it is represented by the abbreviation KE

1.   *Potential energy* has a variety of forms, including chemical and nuclear. When work is done on an object in overcoming its weight, this work is stored as PE (gravity).

Example

A steel forging with a mass of 25kg is raised to a height of 3m. How much work has been done, and how much potential energy is stored in the forging?

m is the forging mass in kg.

g is the acceleration due to gravity is 9.81m/s/s.

$$F \quad = \quad m \times g$$
$$= \quad 25 \times 9.81$$
$$= \quad 245.25\text{N}$$

Work done on the forging $= \quad$ force $\times$ vertical distance moved
$$= \quad 245.25 \times 3\text{m}$$
$$= \quad 735.75\text{Nm or } 735.75\text{J}$$

The forging has stored-up *potential energy* of 735.75J.

2.   *Kinetic energy* is the energy which an object has because of its motion.
Suppose the steel forging mentioned, above with its stored energy of 735.75J fell, and hit the floor. At the moment of impact the forging is moving and has *kinetic energy*.
Potential energy has been converted into *kinetic energy*.
At the mid-point of the fall, the forging still has half of its initial stored energy, as *potential energy*. The remainder has been converted to *kinetic energy*.

3.   *Chemical energy* .
Food which is eaten contains chemical energy. This energy is converted into heat to keep the body fit and healthy. Coal, oil and gas release their chemical energies when they burn: energy is given out as heat.

Note: When friction brake pads rub on the brake drums, heat is produced. Heat energy from the sun can be harnessed using solar panels.

5.   *Electrical energy*
Electrical energy is produced in a variety of ways; normally, using an electrical

generating station where naturally occurring energy is passed through a range of production processes.

Stage 1 Chemical energy (coal) or nuclear energy
Stage 2 Heat energy (combustion)
Stage 3 Steam (water boiler)
Stage 4 Mechanical energy (turbine)
Stage 5 Electrical energy.

6. *Nuclear energy*
Nuclear power stations utilise nuclear energy which is converted to heat energy (under controlled conditions). This is then converted to mechanical energy and subsequently into electrical energy. Nuclear energy is potential energy stored in the nuclei of atoms of (uranium)

Energy Conversion

The Law of Conservation of Energy states:

Energy cannot be created nor destroyed; it can only be changed in form.

8.d   Efficiency in terms of energy input and output

When energy is changed from one form to another, there is always a loss of energy, due to *friction*.

When energy is used in driving a machine, some of it is lost in the form of heat. This can be a high proportion of the energy input.

Even in high efficiency machines, such as electric motors, some energy is lost.

No machine is 100% efficient!

$$Energy\ Output\ =\ Energy\ Input\ -\ Energy\ lost\ in\ overcoming\ resistances$$

By comparing the useful energy produced by a machine with the energy put into driving it, the machine's efficiency can be calculated.

$$Efficiency\ =\ \frac{Energy\ Output}{Energy\ Input}$$

$$Efficiency\ (\%)\ =\ \frac{Energy\ Output}{Energy\ Input}\ \times\ 100\%$$

Example

How much work is done when a force of 100 N moves an object 15 m in the direction of the applied force? If the force is provided by a machine having an input of 4.0 kJ, how efficient is the machine?

The work done by the machine   =   force × distance
                                  =   100N × 15m
                                  =   1500J

$$= \quad 1.5\text{kJ}$$

$$\textit{Efficiency \%} \quad = \quad \frac{\textit{energy input}}{\textit{energy output}} \times 100 \%$$

$$= \quad \frac{1.5}{4.0} \times 100\%$$

$$= \quad 37.5\%$$

8.e   Power

Power is energy under control. Power is the rate of doing work.

$$\textit{Power} \quad = \quad \frac{\textit{Work done}}{\textit{Time taken}}$$

The SI unit for measuring power is the *Watt*. It is represented by the symbol, W

$$1 \textit{ watt} \quad = \quad 1\frac{\textit{joule}}{\textit{second}}$$

$$= \quad 1\frac{\textit{newton metre}}{\textit{second}}$$

NOTE: When solving problems concerning power, use SI units of force, Newtons, and measure distance moved in metres and time taken in seconds.

Example 1

A force of 450 N is applied to an object, moving it smoothly through a distance of 30 m in a time of 2.5 minutes.

Calculate the work done in kJ and the power used in watts.

(Force=450 N; distance=30 m; time=150 s)

Work done	=	force × distance
	=	450N × 30m
	=	1350Nm
	=	1.35kJ
Power	=	$\dfrac{\textit{work done}}{\textit{time taken}}$
Work Done	=	1.35kJ
	=	1.35 × 1000J
Time taken	=	2.5mins
	=	150s
Power	=	$\dfrac{1.35 \times 1000}{150} \dfrac{J}{s}$
	=	9.0J/s
	=	9.0W

Example 2

An object moves at a constant speed of 10 m/s when subjected to force of 250N. Calculate the power (Force = 250 N; distance = 10 m in time 1 s.)

$$\text{Power} = \frac{\textit{work done}}{\textit{time taken}}$$

$$= \frac{\textit{force} \times \textit{distance}}{\textit{time}}$$

$$= \text{force} \times \text{speed}$$

Therefore, Power

$$= 250\text{N} \times 10\text{m/s}$$
$$= 2500\text{J/s}$$
$$= 2500\text{W}$$

9 **Solve problems associated with mass, specific heat capacity and temperature change, showing how materials expand or contract with temperature change, and illustrate positive and negative effects in practical situations. Cover the following:**

- temperature/time graphs for change of state
- sensible and latent heat
- coefficient of linear expansion
- single and composite materials

9.a *Temperature/time graphs for change of state*

Transfer of heat energy

The quantity of heat energy 'retained' by an object depends upon:

- its mass
- its temperature
- the nature of the material.

The quantity of heat Q is proportional to ($m \times dt$.)

Where

Q is the quantity of heat
m is the mass of the material
dt is the temperature range
$Q = m \times dt \times \text{constant}$
The value of the constant depends on the material

Specific heat capacity is the amount of heat energy needed to raise the temperature of 1Kg of a substance by 1 degree Celsius ($^{\circ}$C).

The specific heat capacity is denoted by c.

$$Q = m \times c \times dt$$

Where the units are:

Q is the quantity of heat energy in   kJ
m is the mass of material in   kg
c is the specific heat capacity of the material in   kJ/kg $^{\circ}$C
dt is is the temperature range in $^{\circ}$C

Example 1

Calculate the quantity of heat energy required to raise the temperature of 15kg of steel from 30°C to 900°C if the specific heat capacity of steel is 0.5 kJ/kg$^{\circ}$ C.

$$
\begin{aligned}
Q &= m \times c \times dt \\
&= 15 \times 0.5 \times \text{(range of temperature)} \\
&= 15 \times 0.5 \times (900 - 30) \\
&= 7.5 \times 870 \\
\text{Heat energy} &= 6525 \text{ kJ}
\end{aligned}
$$

Changes of State

Many substances can exist in three states: Solid – Liquid – Gas.

Changes of state, from solid to liquid to gas, are reversible.

When Naphthalene for example, is heated to a liquid state and allowed to cool. At a stage in the cooling, when the naphthalene changes its state from liquid to solid, there is a period of time in which no temperature change is observed. This is the *solidification* point of the naphthalene. It is also the *melting* point of the naphthalene.

Stage A.   Heat gained by the solid naphthalene to raise it to the melting point produces a rise in temperature.

Stage B.   Heat gained by the naphthalene to cause it to change state from solid to liquid is not associated with a change in temperature.

Stage C.   Heat gained by the liquid naphthalene is shown by a rise in temperature.

9.b   Sensible and latent heat

When heat energy is supplied to a substance and causes a rise in temperature, it is called *sensible heat*.

When heat energy is supplied to produce a change of state at constant temperature, it is called *latent heat*.

Two changes of state are possible:

(a)   solid to liquid – known as *fusion* (or melting)

(b)   liquid to gas – known as *evaporation* (or vaporisation).

The *Specific Latent Heat of Fusion* of a substance is the amount of heat energy required to change 1 kg of the substance from solid to liquid at constant temperature.

Substance	Ice	Cast Iron	Tin	Copper	Aluminium

Specific latent heat of fusion (kJ/kg)	335	96	60	180	387

The *specific latent heat of evaporation* of a substance is the amount of heat energy required to change 1kg of the substance from liquid to gas at constant temperature and pressure.

Substance	Water	Alcohol	Turpentine
Specific latent heat of evaporation (kJ/kg)	2260	860	310

Example

If 12 kg of lead at 24^0C is to be melted and its melting temperature is 326^0C, calculate the total heat energy required to melt it. Take the specific heat capacity of the lead as 0.13 kJ/kg and the specific latent heat of fusion of lead as 23 kJ/kg.

Total energy	=	Sensible heat to raise temperature of the lead + latent heat to melt the lead
Sensible heat,	=	$m \times c \times (t_2 - t_1)$
	=	$12 \times 0.13 \times (326 - 24)$
	=	471kJ
Latent heatQ	=	$m \times c$
	=	12×23
	=	276kJ
Total energy required	=	471 + 276
	=	747kJ.

9.c Coefficient of linear expansion

When a solid is heated, it expands. The amount of expansion depends upon the following:

- the change in temperature
- the initial size of the solid
- the nature of the material of the solid.

The amount of expansion is proportional to length and temperature change.

Expansion $\quad = \quad$ a constant $\times L \times \delta t$
(δt, the temperature change, is pronounced 'delta t'.)
The constant is dependent upon the material, and is known as the *coefficient of linear expansion*. It is denoted by α (alpha).
Therefore the expansion $\quad X \quad = \quad L \times \alpha \times \delta t$
$$\frac{X}{\alpha} \quad = \quad L \times \delta t$$

The coefficient of linear expansion for a material is the change in length per unit length per, degree of change in temperature.

Material	Steel Cast iron	Aluminium	Brass	Copper
α (per$^{\circ}$C)	11×10^{-6}	24×10^{-6}	$20 \times 10{-}6$	17×10^{-6}

Example

The coefficient of linear expansion for copper is 17×10^{-6}per$^{\circ}$C

A copper pipe is 20m long at 20°C. Calculate its length when it is carrying steam at 140°C

(L = 20m = 20×10^3mm; δt = 140 − 20 = 120°C)

$$
\begin{aligned}
\text{Expansion} \quad X \quad &= \quad L \times \alpha\,\delta t \\
&= \quad 20 \times 10^3 \times 17 \times 10^{-6} \times 120\text{mm} \\
&= \quad 40.8\text{mm} \\
&= \quad 0.0408\text{m} \\
\text{Length at } 140^{\circ}\text{C} \quad &= \quad 20.0408\text{m}
\end{aligned}
$$

9.d   Single and composite materials

If two materials, which have different coefficients of linear expansion are joined together to form a bi-metallic strip, then the strip will bend when it is heated or cooled, owing to one material expanding or contracting at a greater rate than the other.

Example

A bi-metallic strip is made from a strip of brass and a strip of iron riveted together. If both strips are 6 cm long at 20°C, find the difference in lengths at 60°C. Denote length at 20°C by L_1 and length at 60°C by L_2

$$
\begin{aligned}
L_2 \quad &= \quad L_1(1 + \alpha t) \\
&= \quad L_1 + L_1\alpha t
\end{aligned}
$$

Therefore, the increase in length is $L_1\alpha t$.

Brass strip

$$
\begin{aligned}
L2 \quad &= \quad 6 \times 20 \times 10^{-6} \times (60 - 20) \\
&= \quad 4320 \times 10^{-6}\text{cm}
\end{aligned}
$$

Iron strip

$$
\begin{aligned}
L_2 \quad &= \quad 6 \times 11 \times 10^{-6} \times (60 - 20) \\
&= \quad 2855 \times 10^{-6}\text{cm}
\end{aligned}
$$

The brass strip will be longer by $(4320-2855) \times 10^{-6}$ mm

$$
\begin{aligned}
&= \quad 1465\ 10^{-6} \\
&= \quad 1.465 \times 10^{-3}\text{mm.}
\end{aligned}
$$

This effect is exploited in a number of devices, including thermostats, fire alarms, time-delay switches in electronic circuits.

D Electricity

10   Use waveform diagrams to illustrate the difference between direct current (d.c.) and alternating current (a.c.)

A *direct current* flows at all times in one direction, from the positive pole of a generator, through an external circuit to the negative pole of the battery or generator. Current inside the battery or generator apparently flows from the negative to the positive.

For direct current this flow may appear obvious; for alternating current, it is not so clear.

An *alternating current,* does not always flow in the same direction; it reverses its direction periodically. In most a.c. circuits the current flows for equal periods, first in one direction and then in the other.

Many alternating currents can be represented by a smooth and symmetrical curve. There are no abrupt changes of current, and the wave form is alternately above and below the horizontal axis. The wave form is periodic.

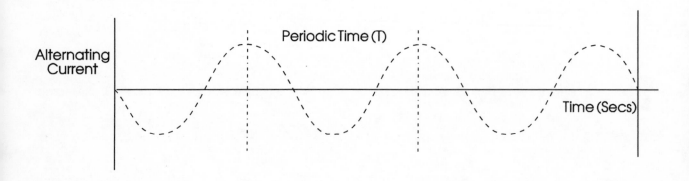

The curve is known as a sinewave. The wave form is completed after a cycle of changes and the time in which this occurs is the *periodic time*.

$$
\begin{aligned}
T &= \text{time (usually in seconds) for one cycle} \\
F &= 1/T \text{ The number of cycles in 1 second is known as} \\
  &\quad \text{the } frequency, \text{ which is measured in cycles/second} \\
  &\quad \text{or, more usually, in Hertz (Hz)}
\end{aligned}
$$

The UK supply frequency of mains electricity is 50Hz

11   Solve problems related to current, potential difference and resistance for simple resistive circuits in parallel and series. Cover the following:

- electromotive force (emf)

- potential difference
- current flow
- use of ammeters and voltmeters
- Ohm's law
- temperature effects

11.a Electromotive force (emf)

An electric current is a flow of electrons in one direction through a conductor. The force necessary to cause the flow of electrons can be achieved by applying a battery across the conductor. This force is referred to as the *electromotive force* (emf)

The quantity of electricity flowing is generally represented by the symbol Q and is measured in *coulombs*. A coulomb is the quantity of electricity carried in one second by a current of one *ampere* (amp).

Therefore, a current of one amp flows through a conductor when one coulomb of electricity passes a given point in one second.

Current is generally reperesented by the symbol, I

$$Q = I \times t$$

where
$$Q = \text{electric quantity in coulombs;}$$
$$I = \text{electric current in amps;}$$
$$t = \text{time in seconds}$$

In order to get electricity to flow at a particular rate, a electromagnetic force has to be exerted. This force is measured in *volts*.

A volt is the unit of electrical pressure which, when applied to a circuit with a resistance of one ohm, produces a current flow of one ampere.

Each material has an in-built opposition to the flow of electrons through it. Materials range from low resistance conductors to high resistance insulators. Resistance is measured in *ohms*.

The relationship between current, voltage and resistance is expressed as:
> *One ampere of current will flow through a conductor having a resistance of one ohm when one volt is applied.*

11.b Potential difference

The analogy of water flow in pipes can be applied to the flow and and rate of flow, of electricity through a conductor. Water tends to move from a position of high potential to a position of low potential, because of the effect of gravity. The greater the drop in level between the input and the output of the pipe, the greater the potential energy difference. The same principle applies to an electrical conductor. In this case the difference in potential energy (supplied by a battery) between the ends of the conductors.

The *potential difference* is the electrical pressure as measured at a particular point in a circuit; the potential difference is called the voltage.

Note: The voltage of a power source, *before* it is connected to a circuit, is referred to as the electromotive force.

The voltage, *after* current is flowing, is referred to as the potential difference, since it can be different at different points in the circuit.

An electric current will flow when there is a potential difference between two points in an electrical conductor. The unit of potential difference is the volt, symbol V.

11.c   Current flow

An electric current is the rate of flow of an electric charge. Current can be measured using an ammeter. The ammeter must part of the circuit through which the current flows.

For electrical current to flow there must be a complete electrical circuit; that is, there must be a closed circuit. The switch shown in the diagram (see 11.e) closes the circuit, allowing electricity to flow.

11.d   Use of ammeters and voltmeters

An instrument that measures current is an *ammeter*.

An instrument that measures voltage is a *voltmeter*.

The most convenient meter to use is the *multimeter* which can measure voltage, current and resistance and which has a variety of scales of measurement and incorporates a selector switch, which can be used to change the meter's range.

An ammeter must be connected in series with the supply voltage and any appliance. The positive terminal of the ammeter must always be connected to the more positive part of the electrical circuit.

To measure the potential difference in a circuit, a voltmeter must be connected so that its terminals are across the points where the voltage is to be measured. The voltmeter acts as an electrical pressure gauge. The positive terminal of the voltmeter is connected to the most positive point in the circuit.

11.e   Ohm's Law

> *In a direct current circuit the current flowing through a conductor is directly proportional to the potential difference applied to the ends, providing the temperature remains constant*
> or
> *In a direct current circuit the current is directly proportional to the voltage and inversely proportional to the resistance at constant temperature.*

That is to say:

The *potential difference between the ends of a circuit* = A constant value × the current flowing in the circuit.

The *electrical resistance* of the conductor is the constant value.

Let	I	=	the current flowing in the conductor (in amperes)
Let	R	=	the resistance of the conductor (in ohms)
Let	V	=	the potential difference across the conductor (in volts)

$$
\begin{aligned}
\text{Resistance, } R &= V/I \\
\text{Voltage, } V &= I \times R \\
\text{Current, } I &= V/R.
\end{aligned}
$$

Resistance R (OHMS)

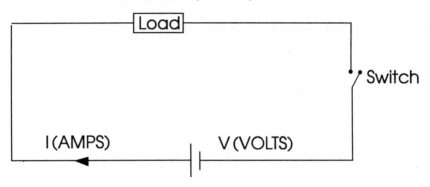

Series circuits

Example 1

What current will flow in a 6 ohm resistor when a potential difference of 24 volts is applied across its ends?

$$
\begin{aligned}
\text{Current } I &= V/R \\
&= 24/6 \\
&= 4 \text{ amps}
\end{aligned}
$$

Example 2

What potential difference must be applied across a wire of 35 ohms in order that a current of 4 amps can flow through it?

$$
\begin{aligned}
\text{Potential difference } V &= I \times R \\
&= 4 \times 35 \\
&= 140 \text{ volts}
\end{aligned}
$$

Example 3

When a potential difference of 15 volts is applied across the ends of a conductor, a current of 3 amps flows through the conductor. What is the resistance of the conductor?

$$
\begin{aligned}
\text{Resistance } R &= V/I \\
&= 15/3 \\
&= 5 \text{ ohms}
\end{aligned}
$$

Parallel Circuits

Components are in parallel in a circuit if the current splits to pass through them; that is to say, there is more than one path in the circuit for the current to flow through.

The current, I $\quad=\quad$ $I_1 + I_2$, flowing through the two resistors

The current, I $\quad=\quad$ $I_1 + I_2 + I_3$, flowing through three resistors.

The potential difference in parallel circuits is the same across all resistors.

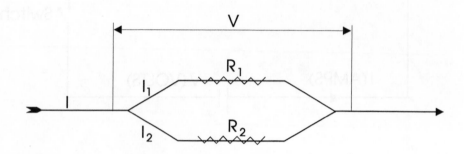

Resistance in parallel

The reciprocal of the resistance of a set of resistors in parallel is equal to the sum of the reciprocals of their individual resistances.

$$\frac{1}{R} \quad=\quad \frac{1}{R_1} + \frac{1}{R_2} + \frac{1}{R_3}.$$

The total resistance, R, of two resistors in parallel is equal to their product divided by their sum

$$R \quad=\quad \frac{R_1 \times R_2}{R_1 + R_2}$$

Example

What is the equivalent resistance of two resistances, 100 ohms and 50 ohms, connected in parallel?

$$R \quad=\quad \frac{100 \times 50}{100 + 50}$$
$$\quad=\quad \frac{5000}{150}$$
$$\quad=\quad 33.33 \text{ ohms}$$

Example 4

A 10 volt battery is connected across two resistors of 12 ohms and 18 ohms connected in parallel. Calculate the current flowing through the battery.

$$R = \frac{R_1 \times R_2}{R_1 + R_2}$$

$$= \frac{12 \times 18}{12 + 18}$$

$$= \frac{216}{30}$$

$$= 7.2 \text{ ohms}$$

The current flowing from the battery is given by:

$$I = \frac{V}{R}$$

$$= \frac{10}{7.2}$$

$$= 1.38 \text{ amps}$$

11.f Temperature effects

The resistance of metals increases with temperature, according to the law:

$$R_t = R_0(1 + \alpha t)$$

Where R_t and R_0 are the resistances of the metal at temperatures of $_t{}^{\circ}$C and $_o{}^{\circ}$C respectively. The constant, α, is called the *temperature coefficient of resistance*.

Example 5

A coil of copper wire has a resistance of 100 ohms when it is at a temperature of 0^0 C. The temperature coefficient of resistance for copper is equal to 0.0043. What is its resistance at 100^0C?

$$R = R_0(1 + \alpha t)$$

$$= 100(1 + 0.0043 \times 100)$$

$$= 100 \times 1.43$$

$$= 143 \text{ ohms.}$$

12 Calculate power in simple electrical circuits, covering the following points:

- $P = IV = I^2R = V^2/R$
- power dissipation
- calculation of fuse values given power rating and voltage of an appliance.

12.a $P = IV = I^2R = V^2/R$

When a current flows through a circuit, energy in the form of heat is dissipated by the circuit. Work is done in overcoming the resistance of the circuit.

Electrical energy is defined as the amount of work done.

When a certain amount of work is done in a specified time interval, the rate at which the work is carried out can be found. Power is defined as the rate of doing work or the rate of consuming energy.

$$\text{Power} \quad = \quad \frac{Energy}{Time}$$

$$= \quad \frac{Joules}{seconds} \text{ or } \frac{J}{s}$$

The unit of power is the watt, where 1 watt is equal to 1 joule per second.

$$\text{Watts} \quad = \quad \frac{Joules}{seconds}$$

$$\text{Joules} \quad = \quad Watts \times seconds$$

Joules Law states that the heat energy developed in a wire is directly proportional to the square of the current, I, (for a given resistance and time); the wire resistance, R, (for a given current and time); the time, t, (for a given resistance and current).

$$\text{Watts} \quad = \quad \text{Power} \times \text{time}$$

$$= \quad P \times t \tag{1}$$

$$\text{Watts} \quad = \quad \text{Current}^2 \times \text{resistance} \times \text{time}$$

$$= \quad I^2 \times R \times t \tag{2}$$

From equations (1) and (2):

$$P \times t \quad = \quad I^2 \times R \times t$$

$$\text{Therefore, } P \quad = \quad I^2 \times R \tag{3}$$

From Ohm's Law :

$$V \quad = \quad I \times R \tag{4}$$

From equations (3) and (4):

$$P \quad = \quad I \times V \tag{5}$$

$$P \quad = \quad V^2/R \tag{6}$$

P is power in watts,

I is the current in amperes,

V is the voltage in volts, and

R is the resistance in ohms.

Example 1

Two resistors of 30 ohms and 60 ohms are connected in series across a 100 volt battery. Calculate the power consumed by each resistor and the total power consumed by the circuit.

$$\text{Total circuit resistance, } R \quad = \quad R_1 + R_2$$

$$= \quad 30 + 60$$

$$= \quad 90 \text{ ohms}$$

$$\text{Current } I \quad = \quad V/R$$

$$= \quad 100/90$$

$$= \quad 1.1 \text{ amps}$$

Power consumed by the 30 ohm resistance

$$= \quad I^2 \times R$$

$$= \quad 1.1^2 \times 30$$

$$= \quad 36.3 \text{ watts}$$

Power consumed by the 60 ohm resistance

$$= I^2 \times R$$
$$= 1.1^2 \times 60$$
$$= 72.6 \text{ watts}$$

Total power consumed by the circuit

$$= 36.3 + 72.6$$
$$= 108.9 \text{ watts}$$

12.b *Power dissipation*

Power dissipation is the power used by the circuit while it is connected to the supply. Power suppliers, that is the Generating Boards, charge for the power in units.

(The charge is typically per kilowatt hour)

Example 2

A 5 kW electric fire switched on for 2 hours will consume:

$$5kW \times 2 \text{ hours} \qquad = \qquad 10 \text{ units (10kWhr)}$$

Assume a rate of 5 pence per unit

The cost will be

$$= \qquad 10 \times 5$$
$$= \qquad 50 \text{ pence.}$$

12.c *Calculation of fuse values given power rating and voltage of an appliance*

The *fuse* in a circuit is a deliberately built in weak link. If a fault occurs and too much current is allowed to flow in the circuit, the fuse wire melts, thereby preventing damage to an appliance.

Example 3

Find the value of a fuse, rated in amperes, which should be used with an electric iron that draws 3 kW from a 240 V supply.

$$\text{Power } P \qquad = \qquad 3kW$$
$$= \qquad 3000W$$
$$P \qquad = \qquad IV$$
$$\text{and} \quad I \qquad = \qquad P/V$$
$$I \qquad = \qquad 3000/240$$
$$= \qquad 12.5 \text{ amps}$$

Since a current of 12.5 amps is being used, the fuse should not be less than this value. A 13 amp fuse would probably be the most appropriate one to use.

13 **Use practical examples to explain the chemical effects of electricity, covering the following points:**

- good and bad conductors
- electrolytes
- electrodeposition

- construction of a simple cell
- primary and secondary cells
- effect of internal resistance

13.a   Good and bad conductors

Every atom comprises a central core, called a *nucleus,* and tiny particles, called *electrons,* which orbit round the nucleus.

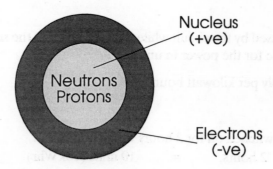

The nucleus of the atom is composed of two particles of matter, *protons,* which are positively charged particles, and *neutrons,* which are electrically neutral particles. This means that the nucleus of the atom is positively charged.

The electrons, which orbit the nucleus, are negatively charged particles.

The electrons furthest away from the nucleus are held less securely than those nearest to the nucleus. The outer electrons can break free, and are known as *free electrons.*

Good electrical conductors have loosely held electrons, since the loss of electrons from the atoms allows an electric current to flow easily through the material (examples are silver and copper).

Good electrical insulators have tightly held electrons, which are not easily detached. Such materials are resistant to the flow of an electric current.

Note See Engineering Fundamentals (K31) for examples of electrical insulator materials.

13.b   Electrolytes

Liquids which conduct electricity are known as *electrolytes.*

Whilst electric current in a solid conductor is due to the flow of free electrons, in a liquid it is due to to the flow of *ions. Ions* are atoms, or groups of atoms, that have either gained or lost one or more of their outermost electrons.

An atom which has gained electrons is called an *anion,* and is *negatively* charged.

An atom which has lost electrons is called *a cation,* and is *positively* charged.

Liquids such as sodium chloride (common salt) solution, which contain cations and anions, are called electrolytes. Strong electrolytes contain a lot of ions, whilst weak electrolytes contain few.

In order to produce a current, two metal rods or plates called *electrodes* are immersed in the electrolyte. They are connected in series with an ammeter, a switch and a battery.

The *positively* charged electrode is called the *anode*.

The *negatively* charged electrode is called the *cathode*.

When electricity flows through the electrolyte, chemical changes take place at each electrode and the electrolyte breaks up into its constituent elements. This process is called *electrolysis*. The apparatus used is called a *voltameter*.

13.c Electrodeposition

Electrodeposition or electroplating metals involves the deposition of a thin layer of a suitable metal on to another metallic surface.

Whereas in other forms of electrolysis the anodes are inert (that is they do not take part in the chemical reaction), in electrodeposition the electrodes not only carry the current but also take part in the chemical reaction. Electroplating is a useful industrial process based on electrodeposition.

In silver plating ,when the current is switched on, silver ions flow to the cathode (possitvely charged metal ions migrate to the cathode), and become attached to the fork. At the same time an equal quantity of silver is detached from the anode and goes into the solution. The thickness of the layer of silver can be regulated by controlling the current and the time of the reaction.

13.d Construction of a simple cell

A *cell* converts chemical energy into electrical energy.

The simplest form of cell consists of two electrodes of different material immersed in an electrolyte. The electrodes react chemically with the electrolyte. Zinc and copper electrodes may be used as electrodes with dilute sulphuric acid as the electrolyte. The zinc develops a negative charge by gradually releasing zinc ions into the solution. Hydrogen ions migrate to the copper electrode, giving it a positive charge. In this way, an electromotive force is set up between the copper anode and the zinc cathode.

13.e Primary and secondary cells

Primary Cells cannot be recharged

Primary cells use the chemicals in them until the energy from them is exhausted. They then have to be scrapped.

Secondary cells can be recharged by passing a current through them. In secondary cells the chemical changes are reversed by passing a current in the opposite direction to that in which it flows when the cell supplies energy.

Since secondary cells can be recharged, they are referred to as either *accumulator batteries* or *storage batteries*.

The most common type of storage battery is the lead-acid type. It has a lead cathode and a lead plate that is coated with lead dioxide to act as its anode. Sulphuric acid is used as the electrolyte.

The lead-acid batteries produce an e.m.f of 2 volts, car batteries consist of six cells in series giving an e.m.f. of 12 volts.

The principle disadvantages of a primary cell compared with a secondary cell are:

- it cannot be recharged
- it needs more maintenance
- it cannot take large currents
- it is more costly
- it contains an acid.

13.f   Effect of internal resistance

All cells have a resistance to the flow of electricity. This is known as the *internal resistance* of the cell. This resistance behaves like a resistor placed in series with the cell. If a 12 ohm resistor is connected across a cell which has an internal resistance of 0.5 ohms, the total resistance of the circuit becomes 12.5 ohms.

Example

When a battery is on load, a current of 240 mA is available from it and the voltmeter shows a reading of 8.75 V. The battery on open circuit gave a 9.0 V reading on the voltmeter. What is the internal resistance of the battery?

$$\text{The voltage drop} = 9.0 - 8.75$$
$$= 0.25V$$
$$V = I \times r$$
$$0.25 = \frac{240}{1000} \times r$$
$$0.25 = 0.24 \times r$$
$$1.04 = r$$

Therefore, its internal resistance is equal to 1.04 ohms.

14   Establish, by experiments, electro-magnetic effects and illustrate simple, practical applications of these covering the following:

- magnetic field
- field patterns produced by bar magnet and solenoid
- effects on current carrying conductors
- moving coil meter
- electromagnetic induction
- generators

14.a   Magnetic field

A *magnetic field* is the region around a magnet where magnetic effects occur (a magnetic field exists). It can be represented by lines of force or flux lines which demonstrate the pattern of the field.

14.b   Field patterns produced by bar magnet and solenoid

For a bar magnet, lines of force can best be demonstrated by placing a sheet of paper over it and sprinkling iron fillings over the paper. When the paper is gently tapped, the iron fillings form the pattern of the force lines. The lines go from a North pole to a South pole.

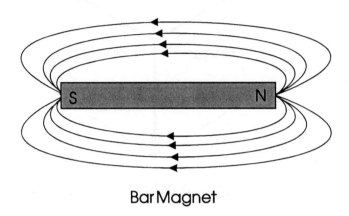

Bar Magnet

If a length of insulated conducting wire is wrapped around an iron bar, and a current is passed through the wire, the bar will behave like a magnet. The iron bar is only a temporary magnet and exists only as long as the current is flowing this form of magnet is called an *electromagnet*. *The coil of an electromagnet is called a solenoid.*

The polarity of an electromagnet depends on the direction of the current flow in the solenoid. When the current flow in a solenoid is clockwise, a *South* pole is formed, when counter-clockwise, a *North* pole is formed. An electromagnet produces a magnetic field similar to that of a bar magnet.

14.c   Effects on current-carrying conductors

A current-carrying conductor experiences a *force* in a magnetic field. The direction of the force on the conductor is at right-angles to both the direction of the current and the magnetic field.

Fleming's Left-hand Rule is used to find the direction of the force. With the thumb and first two fingers of the left hand held at right angles to each other, the first finger pointing in the direction of the magnetic field, north to south, the second finger in the direction of the current, the thumb will be pointing in the direction of the electromotive force.

The force on a conductor carrying a current in a magnetic field is directly proportional to the strength of the current passing through it.

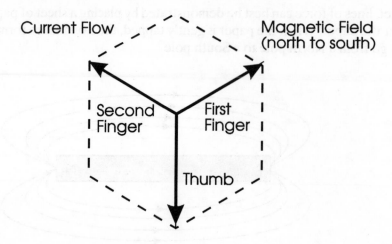

Current Flow

Magnetic Field
(north to south)

Second
Finger

First
Finger

Thumb

Force or Movement

14.d   Moving coil meter

The basis of most electrical measuring instruments is force on a current-carrying conductor in a magnetic field.

A *moving-coil galvanometer* is a sensitive instrument that is used to measure small currents. It is the basic meter from which other meters, such as ammeters and voltmeters, have been developed.

An electric meter is based on the fact that the force on a current-carrying conductor in a magnetic field is directly proportional to the strength of the current flowing through it. The meter has a small coil wound around an aluminium support (which is free to rotate) between an iron core and the poles of a permanent magnet. A small coil spring returns the pointer to zero when the current is shut off. The magnet produces a radial field which is always at right angles to the coil; the coil experiences a force which causes it to move against the spring when current flows through it. The direction of the force can be checked using Fleming's *Left-hand Rule*. Moving coil meters can be constructed so sensitively that they can measure in microamps.

14.e   Electromagnetic Induction

Electromagnetic induction is the production of a current in a conductor which is in the vicinity of a changing magnetic field.

An electromotive force generated by electromagnetic induction increases when:

    (a)   the speed of the relative motion of the magnet or coil increases

    (b)   the number of turns on the coil increases

    (c)   the strength of the magnetic field increases.

That is to say, the induced e.m.f in the circuit is directly proportional to to the rate at which the conductor moves through the magnetic lines of force. Lenz established the direction of the induced currents.

Lenz's Law states that the direction of the induced current is such as to oppose the change causing it.

Fleming's Right-hand Rule states that if the thumb and first two fingers of the *right* hand are held at right-angles to each other, with the first finger pointing in the direction of the field and the thumb pointing in the direction of the thrust, the second finger will point in the direction of the induced current.

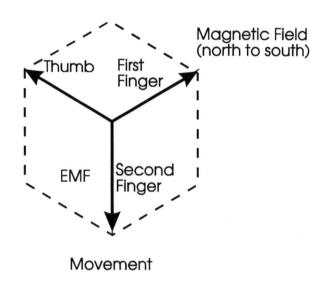

14.f   *Generators*

Electricity is produced by the process of *electromagnetic induction* using electric generators. In power station generators, the coil is fixed and the magnet is rotated using steam turbines, which are themselves powered by nuclear or hydro-carbon fuels.

Introduction to Information Technology

A   Introduction to Information Technology

1   **With the aid of suitable examples, explain the meaning of:**

- information
- message transmission
- quality of information
- information technology

1.a   *Information*

Data comprises facts which may be represented in numerical form, as text, or as a combination of both. For example, someone's age could be expressed as '16', 'sixteen', or '16 years'. When data is needed for a particular purpose it becomes information. Suppose a manager asks his secretary for a customer's telephone number. The secretary will probably search for this item of information in a telephone directory or in another database.

A *database* is a set of records, with each record referring to a particular person or entity. An individual record is made up of a number of *fields*, each of which contains an item of *data*. A telephone directory is a database which comprises records for each subscriber in a particular area of the country. Each record has three fields, containing the subscriber's name, address and phone number.

Many organisations find it convenient to hold records in databases in a computer or on media which computers can read, such as floppy disks. This allows them to take advantage of the speed and accuracy that computers can bring to the processing of data to produce information. Computers can carry out arithmetic operations, such as addition and multiplication, and logical operations, such as sorting and matching, in a tiny fraction of the time that even a genius would need using just his or her own brainpower. Information and the data from which it is derived are valuable assets, because they help people to make the right decisions and take the most appropriate actions. This is equally true in our personal lives as in business. How often do we hear the phrase, "if only I'd known"? The more information we have, and the better the quality of that information, the more likely it is that we will achieve personal and organisational goals.

1.b   *Message transmission*

When we want to communicate information to someone else we have to transmit it as a message. We have to send signals which could simply be spoken or written words but which could also be transmitted as, say, Morse code. Computer users can communicate with one another using electronic mail, sometimes called *e-mail*. This involves connecting one's computer to a 'host' computer using the telephone line. Each user has a unique 'mailbox' into which the host can place messages from other users. If a message is to be sent to a different part of the country, or abroad, the local host computer will forward the message to the nearest host computer to the addressee.

To join an e-mail system you pay a subscription. Some organisations operate their own internal systems. In order to use e-mail your computer must have appropriate communications (comms) software and a modem. The *modem* converts *digital* code, which computers use to process and communicate data, to *analogue* signals which can be transmitted over telephone lines.

1.c Quality of information

The quality of information varies. Some, literally, is not worth the paper it is printed on. To be useful, information should meet the following criteria:

(1) *Accuracy*

In some situations, such as in air traffic control, communicating insufficiently accurate data can endanger peoples' lives . Inaccurate information is misleading and leads to poor decision-making.

(2) *Relevance*

In assignments and examinations, students sometimes pad out their work with information which is true, but is not relevant to the question or task they have been set. Teachers and examiners do not give any credit when this happens. Irrelevant information can be distracting. There is a danger that the person who is presented with a mixture of relevant and irrelevant information will not be able to distinguish between them.

(3) *Timeliness*

This refers to how up-to-date information is. In some businesses, such as dealing in shares or foreign exchange, information situations can change dramatically, so it is essential to get news of new developments as soon as possible. A textbook on mathematics published twenty years ago might still be useful, whereas a book on Information Technology of that vintage would be of little value as so many advances have occurred in IT since then. For example, e-mail systems did not exist at that time.

(4) *Completeness*

Half a loaf may be better than none, but partial information may be as bad as no information at all. Knowing that computer A is cheaper than computer B is, by itself, unlikely to be a sound reason for someone to purchase A. It is quite possible that B is so superior in other respects that it would, in fact, be a better buy.

(5) *Logical structure*

The sequence in which items of information are presented sometimes can be important. If items refer to different periods, presenting them in chronological order may help to identify trends or establish when major changes have occurred.

(6) *Good presentation*

Information which is presented neatly and concisely, using diagrams, charts or tables where appropriate, makes a favourable impression on the reader. If you are required to send a CV when applying for a job, you should ensure that the information is attractively presented. It will improve your chances of being invited to an interview and, ultimately, of getting the job.

1.d   Information Technology

In its broadest sense 'Information Technology' refers to all techniques and equipment used for the processing, storage, accessing and communication of data and information.

Devices that can be used for counting range from fingers through the abacus (invented in ancient China) to electronic calculators and computers. For many centuries, paper has been the most important medium for storing information, and most offices still contain one or more metal filing cabinets. However, other media such as magnetic and compact disks, which computers can use to access or output huge amounts of data at incredible speed, are heralding the arrival of the paperless office.

Thirty years ago few people had seen or knew anything about computers. Computers were extremely expensive and bulky, had to be housed in large air-conditioned and temperature-controlled rooms, and could only be understood and used by 'boffins'. Technological advances have brought us machines, little heavier or bigger than this book, which offer superior performance to their bulky ancestors at a tiny fraction of their cost. Perhaps even more importantly, computers have become much more user-friendly, so that most people, with just a few hours of training, can become effective computer users. It is not surprising, therefore, that the term 'Information Technology' has become synonymous with computers and their peripherals i.e. devices that link to, and work with, computers.

2   Identify practical examples of information technology, and explain their function in:

- The office
- Document storage and retrieval
- Publishing and printing
- Finance and commerce
- Industry
- The home

2.a   The Office

The *typewriter* has occupied a key role in offices for more than a hundred years. However, it is being phased out in many organisations and replaced by wordprocessors or microcomputers. Using typewriters or wordprocessors instead of handwriting documents brings several advantages. Try as we might, most of us would find it difficult to produce handwritten text which is as neat and legible as typewritten text. Skilled typists can operate at speeds in excess of one word per second. Try handwriting a passage of sixty words in less than a minute and you will appreciate that it is not easy to achieve such speeds and still write legibly.

The *telephone* is an essential item in the office and most of us have phones at home. Busy executives carry their portable cellular telephones so that they can keep in touch with developments while they are on the move. The basic function of the telephone has not changed since its invention by Alexander Graham Bell, but modern phones offer additional facilities such as storing commonly used numbers and automatic re-dialling of numbers which are engaged. Answering machines are also widely used to take messages when no-one is available to answer the phone.

Telex machines are keyboard machines which encode the text that is typed onto punched paper tape. The tape is then put through a reading device which converts the code into electrical signals for transmission via telephone lines. The chief advantage that telex offers over the phone is that messages are transmitted more speedily and hence more cheaply, since the telephone line is 'occupied' for a shorter period. Moreover, a hard (printed) copy of the message is made available.

Usage of telex machines has declined in recent years, largely due to the growing popularity of *fax* (facsimile) machines. A fax machine is able to scan a document and produce an exact copy. It can also encode the images into signals for transmission via telephone lines to a fellow machine which will reproduce the document.

For in-house reproduction of documents a *photo-copier* is likely to be used. Sophisticated models offer facilities such as colour reproduction, magnification and size reduction, collation, and stapling of documents.

2.b Document storage and retrieval

We have already noted that computers are able to process and store data. One way of accessing the data is to display it on a screen. This chapter is being written on a micro-computer. As the words are entered they are displayed on the monitor/visual display unit. This facilitates the identification and correction of mistakes. The display is transitory. The sentence that I keyed in five minutes ago has already disappeared to make way for this sentence and others that will follow. When I eventually switch off the computer the monitor will be blank. However, before I do that, I will instruct the computer to save to disk the work that I have done. The computer will store it on its hard disk under the name I have chosen for it, CHAP-TER.DOC. When I wish to resume work on the chapter, I will switch on the computer and instruct it to load or open CHAPTER.DOC.

Should I require a hard copy of CHAPTER.DOC, I can attach a printer to my computer and instruct it to print all or part of the document. The printout is a permanent record or *hard copy*. The day may eventually dawn when we shall all rely principally on computers to access data, and communicate with each other via e-mail. However, hard copy in the form of books, magazines, business documents, and so on, will be with us for the foreseeable future.

If you visit your local library and want to find out whether a copy of a certain publication is available, you may well find yourself using a TV-sized device to enlarge and project extracts from the library's catalogue held on postcard-sized sheets of microfilm known as *microfiches*. Using a technique called *Computer Output on Microfilm* (COM) details of thousands of books can be condensed onto a handful of sheets of microfilm. This offers two advantages: space is saved, and details of publications can be checked quickly and conveniently .

2.c Publishing and printing

Arguably, the most important invention of the Middle Ages was Johan Gutenberg's printing press. This superseded the process of carving each page of a document into a block of wood. Gutenberg's method involved assembling moveable metal blocks, each representing an individual letter. The blocks fitted together to make lines of type. Until relatively recently the publication and printing of books and newspapers usually began with the author or journalist producing his or her work on a typewriter. Subsequently compositors would set up the text for printing, using methods which were basically the same as Gutenberg's. If the editor of a newspaper wanted to change the layout of a page, it would be laborious and time-consuming for the compositors to re-arrange the metal type.

Electronic publishing is now the norm. Authors and journalists typically use word processors and their work is stored on disk. Using desk-top publishing programmes, the basic text can then be embellished with diagrams, pictures or other images, which can be imported from other computer files or scanned into the computer. The finished product can then be printed out on automated machines under the control of the computer.

2.d   Finance and commerce

For many people, no weekend is complete without a visit to their local supermarket. Few of us enjoy this experience. Supermarkets do their best to ensure that customers' purchases are processed as quickly as possible at the check-outs. *Bar codes* on products help to achieve this objective. The cashier passes each item over a scanner which reads the code and prints out the product's description and its price on an itemised receipt.

Moreover, bar codes play a useful role in stock control. For each product, a record is held on a computer file. When the scanner identifies the product, the record is updated. Once the stock level for the product has fallen to its re-order level, an order is automatically placed with the supplier. Stock control is important. Carrying high levels of stock involves high costs for warehousing and wastage. However, if stocks are too low, potential sales may be lost as items go out of stock. Hence, setting appropriate re-order levels and ensuring prompt delivery are vital, not only for supermarkets, but also for many other commercial and industrial concerns.

Banks and other financial institutions often offer their account holders debit cards which can be used to withdraw cash from 'hole in the wall' terminals known as *Automatic Teller Machines* (ATMs). To make a withdrawal, or to check the balance for the account, a confidential combination of numbers referred to as a *Personal Identification Number* (PIN) must be entered on the keypad at the terminal. The terminal is linked to a central computer which confirms that the correct PIN has been entered and that there are sufficient funds in the account to cover the amount that is to be withdrawn.

Each day millions of cheques are issued by individuals and firms holding current accounts with banks and building societies. Computers play a key role in processing these cheques. If you examine a cheque you will see near the bottom a sequence of slightly unusual numerical characters which identify the individual cheque, the branch at which the account is held, and the account on which the cheque is drawn. The characters are encoded in special ink and are input into the banks' computers using a device known as a *Magnetic Ink Character Reader.*

It is sensible to always examine statements from banks, building societies, and credit card companies. A major bank admitted recently that at least 50,000 of its customers had been overcharged by amounts averaging around £50. This resulted from incorrect coding of interest rates into the computer. An error or 'bug' was also identified in a computer program used by several banks and building societies to process credit card accounts. This, too, led to overcharging. If you suspect that you may have been overcharged, or want reassurance, you can approach a firm which specialises in scrutinising statements and recovering over-charges and over-payments for their clients. Their fees are normally charged on a commission basis.

2.e   Communications

Traditionally, telephone lines have comprised metal cables which have been used to transmit analogue signals. In recent decades major advances have been made in the area of telecommunications. *Optical fibres* have been developed which can carry much larger volumes of data with less likelihood of the data being lost or corrupted through interference.

Satellites have also revolutionised communications. Signals can be sent as microwaves through the atmosphere via relay stations and satellites to any destination in the world. For example, scientists in Britain are tracking the movements of African wild dogs, one of that continent's most endangered species, using satellites.

Until quite recently viewers in this country were restricted to watching just four television channels. Now, by purchasing a satellite dish and appropriate decoding equipment, you can tune into any of a multitude of channels originating from various countries. Many TV sets on the market now offer a *teletext* facility. Viewers, using keypads, can access and display on their screens pages of information held on a central computer. For example, they can check sports results or get details of programmes that will be broadcast later in the day.

A *viewdata* system, such as *Prestel* , not only allows subscribers to access information via their telephone and TV set, but also allows them to interact with the central computer. Thus it is possible for someone wishing to travel by air to check flight details and to make a booking . Whilst Prestel has not proved to be particularly popular, in France millions of people have utilised their viewdata system. Children even use it to get help with their homework! *Videophones* , which allow you to see as well as talk with the person at the other end of the line, are now available, and some organisations use *videoconferencing* to allow people in different locations to conduct meetings with one another.

The use of analogue signals and associated equipment is now declining. One of the new buzzwords, or phrases, in Information Technology is *Integrated Services Digital Networks* (ISDN). These systems streamline communications within organisations, and enable people to convey and access information more speedily and efficiently than is possible with traditional systems.

2.f   Industry

There are few industries in which computers have failed to make a significant impact. One industry, in which the potential of computers is just beginning to be realised, is fashion. Consumers' tastes are becoming more fickle, so designers need to make frequent changes to ensure that their clothes will continue to appeal. To achieve this they are, in increasing numbers, making use of *Computer-Aided Design* (CAD) systems. These allow designers to scan images (e.g. sketches they may have made or photographs) into the computer, or they can draw their ideas on screen using a paintbox facility. They can also experiment with millions of colours to achieve the most appropriate combinations. To quote one fashion designer: "The system is great for colourways (colour combinations). If I was doing something by hand I might do a navy or red version, whereas now I can play around with colours and this means I am more adventurous. I think you can be a better designer by using CAD. I'll find a design I like and then play around with it. Previously if I made a decision I was stuck with it because it took too long to change." The clients, usually buyers from high street retailing organisations, can see what garments look like with different combinations of colours and patterns. If they suggest any changes, these can be made in seconds. Hence decisions are made more quickly, and buyers have more choice and influence. Another benefit offered by CAD is that patterns and colours can be printed directly onto fabrics using bubble jet printers. This makes it possible to produce sample garments in less than a day, compared with a period of several weeks that would be needed if traditional techniques were used.

CAD systems are used in the design of a wide range of products, from cars to computers. Computers also play a key role in the areas of planning and monitoring, especially when major projects are being undertaken, such as the construction of an oil-drilling platform or the purchase and installation of a powerful mainframe computer. Such projects may stretch out over many months. Utilising computers, and techniques such as *Critical Path Analysis* (CPA), it is possible to identify the particular tasks which, if delayed, will set back the completion time for the entire project. These critical tasks should be monitored very closely.

Computers perform crucially important monitoring roles in installations such as chemical plants and nuclear power stations. A secondary, back-up computer may be required to guard against the potentially catastrophic effects of a malfunction or breakdown of the main computer.

Computer Integrated Manufacturing (CIM) refers to the application of computers to all aspects of a manufacturing company's operations. Designs produced using CAD may be translated into prototypes and finished products using computer numerically controlled machine-tools and robots. Orders from customers can be logged onto a computer which can check whether items are available in stock or need to be produced to order. The manufacturing process can be scheduled and monitored by computers, which can also be used by the marketing department for sales analysis and market research, and by the finance department for budgeting and accounting purposes.

2.g   The home

Currently, there is an immense range of computer games software available. In the comfort of your own home you can play a round of golf on a famous course or tackle an opponent of grandmaster calibre at chess. Television programmes devoted to computer games are broadcast regularly. This is an indication of the popularity of such games, especially with children and young people. Whilst some simulations are rather crude, others are extremely realistic and sophisticated.

Home computers can also help people with their hobbies and other interests. For example, word processing and desk top publishing packages can be used to produce circulars and newsletters for fellow members of clubs and societies. Collections of music or other items can be catalogued on computer disks. Computers are also used as diaries and for personal budgeting.

With crime levels on an upward trend, a growing number of people are installing *electronic security systems* to protect their homes and possessions from burglars and vandals. Programmable systems can be used to arm or disarm a range of sensing devices located at strategic points. In addition, some systems automatically alert emergency services such as the police or fire brigade.

The traditional way of learning and acquiring academic qualifications has been through attending classes at schools and colleges. Due to logistical and time constraints, many people who would like to follow certain courses and gain the corresponding qualification, are unable to follow this path. *Computer Assisted Learning* (CAL) packages offer an alternative to students who have access to computers at home or at work. These packages typically combine instructional material with diagnostic material, which tests students' understanding and progress.

3   Consider the present and likely future effects of information technology on:

- patterns of employment
- domestic and leisure activities.

3.a *Patterns of employment*

In the second half of the eighteenth century the Industrial Revolution began in Britain. The utilisation of new sources of power and the invention of new machines and processes had profound effects on the lives of people. Until then, working at home was normal, but the introduction and rapid growth in the numbers of mills, factories and foundries resulted in a divorce between place of residence and place of work for most people. Not only did the location of work change, but so too did the nature of the work done.

Adam Smith, the founding father of modern economics, drew attention to the increasing specialisation of labour and to the benefits that resulted in terms of higher productivity. By how much the quality of life of the average person was improved by such developments is a matter of debate. In the longrun living standards did rise, but in nineteenth century British cities, working and living conditions were often appalling. The Luddites smashed machines which they feared, with some justification, would make their skills redundant and would take away their jobs.

Many people argue that we are currently undergoing a computer based revolution, which is having and will continue to have serious consequences for us in terms of work opportunities and lifestyles. The fastest growing sector of the economy in advanced countries such as Britain is the service sector. The number of people employed in services will continue to grow, whilst employment in extractive and manufacturing industries will decline.

Robots and *computer controlled machines* will take over many strenuous and repetitive tasks on the factory floor. Unskilled and semi-skilled jobs will tend to disappear. There should, however, be more opportunities available for people who acquire the skills needed to maintain and diagnose faults with automated systems and equipment.

Previous generations of workers usually gained their skills and qualifications at an early age, and carried out the same basic tasks with no, or relatively little, need for retraining. This is no longer the case. Anyone entering the workforce now can expect to face several career changes and undergo associated training programmes. Familiarity with computer technology and the ability to use computers will be useful and, in many cases, essential skills for a wide range of jobs.

To some extent we are witnessing a reversal of the trend for people to travel out of their homes to work. Currently, about six percent of our working population, some 1.5 million people, are *teleworkers*. This means that they carry out their work at home using personal computers (PCs). Basic requirements are a telephone, a modem and a PC. The likelihood is that many more people will become teleworkers in the future.

3.b *Domestic and leisure activities*

It seems both likely and desirable that technological advances will lead to a reduction in the average number of hours worked, enabling us to devote more time to leisure activities. By the turn of the century, PCs may well be as commonly used in homes as video recorders and hi-fi systems are today. Such items, and high resolution TV sets, on which a great deal of research is currently being undertaken, may be linked together under the overall control of a PC. This convergence and integration of differing types of equipment and technologies is known as *multimedia*. It is likely to revolutionise the way in which people learn such things as foreign languages and musical instruments. For example, using multimedia, someone learning to play the guitar could see on a TV exactly how a set of strings vibrate to produce a particular chord. Or one could call up, and compare in minute detail, renditions of the same piece of music by several famous guitarists.

Whilst people are likely to have more leisure time available in the future, it may be difficult to experience at first-hand many attractive and appealing situations and activities. Many of us would like to go on an African safari to see majestic animals such as lions and elephants in their natural habitats. However, going on safari is expensive, unless you go with hordes of other tourists, in which case you will see many more people than animals. In the near future it should be possible, by donning a set of headphones connected to a computer, to experience, in a very life-like fashion, the sights and sounds and even, perhaps, the smells of the African bush. This kind of experience is known as *virtual reality*.

B Computing

4   Investigate types of digital computer and their function and prepare a report which includes:

- Differences between user programmable and stored program machines

- Advantages and disadvantages of stored program machines

- Typical fields of application for digital computers in both real-time and batch processing modes

4.a   Differences between user programmable and stored program machines

Stored program or *dedicated systems* range from microprocessor chips inside devices, such as watches and washing machines, to computers designed to perform a specific type of task, typically word processing.

User programmable machines offer much more scope. Not only is it possible to use these machines to run standard applications, such as spreadsheet, database and accounting packages, but it is also possible to run programs which will perform non-standard tasks. If the nature of the task changes, the program can be amended or updated to take this into account.

4.b   Advantages and disadvantages of stored program machines

The advantages of stored program systems and machines are that they:

- *are relatively cheap*
  The microprocessors at the heart of these systems are not as sophisticated and expensive as those used in more powerful progammable machines.

- *hold data more securely*
  With general purpose machines there is a greater danger that data may be accidentally erased.

- *carry out the functions for which they have been designed very efficiently*
  The programs controlling them will have been extensively tested and debugged.

The chief disadvantages are:

- *lack of flexibility*
  They can accomplish only a limited range of tasks.

- *need for large volumes of input*
  Fairly large volumes of work are needed to make them cost-effective.

- *Difficulty in upgrading*
  It will probably be difficult, and may be impossible, to upgrade the machines, so they may become obsolete quite quickly.

4.c   *Typical fields of application for digital computers in both real time and batch processing modes*

Real-time processing

This involves frequent or continuous input of data into a computer system and immediate processing of that data. The results of the processing may in turn influence the subsequent data input. Suppose you go into an airline office to make a booking on a flight, the assistant will input the flight details to a central computer and the computer will respond with a message indicating whether or not there are seats available. If the answer is yes, the assistant will make the booking, allocating a smoking or non-smoking seat to you according to your preference.

Another example of real-time processing is the monitoring and control by computer of heating in a building. *Sensing devices* provide constant input to the computer, which responds by switching off the heating when the temperature is above the required level, and switching it back on when necessary. There are many industrial applications of real-time process control, in areas such as engine management systems, automatic production lines, chemical engineering and computer-aided engineering. On car production lines welding is carried out by robots. A sensor detects the exact locations of the two pieces of metal that are to be welded together. Once they are in the required positions, the welding begins. In real-time processing the computer processes the input data and generates the appropriate response very rapidly.

Batch-Processing

In batch processing, the input data is accumulated into a sizeable batch over a period of time, and the entire batch is then processed in one run. The timing and frequency of processing depends on when the output information is required. Payrolls are a typical example of batch processing. Input data relates to hours of work, pay rates etc., while the output comprises payslips. A weekly factory payroll would, naturally, be processed weekly, whereas a monthly staff payroll would be processed on a monthly basis.

Many accounting applications, such as the updating of suppliers' and customers' accounts, involve batch processing. Documents, such as invoices and receipts, are collected together in batches. The data they contain is keyed onto magnetic disks and then input into the computer, which updates the appropriate records. In recent years real-time processing applications have tended to become relatively more important. It is quite common for computers to be used predominantly for real-time applications during the day and for batch processing applications to be run at night.

5   Demonstrate an understanding of the basic structure of a digital computer system and distinguish between the control signal paths and data paths by illustrating the relationship between the central processor and peripheral equipment in terms of:

- Control unit
- Arithmetic unit
- Main store
- Control paths and data paths
- Input and output devices

At the heart of a digital computer is the *Central Processing Unit* (CPU). The CPU gives the computer its characteristics and controls its operations. It comprises two basic components, the *Control Unit* and the *Arithmetic/Logic Unit* (ALU). In a micro-computer, both components can be integrated on the same *chip, to form a microprocessor.*

5.a   Control Unit

This controls the operation of the entire system. It obeys the instructions which are issued to it via *input devices*, such as a keyboard. It also fetches, interprets and executes instructions that have been stored in the main store. It behaves rather like a manager or organiser, making sure that the instructions that have been programmed into the computer are obeyed.

The control unit uses a *system clock* to synchronise its operations. The clock emits regular electrical pulses, and the rate at which these pulses are transmitted determines the speed at which the processor operates. Clock speed is measured in MegaHertz. Top of the range microprocessors can operate at speeds of 66MHz i.e. sixty six million pulses per second.

5.b   The Arithmetic/Logic Unit

The ALU performs arithmetic operations such as addition, subtraction, multiplication, division and exponentiation. It can also make logical comparisons. For example, it can determine whether a given number is less than, greater than or equal to another number. It can also handle text enabling the computer to sort items of data into alphabetic order.

Sometimes a computer is equipped with a second processor called a *maths co-processor*. If the computer has to perform a great many arithmetic calculations this will increase its speed of operation. *Parallel processing* is used in complex tasks, such as weather forecasting, and involves several processors working in conjunction.

5.c   Main store

The memory of the computer stores certain instructions on a permanent basis. Other data is held only temporarily and is eventually replaced. The terms *memory* and *main store* are interchangeable.

Read only Memory (ROM) is used for holding the bootstrap or starting instructions which are executed when the computer is switched on. The instructions are burnt or hardwired into the silicon chip which comprises the ROM. They can be read, but cannot be overwritten. ROM is sometimes referred to as *firmware*. ROM can also be used to store, for example, applications programs and fonts.

Random Access Memory (RAM) holds the programs and the data that the computer is currently working on. RAM is *volatile*. This means that, if the power supply to the computer is interrupted or switched off, the contents of RAM are lost. It is, therefore, advisable to periodically 'save' ones' work to a non-volatile backing storage medium, such as magnetic disk.

5.d   Control paths and data paths

The CPU can only accept and transmit data as pulses of electricity. If over a set (very brief) period of time there is a pulse, this can represent the binary digit 1. Conversely, the lack of a pulse within that period can be interpreted as the binary digit 0. Not surprisingly, digital computers utilise the binary system to represent instructions and data. We are more familiar with the decimal system which uses ten digits, 0 through to 9.

Within a computer, the electrical pulses flow along metallic paths called *buses*. There are three types of bus:

1.   The *control bus* which the CPU uses to send control messages to other components.

2.   The *address bus* which carries information about the addresses/locations of data and instructions within the main store.

3.   The *data bus* which is the highway for data travelling between input and output devices, the ALU and the main store.

5.e   Input and output devices

An *input device* is used to enter data or instructions into the CPU or main store. The most commonly used input device is the keyboard. Once data has been processed, the results can be displayed or printed using a suitable output device. Input and output devices are *peripherals*. They can be attached to, but are separate from, the CPU and memory which are housed together in a single piece of equipment.

Peripheral devices are linked to the CPU via *interface connections*. These are usually sockets located on the box that houses the CPU. There are two types of interface. A *serial interface* accepts information from the CPU in groups of pulses, but transmits it to the peripheral device one pulse at a time. Cheap dot-matrix printers use serial interfaces. More expensive printers can be connected via *parallel interfaces*, because they can handle groups of pulses. As you might expect, they operate at faster speeds than their cheaper serial counterparts.

6   Analyse programming tasks by the use of flowcharts and identify the standard flow symbols for:

- Processing functions
- Input/output operations
- Decisions
- Terminal points
- Connector

In computing, two kinds of flowchart may be drawn. A *systems flowchart* gives an overview of how a certain processing task will be achieved. It makes use of symbols representing peripheral devices such as keyboards, printers and magnetic disks.

A *program flowchart* is used by a programmer to show the logical steps involved in his program. It serves two purposes. It helps the programmer to clarify his or her own ideas before writing the instructions that make up the program. In addition, it documents the work, so that anyone else who wants to understand the program has a guide to refer to.

The following symbols are used in program flowcharts:

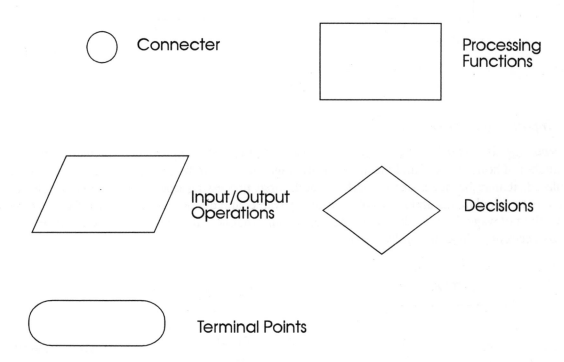

Connecter

Processing Functions

Input/Output Operations

Decisions

Terminal Points

6.a Processing Functions

The *processing symbol* is a rectangular box. It is used to represent an action or operation, such as sorting data into a sequence or performing a calculation. For example, in a program to calculate an employee's wage, the processing symbol could be used for the calculation of gross wage by multiplying hours worked by hourly wage rate.

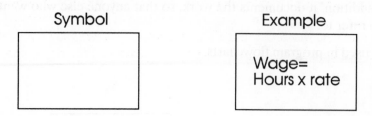

Symbol	Example
	Wage= Hours x rate

6.b   *Input/output operations*

The *input/output symbol* is in the shape of a rhombus. Before the computer can calculate someone's wage, the number of hours worked and the appropriate wage rate have to be input. Once the gross wage has been calculated, it may be necessary to perform additional processing operations. For example, it may be necessary to calculate tax and national insurance payable, and deduct these amounts from the gross wage to give the net wage. Finally, the net wage, the amount that actually goes into the employee's pay packet or bank account, will be output by the program.

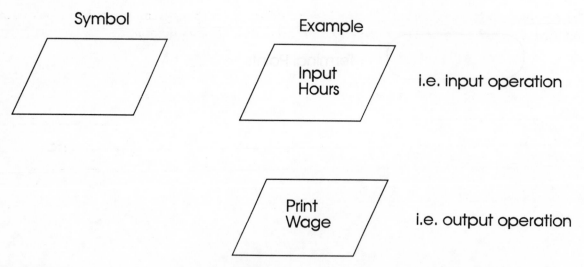

Symbol

Example

Input Hours   i.e. input operation

Print Wage   i.e. output operation

6.c   *Decisions*

At certain stages in a program it may be necessary to make decisions based on the answers to particular questions. A 'yes' will require a certain set of actions to be followed, but if the answer is 'no' a different course will be appropriate. In a wages application, hours worked in excess of 40 might be paid at a special overtime rate. The question 'Do hours worked exceed 40?' would give rise to a calculation of overtime pay, providing the answer is 'yes'. Otherwise an overtime calculation is not appropriate.

When a batch of data is being processed, the same processing operations are performed on each set of data. The programmer sets up a *loop* to achieve this. However, the loop must eventually be exited, otherwise the computer will be frantically looking for additional data to process when there is none! To exit the loop, the computer can be instructed to keep a count of how many sets of data it has processed. Once the count has reached the required number, the program will terminate. If just ten employees' wages are to be calculated, once the count reaches ten there will be no more data to process, so the program should terminate at that stage.

Symbol

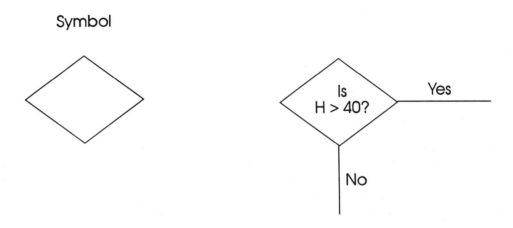

6.d   Terminal points

The *terminal symbol* appears at the beginning and the end of each program. It has the shape of a sausage and usually contains either the word START or the word END as appropriate.

Symbol   Examples

6.e   Connector

If a long and complicated program is represented on a flow diagram, it is unlikely that the entire chart will fit onto a single sheet of paper. The *connector symbol*, a small circle, can be used to indicate the connections that need to be made between the separate sheets of paper.

When a batch of data is being processed, the same procedure or operations are performed on each set of data. The programmer sets up a loop to achieve this. However, the looping procedure didn't be varied, otherwise the computer would be running for infinity and data process. When there is no exit the exit the stop, the computer can be instructed to keep a count of how many sets of data it has processed. Once the count has reached the required number, the process will terminate. If just ten employees' wages are to be calculated, once the count reaches ten there will be more than ten wages, the computer should terminate the program.

Symbol   Example

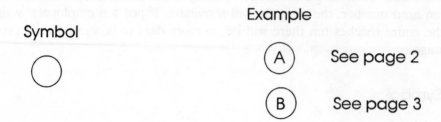

A   See page 2

B   See page 3

The flowchart below incorporates each of the symbols, apart from the connector which is not required as the chart fits onto a single page.

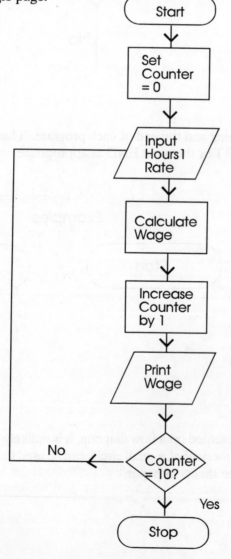

7   Identifies the relative merits of machine level coding and high level language programming and explain the need within an instruction for an address and a function. Writes a simple program, using a flow chart and employing a simple instruction set containing up to 8 instructions such as Load, Store, Add, Decrement, Halt, Conditional and Unconditional Jump, Compare. Enter and execute the program.

Computers can only work with data and instructions which are represented in binary code. A computer program that is written in machine code uses the binary system and communicates with the computer in its own language.

The computer's main store comprises a vast number of electronic cells. Each cell can either be charged or uncharged and is, therefore, a two-state device. A cell can represent a binary digit or *bit*. If it is uncharged, it can represent the binary digit 0, and if charged it can represent 1. Cells are grouped together to make up memory locations or *words* within the main store. In some computers, each word comprises 8 cells. This is known as a *byte*. More powerful machines may have 16 bit, 32 bit or 64 bit sized words. The size of a computer's main store or memory is usually measured in *kilobytes* or *megabytes*. One kilobyte is approximately equal to one thousand bytes, while one megabyte represents slightly more than one million bytes.

Remember that the computer performs calculations using its *arithmetic /logic unit*. The ALU itself contains special locations called *registers*. The most important of these is the *accumulator*. It is the accumulator which stores the results of calculation. An accumulator does not perform arithmetic; it is just a storage device. Suppose register 1 contains a value of 6 and register 2 contains a value of 37. If we want to add the two values together, we have to instruct the computer to load the contents of register 1 into the accumulator. The accumulator now contains the value 6. Next we instruct the computer to 'add to' the accumulator the contents of register 2. This causes the value of 37 to be added to the value of 6 so that the accumulator will contain the value of 37 + 6 = 43. We would probably want to store this result in another register or memory location. The accumulator can then be cleared.

Machine code instructions to carry out the tasks described in the previous paragraph would comprise *strings* of binary digits. For example, the instruction 'load the accumulator' might be represented as 10101001. Writing a program in machine code is very time-consuming for the programmer, who will constantly have to refer to a manual to identify the correct codes to use.

Programming is made easier by the use of *assembly code*. This allows the programmer to use mnemonics such as LDA for 'load the accumulator' and STO for 'store the contents of the accumulator'. Assembly code instructions have to be converted into machine code using a program called an *assembler* which is provided by the computer manufacturer.

Machine code and assembly code are both *low-level languages*. They make very efficient use of the computer and programs written in low-level language usually operate very much faster than those written in high-level languages, which will be described in the next paragraph. However, low-level languages require the programmer to have fairly detailed knowledge about the internal operations of the particular computer he is working with. Machine-code programming is also very prone to error. If a single 0 or 1 is missed out or transposed, this will upset the entire program.

In the early days of computing all programming was written in machine-code. Since then a number of *high-level languages* have been developed which have made the task of programming considerably easier.

These languages incorporate in their vocabulary standard English words and phrases such as IF, GO TO, PRINT and END.

Commonly used high-level programming languages include:

FORTRAN	This is used mainly in scientific and technical applications.
COBOL	This is suitable for commercial batch processing operations such as payroll and accounting procedures.
PASCAL	This is a general purpose language.
BASIC	This language is mainly used for teaching purposes as it is fairly easy to learn.
4GLs,	Fourth generation languages comprise short, easily remembered words and phrases, and are principally used to set up and manipulate databases. They are an integral part of database applications packages such as dBase and Oracle.

The chief advantages of high-level languages are that they are much easier to learn, understand and use. This cuts down the time needed to write, test and debug programs. However, they are much less efficient in terms of the amount of storage/memory used and speed. A program written in a low-level language might well operate as much as ten time faster than an equivalent program in a high-level language.

8   Distinguish between types of storage and recognise their role within the computer system:

8.a   Basic characteristics of storage media and devices.

Data to be processed has to be read into the CPU. The data may be held in the *main store* of the computer or on additional storage media, such as floppy disks, which are referred to as *backing store*. Storage media are held in storage devices. For example, a disk(the medium) must reside in a *disk drive*(the device), in order for its contents to be accessible to the CPU. A disk is a *direct access* medium. The read-write head in the disk drive can move directly to the appropriate track and sector on the disk, to read existing data from, or to write new data onto, the disk. Conversely, magnetic tape is a *serial access* medium. If data to be read into the CPU is located in the middle of the tape, it is necessary to wind the tape on from the beginning, until the appropriate section is found. There is a close analogy between computer storage and hi-fi storage. Musical CDs are a direct access medium, whereas cassette tapes are a serial access medium.

Before a disk can be used to store data or programs, it must be *formatted*. Data is held in concentric tracks on the surface of a disk. Each track is subdivided into several sectors. The arrangement of the disk surface in terms of tracks and sectors is the format of the disk. Formatting a floppy disk is usually quite straightforward, whereas formatting a hard disk is a more complex operation.

8.b   Need for main store

Main store is also called *immediate access storage*. IAS is located within the computer itself and is used to hold programs and data that are currently being processed. The CPU can transfer data to and from main storage at a fast rate. The *access time* for peripheral storage devices such as disk drives and tape drives is considerably longer.

8.c   Volatile and non-volatile storage

The instructions needed to start or boot up the computer when it is switched on are held in main store on a *read-only memory* (ROM) chip. However, the major use of the main store is to hold data and instructions on a temporary basis, while they are needed in a particular processing task. For this purpose, *random access memory* (RAM) is suitable. Data and instructions can be stored in RAM, and they can also be read or accessed in order to be processed or displayed. RAM is held on silicon chips.

Because RAM requires an electrical current to enable it to function as a storage medium, if there is a power cut or the computer is switched off the data is lost. RAM is said to be a *volatile storage medium*. ROM chips are *non-volatile*. The information they hold does not require a constant electricity supply. Backing storage media such as magnetic disks, magnetic tapes and compact disks are also non-volatile.

8.d   Destructive and non-destructive read output

In computers that are based on older technologies, data is stored as electrical charges on *ferrite cores*. When data is accessed the charge is lost, so the contents are consequently lost and have to be re-written to the ferrite cores. With semi-conductor memory, however, which is used in most computers today, data is not destroyed when it is read/accessed.

8.e   Use of the main categories of storage

Main store is limited in terms of capacity and by its volatile nature. Backing storage is much cheaper per byte, and can hold vast amounts of data and programs, which can be accessed by the CPU as and when required. Its main limitation is its relative slowness. Indeed, if a computer is equipped with a powerful processor, even the main memory may be too slow to keep it sufficiently busy. Such computers frequently incorporate high-speed *cache* memory. Instructions and data held in cache can be accessed by the control unit much faster than if they were in main memory. Hence, the function of cache is to hold the most frequently used(by the processor) data and instructions. A typical cache size for a microcomputer is 64Kb.

8.f   Characteristics of devices used in main store

Most computers now utilise semi-conductor memory in the form of RAM or ROM chips.

8.g   Characteristics of backing store

Points to consider with regard to backing store include:

Capacity	Floppy disks can generally hold up to around 1.4 megabytes. Hard disks range in capacity from around 20 megabytes to several hundred megabytes. A compact disk typically holds 500 to 700 megabytes.

Access Time

Access time is the period required to transfer a block of data from disk to main store. To effect the transfer, the read-write head in the disk drive has to be positioned over the appropriate track and sector on the disk. This is achieved by spinning the disk inside the disk drive. On average, the disk has to spin through half a revolution before it is appropriately positioned. The period required to complete half a revolution is known as the *latency* of the disk drive. Latency is one of the principal determinants of overall access time.

If you are using a micro-computer, it will probably be equipped with both a hard disk drive and a floppy disk drive. Should you wish to process a large chunk of data held on a floppy, you might well find that it will be quicker to do so if you copy the contents of the floppy onto the hard disk. This is because the access-time is much shorter for the hard disk drive than for the floppy.

9   Identify the range and differences between current computer system hardware devices and categories of software.

9.a   Mainframe, mini and microcomputers

Mainframe computers are found within the computer or data processing sections of most large organisations. They have high capacity main storage, measured in megabytes or even gigabytes. A gigabyte is approximately 1,000,000,000 bytes! Mainframes can be shared by a large number of users, each equipped with a terminal, through a time-sharing procedure.

Mainframes are susceptible to significant fluctuations in temperature or humidity and can also easily be damaged by dust. Therefore, they are housed in specially controlled air-conditioned rooms.

Minicomputers are basically scaled down versions of mainframes. Not only are they cheaper but they also tend to be more robust, being more tolerant of dust and environmental fluctuations. Another advantage is that they tend to be easier to operate than mainframes. They are used in many commercial and industrial applications.

A great leap forward was made when the first *microcomputers* appeared in the late 1970s. These machines can easily be accommodated on a desk in a house, school or office. Technological advances have brought us to the stage where top of the range microcomputers are now significantly more powerful in terms of their processing speeds and capacities than a main-frame computer of early 1980s vintage. Typically, the main store/memory of a microcomputer is somewhere in the range of 512 kilobytes to 16 megabytes. Microcomputers can be networked together to share common programs and data files. They are comparatively cheap and flexible. If considering the purchase of a microcomputer, it is also wise to consider whether it can be easily upgraded, as technology is advancing so rapidly.

9.b   User application software, support software, system software

Applications packages are individual programs, or suites of programs, which can be used to carry out various tasks. In some cases the task concerned is unique, and a special one-off or bespoke program will have to be commissioned or written. This is an expensive and time-consuming business.

Many *general purpose applications packages* are now available to business and personal users. Most businesses will find that they can make good use of word-processing, spreadsheet and database applications packages. These packages typically cost several hundred pounds each, but less sophisticated versions can be much cheaper. Some computer manufacturers have also struck deals with software companies, allowing them to offer prospective buyers a *bundled* package i.e. a computer plus several applications packages at a very attractive price.

Systems software is the name given to the programs which control the overall operation of the computer system, including devices such as keyboards and disk drives. Such programs are also referred to as the *operating system*(OS). Most microcomputers used in commercial and industrial applications, apart from those manufactured by Apple Inc., use a version of the operating system developed by Microsoft Corporation known as the *Disk Operating System* (DOS). When a computer is purchased, it may arrive complete with an operating system, or the OS may have to be purchased and installed separately.

Support software comprises programs which facilitate the smooth running of the computer. These are sometimes known as *utilities*. They can assist in reorganising files on disks so that storage space is not wasted. They may also be able to detect the presence of viruses which can do considerable damage, corrupting and destroying valuable data.

9.c   Data input/output, image, sound and text

The most common input device is the keyboard. However, a range of other devices may also be used including:

bar code readers	most supermarket check-outs are now equipped with these devices
optical character readers	these recognise shapes and can interpret words and pictures
optical mark readers	these recognise position rather than shape and are used extensively to automate the marking of multiple-choice examinations
magnetic ink character readers	are used to input data encoded on bank cheques
magnetic strips	are found on the back of cash cards and credit cards. If a card is used in an ATM to withdraw cash, data is read from the strip
digitizers	a range of devices, including light pens, computer 'mice', joy sticks and touch-pads, can convert data into digital form for input to a computer
speech recognition devices	computers have the capacity to recognise speech patterns and can generate appropriate responses to fairly simple commands
CD ROM drives	compact disks can store large amounts of data, which may be in the form of text, graphics, pictures or sound.

When text is output from a computer system it may be displayed temporarily on the screen of a *visual display unit* (VDU) or it may be printed out to give a permanent record.

Reference has been made to multimedia, the integration of computers with TV and hi-fi equipment. *Compact disk technology* uses lasers to read information stored in digital form on small aluminium disks. CDs can hold enormous amounts of text, equivalent to around 300,000 pages of print, but can also store pictures, video and audio information. Computers can read the data from the disks and produce still and video pictures on TV or play music through audio systems.

9.d   *Importance of man-machine interface and the demands that input/output makes on the users*

Humans and computers speak different languages. The earliest computers could only be programmed in machine code and the use of computers was very specialised and restricted. Now there are millions of computers in homes, offices and factories. Some people, youngsters in particular, quickly adapt to, and get great benefits from computers.

However, in the business world, there are many managers who have computers sitting on their desks, not because the computer helps them in their work, but because they regard computers as status symbols. Many people, including managers and members of the professions, are rather suspicious and wary of computers. They do not understand how the equipment or *hardware* functions, and are reluctant to use computers unless they really have to.

Computers can improve productivity and people should be encouraged to use them. To do this, the hardware itself and other equipment in the office/work place, such as tables and desks, should be ergonomically designed so that users will not suffer unduly from back strain or neck strain. Software packages should also be user-friendly, with helpful screen displays and well-written manuals.

The computer manufacturer, Apple Inc., prides itself on how easy it is for computer novices to use its machines. Whilst experienced typists find keyboard entry easy, many of us struggle to use them effectively. *Graphical User Interfaces* (GUIs) provide a *WIMP* environment which reduces the need for keyboard entry. WIMP stands for windows, icons, mouse and pointers.

- *Windows* provide an on-screen view of a particular area in the computer's memory. Several windows can be displayed on-screen at the same time and this can make it much easier to switch from one task to another.
- A *mouse* is an electronic device which is used to adjust the position of a *pointer*, called a *cursor*, on the screen. This is done by rolling the mouse in the required direction over the surface of a desk. A mouse can be used to select an appropriate program or data file, using icons or drop-down menus which offer several options. A file drop-down menu, for example, might offer the options of opening, closing, saving or deleting a particular file.
- *Icons* represent activities or physical objects such as a printer. By moving the cursor onto an icon, and clicking on that icon, the desired action (e.g. printing) can be achieved.

Steps should be taken to make computers as easy and as comfortable to use as possible. This is especially true for people who spend most of their working day using a microcomputer or word processor. Prolonged exposure to VDUs can damage one's eyesight, and some research suggests that it can increase the possibility of miscarriage for pregnant women. *Repetitive Strain Injury* (RSI) is another malady to which word processing operators in particular are prone. Those people who do spend a good part of the day working with computers should be allowed to take regular breaks, to avoid the headaches and other problems that otherwise are likely to arise.

10 Explain the need for data protection and distinguish between privacy and security with respect to data, giving an example of each to show how unauthorised access to computerised information can be prevented using codes.

Most of us value our privacy. We do not like the idea that other people should have access to information about our health, beliefs, activities and so on. However, the fact is that many organisations *do* have information about our personal circumstances. They are sometimes willing to share this information, and may even sell it to other interested parties. People who apply to buy goods on credit sometimes find that their application is refused. This may be the result of their name appearing, rightly or wrongly, on a file of bad debtors held in a certain organisation's computer.

To help to allay concerns about privacy, the Data Protection Act was introduced in 1984. This makes it obligatory for any organisation or individual who stores personal information to register and state:

- the kind of data that is held

- why it is being held

- where the data is stored

- how the data was obtained

The individuals to whom the data relates are also entitled, under the Act, to know what data is being held. Moreover, they have the right to inspect the data and have it amended if it is incorrect.

The Act also requires that access to information should be confined to those authorised to hold it, and states that adequate security systems must be set up.

Security of information is not just a matter of personal privacy. Companies also need to protect information about their products, processes and plans from competitors. They also need to guard against fraudulent behaviour by their own employees who, by tampering with computer files, might be able to transfer monies, to which they are not entitled, to their own bank accounts.

Several measures can be taken to protect computer programs and files from unauthorised access. They can be *password protected*. This means that only by keying in the appropriate password can access to the program or file be achieved. The system is not foolproof. A casual glance over the shoulder of someone keying in his password is all that is needed to outwit the system. Computer 'hackers' often spend many hours trying out different combinations of numbers and characters to establish the appropriate password for gaining entry to a computer system. Eventually they may succeed.

By *encrypting data* held on computer files, it can be made indecipherable. If hackers or competitors manage to break into the system, they will not actually be able to interpret and use the data anyway.

Security can also be enhanced by restricting access to the computer hardware itself. Only authorised personnel should be allowed into the room(s) concerned. Also, disks and tapes which hold sensitive data should be locked away.

In recent years the spread of *computer viruses* has also become a significant threat to the security of data held on computer files. Viruses are created by people with a considerable amount of expertise in the field of computers. Viruses are usually introduced unwittingly into computers. Typically, the virus is encoded in machine code on a floppy disk. Once the contents of the disk are loaded into a computer's memory, the computer is at the mercy of the virus. Some viruses are relatively harmless ; they may just display an amusing message on the VDU, but others can cause havoc rendering programs and data files totally useless. To identify and protect against viruses, scanning programmes can be installed into the computer. However, new viruses crop up from time to time, and it is not possible to eliminate completely the threat that they pose.

Finally, it is worth bearing in mind that it is quite easy to lose data and programs accidentally. The memory of a computer consists mainly of *random access memory* (RAM), and if there is an interruption in the power supply, or the machine is accidentally switched off, the contents of the memory will be wiped out. Therefore, if you are working on a particular application over a prolonged period, it is advisable to save your work frequently onto backing store (usually a hard disk). This ensures that if your computer does ' go down', you will not have lost all of your work.

C Information technology applications in the office

11   Outline the basic characteristics of document preparation, and compare their cost effectiveness, with:

- Typewriters with no memory
- Typewriters with limited memory
- Word processor systems

11.a   Typewriters with no memory

Many individuals and small businesses rely on basic typewriters to produce letters and other documents. When the documents are fairly straightforward, consisting mainly of text rather than charts or diagrams, and when the volume of typing to be done is not great, a basic typewriter will be quite adequate and cost effective.

11.b   Typewriters with limited memory

These offer a variety of additional features such as:

1.   Tiny display screens, showing a single line of text.

2.   *Buffers* or memories which store keystrokes before they are printed out so that you can make amendments and correct spelling mistakes.

3.   Spell checks, which help to identify spelling mistakes.

Such typewriters are more expensive to purchase than basic models, but having the ability to manipulate and edit text before it is printed increases the productivity of the typist. This increased efficiency may justify the higher capital cost involved.

11.c   Word processor systems

Here the choice lies between using a word processing applications package on a general purpose computer, or using a dedicated word processor. If the user is involved with other applications, such as spreadsheets or databases, then a general purpose computer should be used. Many word-processing packages are available, such as Wordperfect, Wordstar, and Microsoft Word.

Dedicated word processors cannot be used for other applications. However, they may offer facilities which are not available on general purpose machines. To make them cost effective, there has to be a sufficient volume of work to keep machine and operator busy.

The main considerations to bear in mind when deciding between typewriters and/or word processors are: the type and volume of work to be done; the capital cost; the running cost;the relative reliability of each machine.

12   Identify the components of a stand-alone word processor system as being processor, printer and disk store and explain the function of each

The processor in a stand-alone word-processing system performs the same basic functions as the processor in a general purpose computer. It controls the input of data via keyboard, and the output of information to be stored on disk or printed out. The document that the operator is working on will be held in memory and, for tasks such as sorting and merging, the arithmetic/logic unit will be brought into play.

The printer is used to produce a permanent hard copy of the documents that have been processed. The various types of printer are described and discussed under Competence Objective 14.

Data files are held on disk. One such file might hold details of customers, their names, addresses and so on. Another file might hold similar data for suppliers. If amendments need to be made, such as changing the address of a supplier, the data can be read off the disk, amended and restored to the disk.

13   Identify the components of a communicating word processing system as being processor, disk stores, switching system and control printer, and explain the function of each

In a stand-alone word-processing system, each machine requires its own storage device (typically disk storage) and printer. Greater efficiency may be achieved if two or more operators share such devices. Several microcomputers or word processors can be linked to a single printer via a *switchbox*. Some switchboxes require manual adjustment of a dial to give control of the printer to a particular machine. Other switchboxes operate automatically, picking up signals from the processor in a machine which is ready to print and allocating control of the printer to that processor.

Computers and word processors can also be *networked*. In this case they also share a *print server* and a *file server*. The print server can prioritise print jobs, so that those which are most urgent are given precedence. The file server, which is usually a microcomputer with a poweful processor, controls the exchange of files between network users.

14   Outline the operation and compare the characteristics of the main types of printer in common use. Select the appropriate printer for a specified application, showing an awareness of cost factors and print quality

A wide range of printers are available for use in computer systems. Printers vary considerably in terms of cost, speed of operation, the technology they utilise, and the quality of print they produce.

Dot-matrix printers are generally quite cheap. Their print heads comprise arrays of pins. Each keyboard character corresponds to a particular selection of pins. A 24 pin machine can produce near letter quality print which is sufficiently clear and presentable for most business correspondence. A 9 pin machine can only produce standard quality print which would be suitable for internal notes and memos. Typical print speed for a dot-matrix is 40-100 characters per second (cps). A full page of A4 paper could take a minute or so to print. Dot-matrix machines can also operate in draft mode. Speed is increased considerably, but the quality of print is diminished. They are quite versatile and can handle individual sheets of A4, as well as continuous/tractor fed paper. One drawback is the noise that they make which can be irritating. However, acoustic hoods, which reduce the noise level, are available.

Line printers print a single line at a time. Very high speeds can be achieved. Around 6000 lines per minute is quite typical. These printers are suitable for use with mainframes which generate considerable amounts of print out. Reasonable print quality can be achieved, but they cannot accommodate A4 or A3 sized paper documents.

Ink jet printers spray ink through tiny nozzles to form characters on paper. They are faster and quieter than a dot-matrix. Print quality is good, of letter quality, and printing in different colours is possible if the appropriate cartridges are purchased. They are more expensive than dot-matrix machines, but cheaper than laser printers.

Laser printers produce an extremely fine standard of print. They have their own processors and memory and are often more expensive than the computers with which they work. Typical speeds, for relatively inexpensive lasers, are four to seven pages per minute. Lasers are very quiet in operation, but may only print on A4 size paper. It is important to consider how much work a printer is likely to do. Some printers are cheap because their build-quality is relatively poor and they can quickly wear out if subjected to heavy use. It is advisable to read the accompanying literature before making a purchase. Normally, for laser printers, there will be a specified maximum number of copies per month that the printer can manage.

Whatever type of printer is chosen, it is vital to ensure that the software used by your computer is compatible with the printer.

15 Plan the layout of a document and use a word processor to prepare it

Word processors provide a variety of facilities which enable the user to format his document.

Formatting includes considerations such as:

Justification	usually documents are left justified, which means that the first character on each line appears directly below the first character on the above. Right justification or centring, which gives a more symmetrical appearance, may sometimes be preferable.
Line spacing	single spacing can make text appear very dense. Double spacing may be used throughout an entire document or in certain places to improve legibility and appearance.
Character font and style	sophisticated word processors and printers offer the user a wide variety of fonts. The term font refers to a particular typeface and size of character. Commonly used typefaces include Helvetica, Courier and Times New Roman. Character size is specified in points. Characters can also be emboldened, italicised, or underlined to make certain words stand out.
Margins and tab setting	margins can be set to the desired size at the top, bottom, left- and right-hand sides of the page. Tab settings can be used to indent text from the left-hand margin.
Headers and footers	it may be desirable to have certain information at the top or bottom of a page e.g. title of a chapter or page number.

16   Outline the basic characteristics of document storage and retrieval, comparing such factors as cost, ease of use and storage space, for:

- Paper
- Microform
- Computerised Systems

16.a   Paper

Most of us handle paper documents almost every day of our life. Large organisations often produce vast amounts of paper. For ease of access and retrieval, paper documents may be stored in binders or in dockets within filing cabinets. Paper is relatively expensive to purchase and, being relatively bulky, is expensive to store.

16.b   Microform

Organisations can significantly reduce their storage requirements by using rolls or sheets of microfilm, to store miniaturised versions of documents in photographic form.

Many large organisations use computer output to microform to generate *fiches* directly from a computer. Many thousands of documents could be involved, in which case it may be desirable to number the microfiches and set up a computer database as an index to the fiches. This will make retrieval of a specified document much easier.

16.c   Computerised systems

While the cost of paper rises from year to year, the cost of storing data on media such as floppy disks, hard disks. magnetic tape and compact disks continues to decline. Small laptop computers just slightly larger than this book, may incorporate hard disks with capacities of up to 200 megabytes. A compact disk can hold 500 to 700 megabytes of information, equivalent to the contents of about ten encyclopaedias! Until recently, it has only been possible for computers to read data held on CDs, but we now have *Compact Disk Magneto Optical* (CD-MO) systems, whereby computers can erase or write new data onto CDs.

17   Identify the functions required of any form of filing system and suggest a possible filing system for a given situation, bearing in mind the forms of retrieval required. Retrieve specific information from a database

A *file* is a collection of related records. Each record comprises a group of items of data known as *fields*. For example, a form might have a customer file with one record for each of its customers. The fields for a customer record might be identification number, name, address, telephone number, and so on.

Records can be written or printed on paper or cards. One of the problems with this traditional approach is that it usually involves a considerable amount of unnecessary duplication. The same data appears in different files. Time is wasted because the data is recorded several times, rather than just once, and more storage space is required.

Many firms have turned to computerised *database management systems* (DBMS) as a means of improving their information systems. Ideally, with such a system, each item of data has to be entered and stored only once, and any authorised user has easy and speedy access to the data. A number of database software packages are commercially available. Using such packages to set up and maintain a database will require at least some elementary programming skills. Such packages usually come with their own 4GL programming language.

It is perhaps worth mentioning that the term *file* in computing refers to any piece of work that is stored under a particular name. Thus a computer file may contain data, or perhaps a set of instructions which make up a program.

Whether a firm has traditional paper-based filing systems or whether it has a computerised DBMS, the following points need to be considered:

1. *Ease of accessing particular files and records*
   It is important that each record should have a unique identifier. In computerised systems this function is performed by a key field. Thus in a payroll applications, each employee is allocated a unique number, which is the key field in his or her record.

2. *Need for updating files*
   If a customer changes his or her address, that record will need to be amended. When an employee leaves a company, the appropriate record should be deleted. New records also have to be created at various times.

3. *Data integrity*
   There is a danger that data may be damaged, or corrupted, or even totally destroyed. The potential for this happening is probably greater with a computerised than with a traditional system. Keeping backup copies of important files, and requiring users to rec-onfirm that they actually want to delete a particular record or file, will help to minimise such problems.

4. *Privacy and security*
   These considerations are covered in some detail under Competence Objective 10. While no system can be entirely foolproof, measures such as restricting physical access to rooms and password protecting files, are desirable.

Programme of Integrative Assignments

Integrative Assignment 1

The Manufacture of a Light-Operated Tone-Generator

Introduction

This assignment gives you the opportunity to work as a member of a team, in the manufacture, the testing and the cost analysis of a light-operated tone-generator.

The skills you will use and develop, and the relevant programme objectives, are given on page 195. Read them carefully, and, with the assistance of your tutor and your fellow team-members, make sure that you understand the requirements of the assignment.

Assignment Brief

You are a member of an engineering project team which specialises in the application of oscillators.

Oscillators are used in many pieces of electronic equipment, such as calculators, burglar alarms, radios and TV sets. This particular oscillator used in the generator has several components which fit into all electronic equipment. This Assignment will help you to identify these components and practice your skills in manufacture, development and costing.

Your team has been instructed to:

- construct the circuit
- specify and test the circuit
- using catalogues, determine the overall development costs, including labour costs.

Your team has to produce a joint technical report including a leaflet advertising the qualities of the generator.

This assignment has been divided into five tasks and it is expected that you will be supported in your learning, by a tutor, for approximately 102 hours. To assist you in your time management, each of the assignment tasks have a suggested learning support time given and each objective has a suggested importance weighting. (This is shown on the task data sheet against each of the vocational objectives. The number in brackets indicates the weighting, for example in task 1 of this assignment, objective A3 in Engineering Fundementals has a a weighting of 4 - and so has a relatively low weighting, while objective B5 has a weighting of 20 and so has a relatively high weighting.) This weighting will permit your team to plan your own learning priorities.

You and your colleagues will be continuously assessed and each one of you is encouraged to achieve both the skills and the knowledge requirements of the various tasks of the assignment. These are given in more detail in the Task Data Sheets of the assignment.

The various tasks provide an opportunity for you to achieve all of the selected indicative content and performance criteria associated with the assignment's vocational objectives and common skills. Your tutor will provide learning support for your group and will supply any additional information that you require.

Fact Sheet

Alarm signals are a very common feature of nature and the introduction of micro-electronics has encouraged the development of highly sophisticated automatic sensing devices, providing proximity and alarm signals, for industrial and commercial processes. Your team has the task of manufacturing, testing and marketing a light-operated tone generator. The tone-generator you have to produce is designed to emit an audio alarm when light falls on a variable resistor which is light dependent (Light Dependent Resistor). The generator is an example of the use of an oscillator. This is a commonly-used component in a wide range of electronic equipment such as proximity switches, alarms, radios and televisions.

The time it will take you to manufacture and test the tone generator will vary, depending upon the complexity of its design. The marketing costs will depend on the size of the anticipated sales.

You could employ a range of processes in the manufacture of the tone generator and its container such as soldering, pressing, moulding and encapsulating. The processes you use will depend upon the particular design you adopt.

A number of factors will influence your design of the tone-generator as a finished product. While the basic shape is created by the designer, you will need to make changes to accommodate the manufacturing process.

The materials you should use will depend upon the particular design used and the manufacturing processes employed. For the components you should use see the proposed circuit diagram; other circuits might be used to achieve the same objectives.

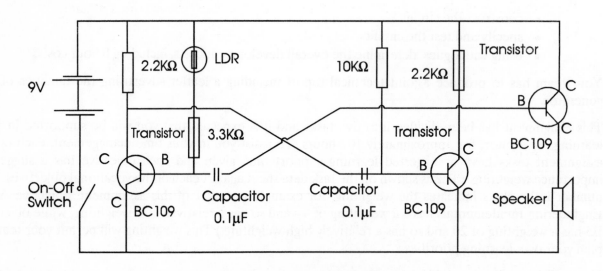

Circuit diagram - Light operated tone-generator

Task 1 – *Generator Construction*

(Suggested support time 29.5 hours)

After the initial briefing by your tutor and working with your team:

(a) Study the given circuit diagram and produce drawings to British Standards. In doing this you should recognise any personal safety problems in the manufacture and operation of the device.

(b) Next organise the various components and carry out tests/measurements on them using ammeters and voltmeters. In this way calculate power in the circuit.

(c) Construct the circuit on veroboard and plan a suitable container. Carry out various joining methods to put the circuit together.

Task 2 – *Testing The Circuit*

(Suggested support time 21.0 hours)

Working with your own team:

(a) Test the completed circuit using suitable instruments. In so doing recognise the difference between conductors and insulators.

(b) Calculate the power requirements of the circuit and then produce the container.

(c) Analyse the task using a flow-chart and standard symbols.

Task 3 – *Generator Specification*

(Suggested support time 18.0 hours)

Working with your own team:

(a) Select a suitable light meter and light source.

(b) Calibrate the generator.

(c) Display you results graphically and use a pictorial presentation of data.

Task 4 – *Research & Development Costs*

(Suggested support time 19.0 hours)

After an initial briefing by your tutor and working with your own team:

(a) Research and select a range of catalogues and publications you judge to be useful for this task. Use reference sources to distinguish between thermoplastic and thermo-setting plastic. Distinguish between the electrical properties of conductors and insulators.

(b) Carry out a series of simple exercises useful in the development of the generator to assess both the material and the labour costs.

(c)   Compare the possible use and relative cost in software and hardware terms of utilising a mainframe, mini or a microcomputer in this type of development.

Task 5 – Marketing The Generator

(Suggested support time 15.0 hours)

After an initial briefing by your tutor and working with your own team:

(a)   Produce a draft advertising leaflet which will describe the product to prospective customers. Produce, using a simple CAD system, final sectioned and dimensioned working drawings. Produce, using a simple CAD system, an electrical circuit diagram.

Assessment

You will be assessed in the following manner:

(a)   How well you contributed to the work of the team. This will be based upon tutor observation and peer-group assessment of your work. You should develop a profile of your achievements during the period of the Assignment.

(b)   Your own understanding and interpretation of the skills and knowledge of the Assignment. This will be assessed at a personal interview with your tutor.

Task Data
Integrative Assignment No. 1

Light Operated Tone Generator

Task No. 1 – Construction

Suggested learning support time – 29 hrs 30 min

Common Skills – Competence Objectives & Performance Criteria

Negotiated Attainment

A Managing and Developing People

A2   Manage own time in achieving objectives
  • plan provided for achieving objectives accepted and implemented ❏

D Managing Tasks and Solving Problems

D13 Deal with a combination of routine and non-routine tasks
  • tasks prioritised and sequenced ❏

D14 Identify and solve routine and non-routine problems
  • nature and extent of problem correctly identified ❏

Vocational – Competence Objectives & Indicative Content
Engineering Fundamentals

A Safety Hazards

A3   Recognises the importance of safe electrical working in protecting life and property and identifies:
  • likely sources of electrical danger (4) ❏

B Hand and Machine Processes

B5   Peforms marking out exercises on plane surfaces, selects the relevant hand tools for a task and uses them, subsequently explaining the following:
  • the function of datum lines and centre lines (20) ❏

D Working in Plastics

D10 Uses and describes the techniques available within conventional workshops to produce shapes in plastic materials and subsequently indicates applications, gives details of techniques used, associated problems and safety measures. Including the following:
  • problems associated with the machining of plastics and the speeds and feeds necessary (10) ❏

E Engineering drawing

E11 Explains with the aid of drawings the meaning of orthographic projection, and produces neat and clear drawings including the use of hidden detail lines, using the following types of projection:
  • points (5) ❏
  • lines (5) ❏
  • areas (5) ❏

E15 Uses conventions shown in appropriate standards to interpret and draw electrical circuit diagrams including:
  • connections, junctions, cables (twin-core, 3-core, screened) (7) ❏
  • circuit elements – resistor (fixed, variable, potential divider), capacitor (fixed, variable), inductor (air-cooled, iron-cored), transformer (double-wound) (7) ❏

F Electrical measuring instruments

F16 Carries out tests/measurements for:
  • resistance, voltage and current, for continuity using multi-range instrument (3) ❏

F17 Uses a cathode ray oscilloscope to measure the amplitude and frequency of sinusoidal signals and for a regular train of pulses and demonstrates the purpose of the following controls:
  • x and y gain (3)

G Electrical connection and termination

G18 Produces soldered joints and explains limitations and precautions (eg close clean surfaces; non-corrosive flux; correct heat from clean source; quality solder; surface flow for tinning) (10)

Mathematics

A Arithmetic

A1 Evaluates expressions involving integer indices and use standard form:
  • standard form eg 1.234 x 10 to the power 5 (10)

B Algebra

B6 Uses basic notation and rules of algebra
  • numbers and letters (22)

C Geometry and trignometry

C12 Calculates areas and volumes of plane figures and common solids using given formulae
  • area of triangle, square, rectangle, parallelogram, circle, semi-circle (30)

D Statistics

D16 Collects, tabulates and summarise statistical data and interprets it descriptively
  • data collection (7)

Science

Motion and Energy

C7 Describes wave motion and solves problems involving wave velocity
  • wavelength (29)

D Electricity

D10 Uses waveform diagrams to illustrate the difference between direct current (d.c.) and alternating current (a.c.) and gives examples of the use of each (11)

D14 Establishes, by experiments, electro-magnetic effects and illustrates simple, practical applications of these
  • magnetic field (8)

Information Technology Studies

A Introduction to Information Technology

A1 Explain information technology using suitable examples
  • information (5)

B Computing

B4 Investigates types of digital computer and their function and prepares a report
  • difference between user programmable and stored program machines (30)

C Information Technology Applications in the Office

C13 Identifies the components of a communicating word processing system as being processor, disk stores, switching system and control printer, and explains the function of each (14)

Task No. 2 – Testing the Circuit

Suggested learning support time – 21 hrs

Common Skills – Competence Objectives & Performance Criteria

A Managing and Developing People

A1   Manage own roles and responsibilities
- personal and work roles and responsibilities to be managed, agreed and accepted ❑

B Working with and relating to others

B7   Work effectively as a member of a team
- importance of teamwork recognised and accepted ❑

Applying Design and Creativity

G17 Apply a range of skills and techniques to develop a variety of ideas in the creation of new/modified products, services or situations
- given opportunities for innovation and creativity recognised ❑

Vocational – Competence Objectives & Indicative Content

Engineering Fundamentals

A Safety Hazards

A1   Studies the 'Health and Safety at Work Act', using practical situations and layouts in the workshop/laboratory to identify the major responsibilities of the employee and hazards including:
- the need for personal hygiene, cleanliness and tidiness in the working situation, highlighting possible hazards arising from untidy working conditions (3) ❑

B Hand and Machine Processes

B6   Uses suitable equipment to measure components, explains the principles and identifies limitations governed by accuracy, robustness, etc. Examines equipment including micrometers; verniers; plunger dial gauges; level type test indicators (23) ❑

F Electrical Measuring Instruments

F16 Carries out tests/measurements
- resistance (in the region 10 to 100 ohms) using a voltmeter and an ammeter (3) ❑

F17 Uses a cathode ray oscilloscope to measure the amplitude and frequency of sinusoidal signals and for a regular train of pulses
- time base (3) ❑

I Electrical Protection

I23 Prepares explanatory notes from given references concerned with adequate protection of electrical installations.
- reasons for protection against excess current and earth leakage current (6) ❑

K Materials

K25 Uses laboratory tests and given reference sources to indicate the general composition, properties of certain engineering materials. The properties should be compared in terms such as strength, rigidity, hardness, elasticity toughness, electrical conductivity, temperature stability, ease of processing and costs.
- tin/lead soldering alloys (11) ❑

Mathematics

A Arithmetic

A5   Performs basic arithmetic operations on a calculator
- numbers to a power (10) ❑

B Algebra

B7 Multiplies and factorises algebraic expressions involving brackets
- multiplying expressions inside brackets by numbers, symbols or expressions within brackets eg $3a(2 + b) = 6a + 3ab$, $(a + b)(2 + c) = 2a + ac + 2b + bc$ (22) ☐

D Statistics

D16 Collects, tabulates and summarise statistical data and interprets it descriptively
- discrete and continuous data (6) ☐

C Science

C Motion and energy

C7 Describes wave motion and solves problems involving wave velocity
- frequency (29) ☐

D Electricity

D11 Solves problems related to current, potential difference and resistance for simple resistive circuits in parallel and series
- electromotive force (e.m.f) (8) ☐

D14 Establishes, by experiments, electro-magnetic effects and illustrates simple, practical applications of these
- generators (8) ☐

Information Technology Studies

A Introduction to Information Technology

A2 Identifies practical examples of information technology, and explains their functions
- the office eg typewriters, telephones, reprographic equipment, calculators, dictating machines, in-house exchanges, electronic mail (7) ☐

B Computing

B6 Analyse programming tasks by the use of flowcharts and identifies the standard flow symbols
- processing functions (30) ☐

C Information Technology Applications in the Office

C11 Outlines the basic characteristics of document preparation, and compare their cost effectiveness
- typewriters with no memory (13) ☐

Task No. 3 – Generator Specifications

Suggested learning support time – 18 hrs

Common Skills – Competence Objectives & Performance Criteria

D Managing Tasks and Solving Problems

D12 Use information sources
- information located and collected from appropriate sources ☐

D13 Deal with a combination of routine and non-routine tasks
- routine and non-routine tasks identified ☐

F Applying Technology

F16 Use a range of technological equipment and systems
- appropriate equipment for task identified ☐

Vocational – Competence Objectives & Indicative Content
Engineering Fundamentals
A Safety Hazards

A1   Studies the 'Health and Safety at Work Act', using practical situations and layouts in the workshop/laboratory to identify the major responsibilities
  - the need for eye protection against sparks and dust (3)   ❏

E Engineering Drawing

E11   Explains with the aid of drawings the meaning of orthographic projection, and produces neat and clear drawings including the use of hidden detail lines
  - principle planes of projection (6)   ❏

I Electrical Protection

I23   Prepares explanatory notes from given references concerned with adequate protection of electrical installations
  - reliability, discrimination, low maintenance costs, protection of the smallest conductor in the circuit, as protection equipment criteria (7)   ❏

J Electronic Systems

J24   Demonstrates and compares different types of input and output waveforms and frequencies
  - d.c. supply operating from an a.c. mains (the term ripple should be introduced) (4)   ❏

Mathematics
A Arithmetic

A1   Evaluates expressions involving integer indices and use standard form
  - indices – multiplication, division, power, reciprocal (10)   ❏

B Algebra

B7   Multiplies and factorises algebraic expressions involving brackets
  - factorising as a reverse of the above (22)   ❏

D Statistics

D16   Collects, tabulates and summarise statistical data and interprets it descriptively
  - pictorial presentation – bar charts, component bar charts, pie charts, pictograms (6)   ❏

Science
A Oxidation

A1   Establishes through experiments, the basic chemical processes involved in burning and rusting as examples of chemical reactions (interactions between substances which result in a rearrangement of their atoms) and applies this knowledge to a variety of practical situations
  - composition of air (9)   ❏

C Motion and Energy

C7   Describes wave motion and solves problems involving wave velocity
  - $v = f$ (29)   ❏

D Electricity

D11   Solves problems related to current, potential difference and resistance for simple resistive circuits in parallel and series
  - potential difference (8)   ❏

Information Technology Studies
B Computing

B4   Investigates types of digital computer and their function and prepares a report
  - advantages and disadvantages of stored program machines (30)   ❏

B8   Distinguishes between types of storage and recognises their role within the computer system
  - basic characteristics of stores ie access and cycle time (30)   ❏

C Information Technology Applications in the Office

C17 Identifies the functions required of any form of filing system and suggests a possible filing system for a given situation, bearing in mind the forms of retrieval required. Retrieve specified information from a database (14)

☐

Task No. 4 – Research & Development Costs

Suggested learning support time – 19 hrs

Common Skills – Competence Objectives & Performance Criteria

B Working with and Relating to Others

B7 Work effectively as a member of a team
  • participation in allocation of team tasks

☐

C Communicating

C8 Receive and respond to a variety of information
  • information clarified as necessary through questioning and enquiry

☐

E Applying Numeracy

E15 Apply numerical skills and techniques
  • use and application of numerical techniques identified

☐

Vocational – Competence Objectives & Indicative Content

Engineering Fundamentals

A Safety Hazards

A1 Studies the 'Health and Safety at Work Act', using practical situations and layouts in the workshop/laboratory to identify the major responsibilities
  • danger associated with electricity in the workshop (3)

☐

E Engineering Drawing

E11 Explains with the aid of drawings the meaning of orthographic projection, and produces neat and clear drawings including the use of hidden detail lines
  • simple 3-dimensional objects (5)

☐

E15 Uses conventions shown in appropriate standards to interpret and draw electrical circuit diagrams
  • electronic devices – semiconductor diode, transistor, LEDs and Zener diode (7)

☐

J Electronic Systems

J24 Demonstrates and compares different types of input and output waveforms and frequencies
  • oscillators giving sinusoidal, square and sawtooth outputs (4)

☐

K Materials

K28 Carries out simple tests to discover the differences between thermoplastics and thermo-setting plastics, uses reference sources to list engineering applications and properties of these materials (11)

☐

K31 Distinguishes between the electrical properties of conductors and insulators and gives examples of materials in each class of material (11)

☐

Mathematics

A Arithmetic

A3 Ensures the answers to numerical problems are reasonable
  • significant figures, validity and feasibility of solutions, approximations, checking results (15)

☐

A4 Understands and uses, tables and charts
  • conversion tables (10)

☐

B Algebra

B9 Evaluate and transform formulae
- substitution of given data (22) ❏

Science

A Oxidation

A1 Establishes through experiments, the basic chemical processes involved in burning and rusting as examples of chemical reactions (interactions between substances which result in a rearrangement of their atoms) and applies this knowledge to a variety of practical situations
- mass gain of metals such as copper, brass, iron and steel (8) ❏

D Electricity

D11 Solves problems related to current, potential difference and resistance for simple resistive circuits in parallel and series
- current flows (8) ❏

D12 Calculates power in simple electrical circuits
- $P = I V = I^2 R = V^2/R$ (8) ❏

Information Technology Studies

A Introduction to Information Technology

A1 Explain information technology using suitable examples
- quality of information (7) ❏

B Computing

B9 Identifies the range and differences between current computer system hardware devices and categories of software
- mainframe, mini and microcomputers (30) ❏

C Information Technology Applications in the Office

C16 Outlines the basic characteristics of document storage and retrieval, comparing such factors as cost, ease of use and storage space
- paper (13) ❏

Task No. 5 – Marketing the Generator

Suggested learning support time – 15 hrs

Common Skills – Competence Objectives & Performance Criteria

B Working with and Relating to Others

B6 Relate to and interact effectively with individuals and groups
- experience, skills and knowledge of others identified and valued ❏

C Communicating

C10 Communicate in writing
- correct sources of information identified and consulted ❏

G Applying Design and Creativity

G18 Use a range of thought processes
- ways of thinking identified and stated ❏

Vocational – Competence Objectives & Indicative Content

Engineeering Fundamentals

A Safety Hazards

A3 Recognises the importance of safe electrical working in protecting life and property
- personal safety precautions regarding clothing, dampness, tools (5) ❏

C Fastening and Joining of Materials

C9   Carries out various joining methods for materials, identifies their applications, advantages and disadvantages
- adhesives, resins and solvents, with particular attention to safety hazards (15)   ❑

E Engineering Drawing

E14   Uses the conventions shown in the British Standards to produce sectioned and dimensioned working drawings
- components from electrical/mechanical devices (7)   ❑

E15   Uses conventions shown in appropriate standards to interpret and draw electrical circuit diagrams
- power supplies – battery, earth, a.c. mains, d.c. mains (7)   ❑

F Electrical Measuring Instruments

F16   Carries out tests/measurements
- insulation resistance using IR tester (multi-meter) (3)   ❑

J Electronic Systems

J24   Demonstrates and compares different types of input and output waveforms and frequencies
- using, for example a CRO and in addition measures the gain of a simple a.c. amplifier (4)   ❑

Mathematics

A Arithmetic

A4   Understands and uses, tables and charts
- applications to practical problems (10)   ❑

A5   Performs basic arithmetic operations on a calculator
- checking of results (10)   ❑

D Statistics

D16   Collects, tabulates and summarise statistical data and interprets it descriptively
- sample and population (6)   ❑

Science

A Oxidation

A1   Establishes through experiments, the basic chemical processes involved in burning and rusting as examples of chemical reactions (interactions between substances which result in a rearrangement of their atoms) and applies this knowledge to a variety of practical situations
- analysis of oxides (8)   ❑

D Electricity

D11   Solves problems related to current, potential difference and resistance for simple resistive circuits in parallel and series
- use of ammeters and voltmeters (8)   ❑

D12   Calculates power in simple electrical circuits
- power dissipation (8)   ❑

Information Technology Studies

A Introduction to Information Technology

A2   Identifies practical examples of information technology, and explains their functions
- finance and commerce eg bar codes on goods in shops, computer controlled stock, electronic payment services, debit-card terminals, cash points (7)   ❑

A3   Considers the present and likely future effects of information technology on
- patterns of employment (7)   ❑

C Information Technology Applications in the Office

C16   Outlines the basic characteristics of document storage and retrieval, comparing such factors as cost, ease of use and storage space
- microform (microfilm and microfiche) (13)

Integrative Assignment 2

Energy Conservation

Introduction

This assignment gives you the opportunity to work as a member of a team, to gain understanding of the cost, properties and quality of services and materials necessary for maintaining a measurements laboratory. The skills you will use and develop, and the relevant vocational objectives, are given on page 207. Read them carefully and, with the assistance of your tutor and your team-members, ensure that you understand the basis of the assignment.

Assignment Brief

You are a member of an engineering design team, which specialises in the field of clean rooms for industrial purposes. The control of temperature, pressure and air cleanliness has to conform to standards agreed with the customer and those set down by the Government in the Health and Safety at Work Act. The financial cost of achieving the set standards is very high.

Considerable savings in both financial cost and in energy conservation can be achieved by the proper use of insulating material. This assignment will allow you to examine the heat losses of an existing laboratory, to calculate the amount of heat wasted and to investigate methods of converting it into a 'clean room'.

Your team has been instructed to:

- examine an existing laboratory
- assess areas of heat loss
- calculate total heat loss

Using the technical information provided:

- consider methods and the effects of insulation
- consider the costs and benefits of insulation
- use computer technology to control and monitor the environment of the laboratory.

Your team has to produce a final joint technical report and also prepare and present a 10 minute account of your team's progress in this assignment to the other teams in the group at some time during the period of the assignment. This assignment has been divided into four tasks, as outlined below, and it is expected that you will be supported in your learning by a tutor for approximately 106 hours. To assist you in your time management, each assignment-task has a suggested learning support time given and each objective has an importance weighting, decided by a tutor group. This will permit your team to plan your own learning priorities. You and your team will be continuously assessed and each member needs to achieve both the skills and the knowledge involved in the various tasks of the assignment. The task data sheets give more specific details of this. The various tasks provide you with the opportunity to achieve all of the selected indicative content and performance criteria associated with the assignment's vocational objectives and common skills. Your tutor should provide learning support for your group and will supply any additional information that you require.

Fact Sheet

The control, monitoring and use of energy is extremely important at all levels of the national economy. The amount of energy used for any particular facility has to be considered both for its financial cost to the user and for its cost in terms of the available fuel reserves. The control of the environment depends on the nature of the process and its degree of sophistication. Clean rooms with their own particular control problems are a familiar facility in a wide range of industrial applications.

The clean room in this assignment has to be assessed on both counts. The purpose of this assignment is to assess, monitor and control the environment of an industrial clean room for temperature, lighting and atmospheric pressure.

You will have to determine the financial cost of insulating the clean room in the short-term and to measure this against the price of monitoring and controlling the room's environment and the energy saving over the longer term. There are many sources of information available to you to assess the effectiveness of insulating materials and to allow you to calculate the heat losses through structures. The degree of sophistication in measurement and control is being achieved by using equipment designed around micro-technology.

The design of any work area has, first, to be functional, but a clean room, because of its isolation, does require additional planning with respect to design and colour decoration. A number of factors influence the final selection of the room to be converted into the clean room: the cost of conversion; the use to be made of it; the additional services needed; and the control tolerances required.

In completing this task you will have to specify a wide range of materials for wall, ceiling and floor insulation and select instruments to measure the temperature difference across the various wall thicknesses; to measure the energy input into the room over a period of time; to maintain an atmospheric pressure difference; and to measure the light intensity in the room.

Task 1 – Building Specifications

(Suggested support time 27 hours)

After the initial briefing by your tutor, you should work with your team and undertake the following:

(a) Measure and sketch isometrically the selected laboratory. Sketch an isometric view without an isometric scale. Calculate the areas and volumes involved.

(b) Produce, in orthographic projection, a detailed drawing, including dimensions of all areas and openings. Use British Standards conventions to produce sectioned and dimensioned drawings and demonstrate an understanding of lighting and power circuits.

(c) Consider the atmosphere of the workshop and its effects on the various materials involved in its construction.

(d) Consider the situation where the workshop has to be kept with an air pressure slightly above atmospheric pressure, and use experimental methods to establish that fluid pressure is equal in all directions.

(e) To combat the effects of external weather conditions, measure the destructive effects on building materials of water freezing and show that materials expand and contract with temperature change. Use tables and calculators to ensure that answers to problems are reasonable.

Task 2 – Heat Loss Areas

(Suggested support time 29 hours)

Working with your own team undertake the following:

(a) List, in priority order, regions where heat losses occur. Produce neat and clear drawings and investigate energy conservation methods.

(b) Recognise the importance of safe electrical working and draw an electrical circuit diagram which describes the layout of lighting and power circuits.

(c) Consider the pressure/volume output of the compressor which supplies air to the clean room to maintain the pressure differential. Establish experimentally, absolute and gauge pressure.

(d) Consider the energy requirements for all services to the clean room. Identify possible dangers from compressed air, fumes, liquids, gases and dust.

(e) Use computer storage and retrieval systems for information to complete this task and analyse this task using a flowchart. Identify practical applications of IT in this task and consider the cost of using an IT approach.

Task 3 – Evaluate Heat Losses

(Suggested support time 27 hours)

Working with your own team:

(a) Calculate the surface areas where heat losses occur. In this, use conversion tables and a calculator to perform basic arithmetic operations. Use British Standards to produce drawing assemblies.

(b) Calculate the heat losses from these surfaces.

(c) Identify a variety of insulating materials and examine the problems associated with using asbestos. Identify the need to protect materials from atmospheric attack and carry out tests/measurements for insulation resistance.

(d) Calculate the heat losses from insulated surfaces using a range of insulating materials.

(e) Trace the heating and lighting circuits of the chosen room and carry out a series of tests to ascertain any additional power requirement. Demonstrate an understanding of lighting and power circuits. Build and test a lighting circuit and calculate fuse values.

(f) Identify and use information technology techniques in planning this task and extend the use of the flowchart you have already prepared to consider decisions.

Task 4 – *Insulating Costs/Report*

(Suggested support time 22 hours)

After the initial briefing by your tutor and working with your own team undertake the following:

(a) Estimate the costs involved in insulating the laboratory. Prepare a final drawing and calculate the saving over a one-year period.

(b) Consider how a digital computer system could be used to control and monitor the various clean room parameters. Cost the equipment and software necessary.

(c) Prepare a final report and make a 10-minute team presentation of your progress in this assignment.

Assessment

You will be assessed in the following way:

(a) How well you contributed to the work of the team. This will be based upon tutor observation and peer-group assessment of your work. You should keep a profile of your achievements during the period of the assignment.

(b) Your own understanding and interpretation of the skills and knowledge of the assignment. This will be based upon a personal interview with your tutor.

Task Data
Integrative Assignment No. 2

Energy Conservation

Task No. 1 – Building Specifications

Suggested learning support time – 27 hrs

Common Skills – Competence Objectives & Performance Criteria

A Managing and Developing People

A2   Manage own time in achieving objectives
  • prescribed techniques used and planned objectives achieved within an agreed timescale ❑

A3   Undertakes personal and career development
  • areas for development identified and an action plan agreed and produced ❑

C Communicating

C8   Receive and respond to a variety of information
  • received information accurately interpreted and summarised ❑

D Managing Tasks and Solving Problems

D14 Identify and solve routine and non-routine problems
  • plan of action devised and implemented using suitable problem solving techniques ❑

Vocational – Competence Objectives & Indicative Content

Engineering Fundamentals

A Safety Hazards

A4   Carries out simulation exercises successfully and outlines procedures to be followed in cases of electric shock, respiratory or cardiac failure; outlines likely effects, identifying symptoms. Explains procedure when a person is in contact with a live line (3) ❑

E Engineering Drawing

E11 Explains with the aid of drawings the meaning of orthographic projection, and produces neat and clear drawings including the use of hidden detail lines
  • principle planes of projection (5) ❑
  • simple 3-dimensional objects (5) ❑

E13 Draws, from given orthographic drawings and orthographic views
  • isometric views with no isometric scale (5) ❑

E14 Uses the conventions shown in the British Standards to produce sectioned and dimensioned working drawings
  • assemblies (not more than 6 parts) (5) ❑

H Lighting and Power Circuits

H21 Demonstrates an understanding of the layout of lighting and power circuits
  • defining a final sub-circuit as an assembly of conductors and accessories emanating from a final distribution board (10) ❑

Mathematics

A Arithmetic

A1   Evaluates expressions involving integer indices and use standard form
  • base, index, power. reciprocal in terms of a to the power of n (8) ❑

A3   Ensures the answers to numerical problems are reasonable
- significant figures, validity and feasibility of solutions, approximations, checking results (10)   ☐

C Geometry and Trigonometry

C12   Calculates areas and volumes of plane figures and common solids using given formulae
- volume of cubes, prisms, cylinders (21)
- surface area of cubes, prisms, cylinders (21)   ☐☐

C15   Solves right-angled triangles for angles and lengths of sides using sine, cosine and tangent functions
- use of tables or calculators (20)   ☐

Science

A Oxidation

A1   Establishes through experiments, the basic chemical processes involved in burning and rusting as examples of chemical reactions (interactions between substances which result in a rearrangement of their atoms) and applies this knowledge to a variety of practical situations
- effects of oxygen and water (13)
- preventative treatments (12)   ☐☐

B Statics

B4   Establishes by experiments that fluid pressure at any level is equal in all directions, is normal to its containing surface, and is dependent on density and head of liquid
- definition of pressure (42)   ☐

C Motion and Energy

C9   Solves problems associated with mass, specific heat capacity and temperature change, showing how materials expand or contract with temperature change, and illustrates positive and negative effects in practical situations
- temperature/time graphs for change of state (22)   ☐

Information Technology Studies

A Introduction to Information Technology

A1   Explain information technology using suitable examples
- message transmission (7)   ☐

A3   Considers the present and likely future effects of information technology on
- domestic and leisure activities (5)   ☐

B Computing

B8   Distinguishes between types of storage and recognises their role within the computer system
- basic characteristics of stores ie access and cycle time (25)   ☐

B9   Identifies the range and differences between current computer system hardware devices and categories of software
- user application software, support software, system software (25)   ☐

Task No. 2 – Areas of Heat Loss

Suggested learning support time – 29 hrs

Common Skills – Competence Objectives & Performance Criteria

A Managing and Developing People

A1   Manage own roles and responsibilities
- constraints of roles and responsibilities identified   ☐

B Working with and Relating to Others

B7   Work effectively as a member of a team
  • strengths and weaknesses of team members identified ❑

D Managing Tasks and Solving Problems

D13 Deal with a combination of routine and non-routine tasks
  • tasks prioritised and sequenced ❑

F Applying Technology

F16 Use a range of technological equipment and systems
  • initial preparation procedures for equipment completed ❑

Vocational – Competence Objectives & Indicative Content
Engineering Fundamentals

A Safety Hazards

A1   Studies the 'Health and Safety at Work Act', using practical situations and layouts in the workshop/laboratory to identify the major responsibilities
  • possible dangers from: compressed air; noxious fumes and liquids; explosive gases and dust (3) ❑

A3   Recognises the importance of safe electrical working in protecting life and property (3)
  • likely damage to property (3) ❑ ❑

E Engineering Drawing

E11 Explains with the aid of drawings the meaning of orthographic projection, and produces neat and clear drawings including the use of hidden detail lines
  • areas (5) ❑

E12 Produces neat and clear drawings using pictorial projection
  • isometric projection (13) ❑

E15 Uses conventions shown in appropriate standards to interpret and draw electrical circuit diagrams
  • power supplies – battery, earth, a.c. mains, d.c. mains (5)
  • electronic devices – semiconductor diode, transistor, LEDs and Zener diode (5) ❑ ❑

H Lighting and Power Circuits

H21 Demonstrates an understanding of the layout of lighting and power circuits
  • describing the following circuit arrangements – 15 amp radial circuit – 30 amp ring circuit supplying 13 amp socket outlets (10) ❑

K Materials

K31 Distinguishes between the electrical properties of conductors and insulators and gives examples of materials in each class of material (9) ❑

Mathematics

A Arithmetic

A2   Evaluates expressions involving negative and fractional indices and logarithms
  • logarithms of numbers (9) ❑

A5   Performs basic arithmetic operations on a calculator (8) ❑

B Algebra

B9   Evaluate and transform formulae
  • transformation to change subject of formula (22) ❑

Science

B Statics

B4   Establishes by experiments that fluid pressure at any level is equal in all directions, is normal to its containing surface, and is dependent on density and head of liquid
  • absolute and gauge pressure (42) ❑

C Motion and Energy

C8   Carries out tests and solves problems associated with energy
   - identification of forms of energy (21)   ❑

D Electricity

D12 Calculates power in simple electrical circuits
   - $P = I V = I^2 R = V^2/R$ (11)   ❑

Information Technology Studies

A Introduction to Information Technology

A2   Identifies practical examples of information technology, and explains their functions
   - industry eg design, manufacturing, planning, process automation, monitoring and control (7)   ❑

B Computing

B6   Analyse programming tasks by the use of flowcharts and identifies the standard flow symbols
   - input/output operations (25)   ❑

C Information Technology Applications

C16 Outlines the basic characteristics of document storage and retrieval, comparing such factors as cost, ease of use and storage space
   - computerised systems (67)   ❑

Task No. 3 – Evaluate Heat Losses

Suggested learning support time – 27 hrs

Common Skills – Competence Objectives & Performance Criteria

A Managing and Developing People

A4   Transfer skills gained to new and changing situations and contexts
   - new skills and knowledge to be developed identified in cooperation with others   ❑

B Working with and Relating to Others

B6   Relate to and interact effectively with individuals and groups
   - others listened to and observed appropriately   ❑

C Communicating

C9   Present information in a variety of visual forms
   - appropriate visual methods of presentation identified and selected   ❑

G Applying Design and Creativity

G17 Apply a range of skills and techniques to develop a variety of ideas in the creation of new/modified products, services or situations
   - use and combination of skills and techniques explored   ❑

Vocational – Competence Objectives & Indicative Content
Engineering Fundamentals

A Safety Hazards

A3   Recognises the importance of safe electrical working in protecting life and property
   - likely sources of electrical danger (3)   ❑

E Engineering Drawing

E14 Uses the conventions shown in the British Standards to produce sectioned and dimensioned working drawings
   - assemblies (not more than 6 parts) (5)   ❑

E15 Uses conventions shown in appropriate standards to interpret and draw electrical circuit diagrams
   - connections, junctions, cables (twin-core, 3-core, screened) (5)   ❑

F Electrical Measuring Instruments

F16 Carries out tests/measurements for
- insulation resistance using IR tester (multi-meter) (21) ❏

H Lighting and Power Circuits

H21 Demonstrates an understanding of the layout of lighting and power circuits
- sketching the circuit diagrams for one-way and two-way lighting circuits (10) ❏
- studying and listing the IEE Regulations for the limitations of the number of lighting points and circuit ratings (10) ❏

H22 Carries out an assignment involving the building and testing of a lighting circuit: (For safety reasons the circuit must not be connected to the mains supply) (10) ❏

K Materials

K30 Discusses the safety hazards in the use of asbestos (8) ❏

K32 Discovers the reason for and methods of protecting materials from atmospheric attack
- the need for the protection of metallic materials from atmospheric corrosion (8) ❏

Mathematics

A Arithmetic

A4 Understands and uses, tables and charts
- conversion tables (8) ❏

A5 Performs basic arithmetic operations on a calculator
- numbers to a power (8) ❏

B Algebra

B6 Uses basic notation and rules of algebra
- numbers and letters (22) ❏

B10 Illustrates direct and inverse proportionality
- dependent and independent variables (22) ❏

Science

C Motion and Energy

C8 Carries out tests and solves problems associated with energy
- efficiency in terms of energy input and output (22) ❏

D Electricity

D12 Calculates power in simple electrical circuits
- calculation of fuse values given power rating and voltage of an appliance (11) ❏

Information Technology Studies

A Introduction to Information Technology

A1 Explain information technology using suitable examples
- information technology (7) ❏

A2 Identifies practical examples of information technology, and explains their functions
- document storage and retrieval eg computer systems, microfiche (7) ❏

B Computing

B6 Analyse programming tasks by the use of flowcharts and identifies the standard flow symbols
- decision (25) ❏

Task No. 4 – Insulating Costs/Report

Suggested learning support time – 22 hrs 30 min

Common Skills – Competence Objectives & Performance Criteria

B Working and Relating to Others

B5   Treat other's values, beliefs and opinions with respect
- own values, beliefs and opinions identified, reflected upon and described   ☐

D Managing Tasks and Solving Problems

D12   Use information sources
- information sorted into a useable and effective format   ☐

E Applying Numeracy

E15   Apply numerical skills and techniques
- appropriate techniques selected and applied   ☐

Vocational – Competence Objectives & Indicative Content

Engineering Fundamentals

A Safety Hazards

A1   Studies the 'Health and Safety at Work Act', using practical situations and layouts in the workshop/laboratory to identify the major responsibilities
- the need for personal hygiene, cleanliness and tidiness in the working situation, highlighting possible hazards arising from untidy working conditions (3)   ☐

A2   Simulates the appropriate procedures which should be adopted in the event of workshop accidents
- physical injury (3)   ☐

E Engineering Drawing

E13   Draws, from given orthographic drawings and orthographic views
- oblique views (5)   ☐

E14   Uses the conventions shown in the British Standards to produce sectioned and dimensioned working drawings
- functional and non-functional dimensions (5)   ☐

I Electrical Protection

I23   Prepares explanatory notes from given references concerned with adequate protection of electrical installations.
- construction advantages and disadvantages of rewireable fuses and cartridge fuse element (13)   ☐

K Materials

K32   Discovers the reason for and methods of protecting materials from atmospheric attack
- how painting, anodising, plating can be used to protect against atmospheric corrosion (8)   ☐

Mathematics

A Arithmetic

A1   Evaluates expressions involving integer indices and use standard form
- four basic operations using standard form (8)   ☐

A4   Understands and uses, tables and charts
- applications to practical problems (8)   ☐

A5   Performs basic arithmetic operations on a calculator
- checking of calculations (8)   ☐

B Algebra

B6   Uses basic notation and rules of algebra
- simplification of expressions (22)   ☐

Science

C Motion and Energy

C8 Carries out tests and solves problems associated with energy
- power (22)   ❑

D Electricity

D11 Solves problems related to current, potential difference and resistance for simple resistive circuits in parallel and series
- Ohm's Law (10)   ❑
- temperature effect (10)   ❑
- practical applications (10)   ❑

D12 Calculates power in simple electrical circuits
- power dissipation (11)   ❑

D13 Uses practical examples to explain the chemical effects of electricity
- construction of a simple cell (12)   ❑

Information Technology Studies

B Computing

B5 Demonstrates an understanding of the basic structure of a digital computer system and distinguishes between the control signal paths and data paths by illustrating the relationship between the central processor and peripheral equipment
- input unit (25)   ❑

B9 Identifies the range and differences between current computer system hardware devices and categories of software
- data input/output, image, sound and text (25)

Integrative Assignment 3

An Alignment Device

Introduction

This assignment gives you the opportunity to work with a team to investigate the alignment of heavy gauge material during a machining operation, and to design and manufacture an alignment device necessary to support and locate a piece of heavy steel plate.

The skills you will use and develop and the relevant programme objectives, are given on page 218. Read them carefully, and, with the assistance of your tutor and your team-members, make sure that you understand the basis of the assignment.

Assignment Brief

You are a member of a heavy engineering production team, which specialises in the machining of large components to very close tolerances. This type of work has to be carried out with great care and attention to avoid accidents to the people involved, and to prevent damage to the machine tools or other equipment being used. The financial costings for this work have to be recorded. They will include time, labour and materials. The Assignment will allow each member of the team to design and manufacture an adjustable device which can be used safely to support and align an item of steel plate during a machining operation.

Your team has been instructed to:

- consider and record the safety problems involved
- produce a neat sketch of your device with full dimensions
- manufacture the device after considering
    the materials and equipment to be used
    the estimated times for each stage of manufacture
- record the actual time necessary for each stage of its manufacture
- calculate the cost of the design and manufacture of the alignment device.

Your team has to produce a joint report, using a word processor, recording any problems you have met and how you solved them. You will also have to select, from your team's work, the best design of an alignment device and give your reasons for your selection.

This assignment has been divided into four tasks, as outlined below, and it is expected that you will be supported in your learning by a tutor for approximately 115 hours. To assist you in your time management, each assignment task has a suggested learning support time and each of the indicative content items has an importance weighting. This should permit your team to establish its own learning priorities.

You and your colleagues will be continuously assessed. Each of you is encouraged to achieve both the skills and the knowledge involved in the various tasks of the assignment. These are explained in more detail in the task data sheets. The various tasks provide the opportunity for you to achieve all of the selected indicative content and performance criteria associated with the assignment's vocational objectives and common skills. Your tutor will provide learning support for your group and will supply any additional information required.

Fact Sheet

The alignment of large components prior to machining has always involved the use of wedges and metal spacers, as well as adjustable alignment devices to position the component. The machining of large engineering components can be extremely difficult, mainly as a result of the shape and size of the component. The cutting tool of the machine has to be aligned with the surface being shaped, milled, drilled, turned, or burned. The accurate location of the machine tool with the surface can be achieved using an adjustable alignment device.

Your task in this assignment is to produce a screw-threaded adjustable device to align a piece of heavy steel plate during a machining operation. You will need to calculate the overall costing for the design and manufacture of the device. You will be involved in a number of production processes in the manufacture of the device, all of which depend on the particular design you choose.

A number of factors influence the final shape and form of the alignment device and changes are often made to an existing design in order to accommodate the manufacturing process. Your design may use adjustable screw-threads or a combination of plates and wedges. The alignment device for this application should have a base which is internally threaded and a central, externally-screwed pillar, supporting a weight-carrying plate, through a ball and socket joint.

Your devices can be manufactured from a variety of materials. Your choice of materials will depend upon the machining process and the material of the load being supported.

Task 1 – Device Design

(Suggested support time 32.5 hours)

After the initial briefing by your tutor and working with your team:

(a) Study the general safety information and other aspects of working in a machine shop with heavy duty materials and machine-tools, and identify responsibilities under the Health and Safety at Work Act. Perform marking-out exercises.

(b) Study the particular problem of aligning the steel plate in the machine tool and also establish through experiments, damage caused through rusting. Design and sketch your own ideas of an adjustable device to support and accurately position the steel plate and discuss it with your tutor. Use conventions shown in the British Standards to sketch freehand in oblique projection and calculate the areas and volumes involved. Use tests and reference sources to provide examples of damage caused by rusting and establish the effect of a force rotating about a point

(c) Draw and fully dimension your alignment device, include suitable measuring equipment. Use first angle projection. Use tests and reference sources to indicate properties of materials and show how materials expand and contract with temperature change.

(d) Estimate the times necessary for each stage of manufacture. Produce graphs from results obtained.

Task 2 – *Device Manufacture*

(Suggested support time 28.0 hours)

Working with your own team

(a)   Analyse the task using a flowchart. Select machines and appropriate tools. Outline the problems involved.

(b)   Negotiate the availability of machine-tools and select appropriate tools and cutting fluids.

(c)   Under the supervision of your tutor and observing all the workshop safety regulations, select materials and manufacture the alignment device to the set tolerances. Use digital computer measuring systems wherever possible. Perform marking-out exercises and use suitable equipment to measure components. Carry out various joining methods. Carry out heat treatment exercises and show how materials expand or contract with temperature change.

(d)   Record the time each stage of the manufacture takes and analyse the stages of the task.

Task 3 – *Device Costings*

(suggested support time 24.5 hours)

Working with your team, use the estimated and recorded times from each stage of your design, manufacture and research to complete the following tasks:

(a)   Calculate the overall costings for this assignment and carry out a series of alternative investigations that might have been useful in this assignment, using various items of equipment and types of material.

(b)   Assume that the alignment device also has to be used to maintain the steel plate's position during a profile-burning operation and consider the temperature effects on any materials or electrical sensing equipment. Carry out tests on thermoplastic, thermo-setting plastic, ceramics, single and composite materials. Examine the temperature effects on simple resistive circuits and define good and bad conductors, using practical examples.

(c)   Using appropriate computer software, calculate and present a financial statement for both the estimated and actual final costs for this assignment.

Task 4 – *Report & Recommendations*

(Suggested support time 31.0 hours)

Working with your own team:

(a) Consider the possible use of plastics in the design and manufacture of location devices (fabricated or machined). Use encapsulation techniques and carry out various joining methods. Carry out tests to discover the mechanical properties of various plastic materials. Calculate areas and volumes of surfaces and common solids.

(b) Consider how air pressure could be used to support the steel plate. Sketch your proposed design and draw it, using isometric views. Describe this application of gas pressure and carry out tests, draw graphs, and tabulate data.

(c) Recommend ways of improving the design, and the cost of production of your device.

(d) Using a word processing package, and, assuming a degree of privacy and security, prepare a joint report for this Assignment.

Assessment

You will be assessed in the following manner:

(a) how well you contributed to the work of the team. This will be based upon tutor observation and peer-group assessment of your work. You should keep a profile of your achievements during the period of the assignment.

(b) your own understanding and interpretation of the skills and knowledge of the assignment. This will be based upon a personal interview with your tutor.

Task Data
Integrative Assignment No. 3

An Alignment Device

Task No. 1 – Device Design

Suggested learning support time – 32 hrs 30 min

Common Skills – Competence Objectives & Performance Criteria
B Working with and Relating to Others

B7   Work effectively as a member of a team
- accuracy of own interpretation of brief/allocated tasks agreed with team   ❑

C Communicating

C11   Participate in oral and non-verbal communication
- appropriate vocabulary, language, tone and techniques used to give and receive messages   ❑

D Managing Tasks and Solving Problems

D14   Identify and solve routine and non-routine problems
- realistic solution selected and used   ❑

GApplying Design and Creativity

G18   Use a range of thought processes
- ideas mixed in usual and unusual ways to provide creative approaches and solutions   ❑

Vocational – Competence Objectives & Indicative Content
Engineering Fundamentals
A Safety Hazards

A1   Studies the 'Health and Safety at Work Act', using practical situations and layouts in the
workshop/laboratory to identify the major responsibilities
- the need for personal hygiene, cleanliness and tidiness in the working situation, highlighting
possible hazards arising from untidy working conditions (4)   ❑
- dangers associated with unsuitable clothing and hair (4)   ❑

B Hand and Machine Processes

B5   Performs marking out exercises on plane surfaces, selects the relevant hand tools for a task
- the function of datum lines and centre lines (4)   ❑
- how to maintain hand tools in good condition (4)   ❑

B7   Uses machines and outlines problems and limitations which could arise; also identifying design
and operational features and safety precautions
- sensitive drilling machine, centre lathe (4)   ❑
- cutting speeds for common tool/workpiece material combinations (4)   ❑

B8   Selects appropriate tools and cutting fluids for various machining operations and describes
suitable tool maintenance
- the advantages of using cutting fluids (3)   ❑

C Fastening and Joining of Materials

C9   Carries out various joining methods for materials, identifies their applications, advantages and
disadvantages
- screws, bolts, nuts and washers commonly available and types of thread (7)   ❑

E Engineering Drawing

E11 Explains with the aid of drawings the meaning of orthographic projection, and produces neat and clear drawings including the use of hidden detail lines
- first angle projection (15) ❏

E12 Produces neat and clear drawings using pictorial projection
- oblique projection (15) ❏

E14 Uses the conventions shown in the British Standards to produce sectioned and dimensioned working drawings
- functional and non-functional dimensions (9) ❏

K Materials

K25 Uses laboratory tests and given reference sources to indicate the general composition, properties of certain engineering materials. The properties should be compared in terms such as strength, rigidity, hardness, elasticity toughness, electrical conductivity, temperature stability, ease of processing and costs
- low, medium and high carbon steel and cast iron (5) ❏

K27 Identifies the bearing properties of phosphor bronze, cast iron, PTFE, nylon and graphite (6) ❏

Mathematics

A Arithmetic

A3 Ensures the answers to numerical problems are reasonable
- significant figures, validity and feasibility of solutions, approximations, checking results (3) ❏

A4 Understands and uses, tables and charts
- logarithms, squares, cubes, square roots, cube roots, sine, cosine, tangent, reciprocals (5) ❏

B Algebra

B8 Solves, algebraically, simple equations and linear simultaneous equations
- maintenance of equality (6) ❏

B10 Illustrates direct and inverse proportionality
- applications eg Boyle's Law, Charles' Law, Hooke's Law, Ohm's Law (6) ❏

B11 Determines the equation of a straight-line graph
- three or more points from coordinates of equation of form $y = mx + c$ (6) ❏

C Geometry and Trigonometry

C12 Calculates areas and volumes of plane figures and common solids using given formulae
- area of triangle, square, rectangle, parallelogram, circle, semi-circle (7) ❏
- proportionality (7) ❏

C13 Recognises the types and properties of triangles
- acute-angled, right-angled, obtuse-angled, equilateral, isosceles (7) ❏
- Pythagoras – 3, 4, 5 and 5, 12, 13 triangles (7) ❏
- construction of triangle given limited information (7) ❏

C14 Identifies the geometric properties of a circle
- relationship of angles (7) ❏

C15 Solves right-angled triangles for angles and lengths of sides using sine, cosine and tangent functions
- construction of right-angled triangles (6) ❏
- applications to technical problems (7) ❏

Science
A Oxidation

A1 Establishes through experiments, the basic chemical processes involved in burning and rusting as examples of chemical reactions (interactions between substances which result in a rearrangement of their atoms) and applies this knowledge to a variety of practical situations
- examples of damage caused by rusting (25) ❏

B Statics

B2 Produces graphs from results obtained experimentally to determine the relationship between force and extension for different given materials and subsequently verify Hooke's Law relating to elasticity by solving practical problems (8) ❏

B3 Establishes the effect of a force rotating about a point and solves simple problems related to static equilibrium
- principle of moments (8) ❏
- centre of gravity (8) ❏

C Motion and Energy

C8 Carries out tests and solves problems associated with energy
- work in terms of force applied and distance moved (11) ❏

C9 Solves problems associated with mass, specific heat capacity and temperature change, showing how materials expand or contract with temperature change, and illustrates positive and negative effects in practical situations
- temperature/time graphs for change of state (8) ❏

Information Technology Studies
A Introduction to Information Technology

A1 Explain information technology using suitable examples
- quality of information (8) ❏

A2 Identifies practical examples of information technology, and explains their functions
- publishing and printing eg author editing-printing-warehousing-marketing, electronic publishing (8) ❏

B Computing

B4 Investigates types of digital computer and their function and prepares a report
- typical fields of application for digital computers in both real time and batch processing modes (10) ❏

B8 Distinguishes between types of storage and recognises their role within the computer system
- volatile and non-volatile storage (10) ❏

Task No. 2 – Device Manufacture

Suggested learning support time – 28 hrs

Common Skills – Competence Objectives & Performance Criteria
A Managing and Developing People

A4 Transfer skills gained to new and changing situations and contexts
- existing skills and concepts applied to differing situations and contexts ❏

D Managing Tasks and Solving Problems

D13 Deal with a combination of routine and non-routine tasks
- where appropriate, advice identified, sought and used ❏

F Applying Technology

F16 Use a range of technological equipment and systems
- equipment used effectively
- operating, safety and security procedures followed at all times

Vocational – Competence Objectives & Indicative Content
Engineering Fundamentals
A Safety Hazards

A1 Studies the 'Health and Safety at Work Act', using practical situations and layouts in the workshop/laboratory to identify the major responsibilities
- importance of machine guards (4)

A3 Recognises the importance of safe electrical working in protecting life and property
- likely sources of electrical danger (5)

B Hand and Machine Processes

B5 Performs marking out exercises on plane surfaces, selects the relevant hand tools for a task
- which equipment is required for simple tasks to mark out profiles (4)

B6 Uses suitable equipment to measure components, explains the principles and identifies limitations governed by accuracy, robustness, etc. Examines equipment including micrometers; verniers; plunger dial gauges; level type test indicators (4)

B7 Uses machines and outline problems and limitations which could arise, also identies design and operational features and safety precautions
- twist drills, trepanning tools, reamers, cutting angles, holding and clamping methods (4)
- three methods of taper turning (4)

B8 Selects appropriate tools and cutting fluids for various machining operations and describes suitable tool maintenance
- identification of relevant angles on common cutting tools (3)

C Fastening and Joining of Materials

C9 Carries out various joining methods for materials, identifies their applications, advantages and disadvantages
- screws, bolts, nuts and washers commonly available and types of thread
- techniques employed in various locking devices, such as spring washers, self-locking nuts, castle nuts (7)

K Materials

K26 Carries out examples of heat treatment and records the individual stages of annealing; normalising; hardening and tempering as applied to commonly used metals and alloys; identifying their effects on the properties (6)

Mathematics
A Arithmetic

A1 Evaluates expressions involving integer indices and use standard form
- base, index, power. reciprocal in terms of a to the power of n (5)
- four basic operations using standard form (5)

A2 Evaluates expressions involving negative and fractional indices and logarithms
- logarithms of numbers (5)

A4 Understands and uses, tables and charts
- conversion tables (5)

A5 Performs basic arithmetic operations on a calculator
- four basic operations (5)

B Algebra

B6 Uses basic notation and rules of algebra
- numbers and letters (6)

B7   Multiplies and factorises algebraic expressions involving brackets
- multiplying expressions inside brackets by numbers, symbols or expressions within brackets eg $3a(2 + b) = 6a + 3ab, (a + b)(2 + c) = 2a + ac + 2b + bc$ (6)   ☐

B8   Solves, algebraically, simple equations and linear simultaneous equations
- linear equations with one unknown (5)   ☐
- construction of equations from derived data (5)   ☐

B9   Evaluate and transform formulae
- substitution of given data (5)   ☐
- transformation to change subject of formula (6)   ☐

B10   Illustrates direct and inverse proportionality
- coefficient of proportionality from given data (6)   ☐

B11   Determines the equation of a straight-line graph
- intercept with the y axis (6)   ☐
- gradient of the straight line (6)   ☐

C Geometry and Trigonometry

C14   Identifies the geometric properties of a circle
- radius, diameter, circumference, chord, tangent, secant, sector, segment, arc (7)   ☐
- applications relating radius, circumference and diameter (7)   ☐

C15   Solves right-angled triangles for angles and lengths of sides using sine, cosine and tangent functions
- trigonometric functions (6)   ☐
- applications to technical problems (6)   ☐

D Statistics

D16   Collects, tabulates and summarise statistical data and interprets it descriptively
- data collection (3)   ☐
- discrete and continuous data (3)   ☐
- pictorial presentation – bar charts, component bar charts, pie charts, pictograms (4)   ☐

Science

C Motion and Energy

C8   Carries out tests and solves problems associated with energy
- identification of forms of energy (11)   ☐
- efficiency in terms of energy input and output (11)   ☐

C9   Solves problems associated with mass, specific heat capacity and temperature change, showing how materials expand or contract with temperature change, and illustrates positive and negative effects in practical situations
- sensible and latent heat (8)   ☐
- coefficient of linear expansion (8)   ☐

Information Technology Studies

B Computing

B5   Demonstrates an understanding of the basic structure of a digital computer system and distinguishes between the control signal paths and data paths by illustrating the relationship between the central processor and peripheral equipment
- main store (10)   ☐
- output unit (10)   ☐

B6   Analyses programming tasks by the use of flowcharts and identifies the standard flow symbols
- terminal point (10)   ☐
- connector (10)   ☐

B8 Distinguishes between types of storage and recognises their role within the computer system
- need for main stores and immediate access stores (10)
- destructive and non-destructive read output (10)
- use of the main categories of storage ie scratchpad, main store, abcking store (10)

Task No. 3 – Device Costing

Suggested learning support time – 24 hrs 30 mins

Common Skills – Competence Objectives & Performance Criteria

A Managing and Developing People

A1 Manage own roles and responsibilities
- given criteria for achievement accepted, monitored and adjustments agreed

B Working with and Relating to Others

B6 Relate to and interact effectively with individuals and groups
- help and support offered to and received from others

C Communicating

C9 Present information in a variety of visual forms
- relevant visual information presented in a clear and easily assimilated manner

E Applying Numeracy

E15 Apply numerical skills and techniques
- numerical information correctly interpreted

Vocational – Competence Objectives & Indicative Content
Engineering Fundamentals

B Hand and Machine Processes

B5 Performs marking out exercises on plane surfaces, selects the relevant hand tools for a task
- the relative merits of powered and non-powered tools, in terms of speed of production, cost, accuracy, human fatigue (4)

B6 Uses suitable equipment to measure components, explains the principles and identifies limitations governed by accuracy, robustness, etc. Examines equipment including micrometers; verniers; plunger dial gauges; level type test indicators (4)

J Electronic Systems

J24 Demonstrates and compares different types of input and output waveforms and frequencies
- amplifiers,voltage amplifiers, current amplifiers, power amplifiers, d.c. and a.c. amplifiers (6)
- using, for example a CRO and in addition measures the gain of a simple a.c. amplifier (6)

K Materials

K28 Carries out simple tests to discover the differences between thermoplastics and thermo-setting plastics, uses reference sources to list engineering applications and properties of these materials (5)

K29 Uses given reference sources to list the engineering application
- ceramics (5)

K32 Discovers the reason for and methods of protecting materials from atmospheric attack
- the need for the protection of metallic materials from atmospheric corrosion (5)

Mathematics

A Arithmetic

A3 Ensures the answers to numerical problems are reasonable
- significant figures, validity and feasibility of solutions, approximations, checking results (3)

A4   Understands and uses, tables and charts
- applications to practical problems (5)

A5   Performs basic arithmetic operations on a calculator
- numbers to a power (5)
- reciprocals (5)
- checking of calculations (5)

B Algebra

B8   Solves, algebraically, simple equations and linear simultaneous equations
- simultaneous equations with two unknowns (6)

B10 Illustrates direct and inverse proportionality
- dependent and independent variables (6)

D Statistics

D16 Collects, tabulates and summarise statistical data and interprets it descriptively
- range and density of data (3)

Science

B Statics

B2   Produces graphs from results obtained experimentally to determine the relationship between force and extension for different given materials and subsequently verify Hooke's Law relating to elasticity by solving practical problems (8)

B3   Establishes the effect of a force rotating about a point and solves simple problems related to static equilibrium
- use of calculation, practical and vector diagram techniques (8)

B4   Establishes by experiments that fluid pressure at any level is equal in all directions, is normal to its containing surface, and is dependent on density and head of liquid
- measurement of pressure (8)

C Motion and Energy

C8   Carries out tests and solves problems associated with energy
- power (11)

C9   Solves problems associated with mass, specific heat capacity and temperature change, showing how materials expand or contract with temperature change, and illustrates positive and negative effects in practical situations
- single and composite materials (9)

D Electricity

D11 Solves problems related to current, potential difference and resistance for simple resistive circuits in parallel and series
- temperature effect (25)

D13 Uses practical examples to explain the chemical effects of electricity
- good and bad conductors (25)

D14 Establishes, by experiments, electro-magnetic effects and illustrates simple, practical applications of these
- moving coil meter (25)

Information Technology Studies

A Introduction to Information Technology

A3   Considers the present and likely future effects of information technology
- patterns of employment (8)

B Computing

B5 Demonstrates an understanding of the basic structure of a digital computer system and distinguishes between the control signal paths and data paths by illustrating the relationship between the central processor and peripheral equipment
- control unit (10)   ❑

B9 Identifies the range and differences between current computer system hardware devices and categories of software
- user application software, support software, system software (10)   ❑
- importance of man-machine interface and the demands that input/output make on the user (10)   ❑

Task No.4 – Report and Recommendations

Suggested learning support time – 31 hrs

Common Skills – Competence Objectives & Performance Criteria

A Managing and Developing People

A3 Undertakes personal and career development
- own performance improved in line with action plan   ❑

B Working with and Relating to Others

B5 Treat other's values, beliefs and opinions with respect
- other's values, beliefs and opinions identified, reflected upon and described   ❑

B7 Work effectively as a member of a team
- personal contribution is adjusted in response to constructive feedback   ❑

C Communicating

C10 Communicate in writing
- relevant information extracted from a variety of sources   ❑

Vocational – Competence Objectives & Indicative Content
Engineering Fundamentals

B Hand and Machine Processes

B6 Uses suitable equipment to measure components, explains the principles and identifies limitations governed by accuracy, robustness, etc. Examines equipment including micrometers; verniers; plunger dial gauges; level type test indicators (4)   ❑

B7 Uses machines and outline problems and limitations which could arise, also identies design and operational features and safety precautions
- machine spindle speeds for turning, boring and drilling (4)   ❑

C Fastening and Joining of Materials

C9 Carries out various joining methods for materials, identifies their applications, advantages and disadvantages
- adhesives, resins and solvents, with particular attention to safety hazards (7)   ❑

D Working in Plastics

D10 Uses and describes the techniques available within conventional workshops to produce shapes in plastic materials and subsequently indicates applications, gives details of techniques used, associated problems and safety measures
- the use of casting to form plastic materials with special reference to encapsulation techniques for electrical components (16)   ❑

E Engineering Drawing

E13 Draws, from given orthographic drawings and orthographic views
- isometric views with no isometric scale (9)   ❑

- isometric views (9) ❑

E14 Uses the conventions shown in the British Standards to produce sectioned and dimensioned working drawings
  - fastenings, locking devices, threads, knurling, square on shaft, related holes, bearings, springs, gears, matching symbols, welding symbols (10) ❑

G Electrical Connection and Termination

G19 Identifies different types of connection method, recognise their characteristics, and selects a method of connection for a given job, giving reasons for the choice
  - mechanical clamping (5) ❑

K Materials

K28 Carries out simple tests to discover the differences between thermoplastics and thermo-setting plastics, uses reference sources to list engineering applications and properties of these materials (5) ❑

Mathematics

A Arithmetic

A2 Evaluates expressions involving negative and fractional indices and logarithms
  - index rules for negative and fractional indices (5) ❑

A3 Ensures the answers to numerical problems are reasonable
  - significant figures, validity and feasibility of solutions, approximations, checking results (4) ❑

A4 Understands and uses, tables and charts
  - applications to practical problems (5) ❑

A5 Performs basic arithmetic operations on a calculator
  - checking of results (5) ❑

B Algebra

B11 Determines the equation of a straight-line graph
  - positive, negative and zero gradients (6) ❑

C Geometry and Trigonometry

C12 Calculates areas and volumes of plane figures and common solids using given formulae
  - volume of cubes, prisms, cylinders (7) ❑
  - surface area of cubes, prisms, cylinders (7) ❑

D Statistics

D16 Collects, tabulates and summarise statistical data and interprets it descriptively
  - pictorial presentation – bar charts, component bar charts, pie charts, pictograms (4) ❑
  - histogram, frequency polygon, ogive-interpretation (8) ❑

Science

B Statics

B2 Produces graphs from results obtained experimentally to determine the relationship between force and extension for different given materials and subsequently verify Hooke's Law relating to elasticity by solving practical problems (8) ❑

B3 Establishes the effect of a force rotating about a point and solves simple problems related to static equilibrium
  - co-planar forces (8) ❑
  - scalar and Vector quantities (8) ❑

B4 Establishes by experiments that fluid pressure at any level is equal in all directions, is normal to its containing surface, and is dependent on density and head of liquid
  - application to simple problems (including gas pressure) (8) ❑

C Motion and Energy

C8   Carries out tests and solves problems associated with energy
- graphs (11) ☐

Information Technoliogy Studies

A Introduction to Information Technology

A2   Identifies practical examples of information technology, and explains their functions
- communications eg telephone service, broadcasting, cellular radio (8) ☐

B Computing

B5   Demonstrates an understanding of the basic structure of a digital computer system and distinguishes between the control signal paths and data paths by illustrating the relationship between the central processor and peripheral equipment
- arithmetic unit (10)

B7   Identifies the relative merits of machine level coding and high level language programming and explains the need within an instruction for an address and a function. Writes a simple program, using a flow chart and employing a simple instruction set containing up to 8 instructions such as Load, Store, Add, Decrement, Halt, Conditional and Unconditional Jump, Compare. Enter and execute the program (10)

B10   Explains the need for data protection and distinguishes between privacy and security with respect to data, giving an example of each to show how unauthorised access to computerised information can be prevented using codes (10) ☐

C Information Technology Applications in the Office

C12   Identifies the components of a stand-alone word processor system as being processor, printer and disk store and explains the function of each (34) ☐

C16   Outlines the basic characteristics of document storage and retrieval, comparing such factors as cost, ease of use and storage space
- paper (34)

Integrative Assignment 4

An Impact Vehicle

Introduction

This assignment gives you the opportunity to work as a member of a team, in the design, manufacture and the testing of a piece of engineering laboratory equipment. The skills you will use and develop, and the relevant programme objectives, are given in on page 233. Read them carefully, and, with the assistance of your tutor and your team-members, make sure that you understand the basis of the assignment.

Assignment Brief

You are a member of an engineering project team. Your team has been instructed to design and develop a multi-purpose materials testing rig, which is an item of laboratory equipment. You will use the materials provided to produce a prototype. If the rig proves to be a success, it will be considered for commercial production. The tasks set out in this assignment will encourage your inventiveness and allow you to practice your own skills in design, manufacture and development. Your team has been instructed to consider the following:

- safe working
- team work
- energy conversion
- friction
- properties of materials
- electronic sensing.

Your team has to produce a joint technical report containing a specification for a production test rig. This assignment has been divided into five tasks, as outlined below, and it is expected that you will be supported in your learning by a tutor for approximately 135 hours. To assist you in your time management, each assignment task has a suggested learning support time given and each objective has an importance weighting decided by a tutor group. This information should allow your team to plan its own learning priorities. Before starting the assignment, it is essential that your student group provides your tutor with an action plan demonstrating how, while completing the tasks, you intend to achieve the specific skills and objectives relating to the assignment. You and your team will be continuously assessed and each member of the team needs to achieve both the skills and knowledge involved in the various tasks of the assignment. The task data sheets give more specific details of this. The various set tasks provide you with the opportunity to achieve all of the selected indicative content and performance criteria associated with this assignment's vocational objectives and common skills. Your tutor should provide learning support for your group and will supply any additional information that you require.

Fact Sheet

The impact vehicle, which you have to design and manufacture, is a piece of equipment used in the testing of the properties of materials. The energy to carry out the tests is restricted to that available from a known mass falling through a set distance.

Your group's function is to construct and calibrate the vehicle. You will then need to measure the properties of a range of materials for hardness (impact testing) and friction between various surfaces. You will then calculate the energy conversion (potential-kinetic-friction) for a range of masses. To do this, you will need to select appropriate measuring equipment. The time you will need to manufacture the impact vehicle will vary, depending on the complexity of your design; and the production costs involved will depend on the materials you use and the production processes involved. You could use a variety of production processes to manufacture the vehicle, but the process you use will depend clearly upon the design you have chosen.

You should improve the technical processes involved by introducing an accurate sensing device. This could involve the introduction of:

(i)   an impact plate at the base of the inclined plane. This will allow you to measure the hardness of a range of materials. You can then compare your results with those available from a published set of hardness tables.

(ii) if you have a range of materials on the surface of the inclined plane, this will allow you to measure friction between a wide range of surfaces.

The final design of your impact vehicle should be an inclined plane with a support structure which you have designed to accommodate a range of manufacturing processes.

You can use a variety of materials to manufacture your impact vehicle. For example, you might use a wooden structure for cheapness and ease of manufacture; a steel (Dexion Type) structure would permit easy adjustment and flexibility of design. A welded steel structure may prove expensive to manufacture and make modifications relatively difficult.

Your component parts should be as follows:

An *inclined plane*, *pulley wheels*, *cord*, *selected masses* and *timing equipment*.

A *trolley* designed to carry a variable load with the facility to accept a pointed dart on its 'impact face'.

A range of *impact darts* with different point shapes.

An *impact plate* set at the base of the incline, capable of accepting a range of materials for impact testing.

A range of *friction pads* to be fitted to the base of the trolley and the surface of the inclined plane.

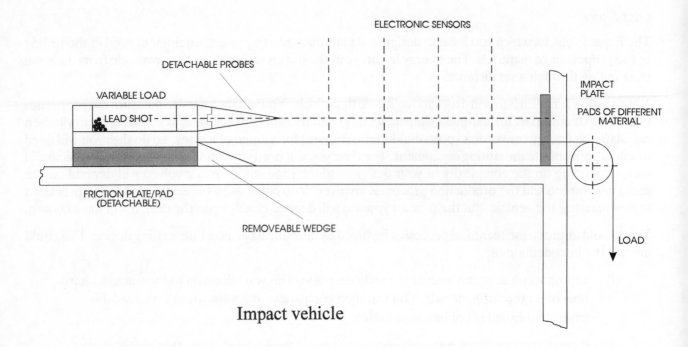

Impact vehicle

Task 1 – *Planning and Preparation*

(Suggested support time 22.0 hours.)

After the initial briefing by your tutor, you should work with your team and undertake the following:

(a)   Study the given outline diagram and analyse the assignment tasks. Use a flowchart to show how you will carry them out. Produce neat and clear drawings.

(b)   Consider the various materials and equipment involved and select various materials for testing.

(c)   Consider the situation where the only energy available for the materials testing is that available from a falling weight and carry out tests associated with energy. Produce graphs from results obtained experimentally.

(d)   Consider the possible application of computer-based systems to the solution of this assignment.

Task 2 – *Design and Manufacture of the Impact Vehicle*

(Suggested support time 33.5 hours)

Working with your own team:

(a)   Analyse the task using a flowchart with standard symbols and extend the use of the flowchart with task details.

(b) Utilising the given diagram, or using your own design, produce working drawings for the impact vehicle. Produce neat and clear drawings in orthographic projection. Produce isometric views from the orthographic drawings.

(c) Manufacture the vehicle, demonstrating the highest possible safety standards, recognising the importance of safe working practices. Perform marking-out exercises. Use suitable measuring equipment and suitable machine-tools.

(d) Consider the use of information technology in the collection and analysis of the test data.

(e) Test prototypes and identify need for instrumentation, including both sensors and recorders. Prepare trial plot graphs for distance/time and trial velocity time graphs from data.

Task 3 – Sensors and Measurement

(Suggested support time 45.0 hours)

Working with your own team:

(a) Test and select suitable sensing and measurement equipment. Carry out measurements using a CRO. Carry out tests and measurements using a variety of meters and use suitable equipment to measure components.

(b) Select and locate instrumentation on the test vehicle rig. While recognising the importance of safe working use machines and outline their limitations. Select appropriate tools and carry out various joining methods.

(c) Test sensing and recording equipment in place. Draw electrical circuit diagrams and carry out the electrical jointing. Identify different types of connection methods.

(d) Write a simple computer program to analyse test results. Use a flowchart.

Task 4 – Properties of Materials

(Suggested support time 15.0 hours)

After an initial briefing by your tutor and working with your own team:

(a) Calibrate the impact vehicle by testing it against commercially available hardness-testing equipment. Determine the relationship between force and extension for different materials. Carry out tests and solve problems associated with energy and ensure that the answers to numerical problems are reasonable.

(b) Carry out a series of simple hardness tests, using as wide a range of materials as possible. Carry out examples of heat treatment. Use laboratory tests and given reference sources. Calculate areas and volumes.

(c)   Carry out a series of friction tests, using a wide range of materials and surfaces. Carry out tests and solve problems associated with energy. Identify the bearing properties of various materials.

(d)   Tabulate your results and produce graphs of energy/hardness and energy/friction for a range of materials. Produce graphs from results obtained experimentally and collect, tabulate and summarise your statistical data.

Task 5 – *Report and Recommendations*

(Suggested support time 19.0 hours)

After an initial briefing by your tutor and working with your own team:

(a)   Consider the viability of the multi-purpose test rig. Draw the fully assembled rig using a simple CAD system.

(b)   Describe the product to prospective customers.

(c)   Use a range of communication techniques in preparing and presenting a final report. Outline the basic characteristics of the report. Plan the layout of the report and use a word-processor to prepare it.

Assessment

You will be assessed in the following way:

(a)   how well you contributed to the work of the team. This will be based upon tutor observation and peer-group assessment of your work. You should keep a profile of your achievements during the period of the assignment.

(b)   your own understanding and interpretation of the skills and knowledge of the assignment. This will be based upon a personal interview with your tutor.

Task Data
Integrative Assignment No. 4

Impact Vehicle

Task No. 1 – Planning & Preparation

Suggested learning support time – 22 hrs

Common Skills – Competence Objectives & Performance Criteria

A Managing and Developing People

A1 Manage own roles and responsibilities
- opportunities for developing own roles and responsibilities agreed ☐

D Managing Tasks and Solving Problems

D13 Deal with a combination of routine and non-routine tasks
- tasks prioritised and sequenced ☐

D14 Identify and solve routine and non-routine problems
- solution checked and action adjusted as necessary ☐

G Applying Design and Creativity

G18 Use a range of thought processes
- use of ideas and results produced, reviewed and evaluated ☐

Vocational – Competence Objectives & Indicative Content
Engineering Fundamentals

A Safety Hazards

A1 Studies the 'Health and Safety at Work Act', using practical situations and layouts in the workshop/laboratory to identify the major responsibilities
- the need for personal hygiene, cleanliness and tidiness in the working situation, highlighting possible hazards arising from untidy working conditions (1) ☐

A2 Simulates the appropriate procedures which should be adopted in the event of workshop accidents
- mouth to mouth resuscitation, using dummies (1) ☐

A3 Recognises the importance of safe electrical working in protecting life and property
- likely damage to property (1) ☐

A4 Carries out simulation exercises successfully and outlines procedures to be followed in cases of electric shock, respiratory or cardiac failure; outlines likely effects, identifying symptoms. Explains procedure when a person is in contact with a live line (5) ☐

B Hand and Machine Processes

B5 Performs marking out exercises on plane surfaces, selects the relevant hand tools for a task
- the function of datum lines and centre lines (3) ☐

E Engineering Drawing

E11 Explains with the aid of drawings the meaning of orthographic projection, and produces neat and clear drawings including the use of hidden detail lines
- areas (3) ☐

E12 Produces neat and clear drawings using pictorial projection
- isometric projection (6) ☐
- oblique projection (7) ☐

E13   Draws, from given orthographic drawings and orthographic views
- oblique views (3)   ❑

E14   Uses the conventions shown in the British Standards to produce sectioned and dimensioned working drawings
- components from electrical/mechanical devices (3)   ❑
- assemblies (not more than 6 parts) (3)   ❑
- functional and non-functional dimensions (3)   ❑

G Electrical Connection and Termination

G19   Identifies different types of connection method, recognise their characteristics, and selects a method of connection for a given job, giving reasons for the choice
- pinched screw (4)   ❑
- bolted connections (4)   ❑

J Electronic Systems

J24   Demonstrates and compares different types of input and output waveforms and frequencies
- d.c. supply operating from an a.c. mains (4)   ❑

K Materials

K27   Identifies the bearing properties of phospher bronze, cast iron, PTFE, nylon and graphite (1)   ❑

K28   Carries out simple tests to discover the differences between thermoplastics and thermo-setting plastics, uses reference sources to list engineering applications and properties of these materials (1)   ❑

K29   Uses given reference sources to list the engineering application
- rubber (1)   ❑

K31   Distinguishes between the electrical properties of conductors and insulators and gives examples of materials in each class of material (2)   ❑

K32   Discovers the reason for and methods of protecting materials from atmospheric attack
- the need for the protection of metallic materials from atmospheric corrosion (2)   ❑

Mathematics
A Arithmetic

A4   Understands and uses, tables and charts
- logarithms, squares, cubes, square roots, cube roots, sine, cosine, tangent, reciprocals (5)   ❑

B Algebra

B6   Uses basic notation and rules of algebra
- numbers and letters (4)   ❑
- simplification of expressions (4)   ❑

B9   Evaluate and transform formulae
- substitution of given data (5)   ❑

Science
B Statics

B2   Produces graphs from results obtained experimentally to determine the relationship between force and extension for different given materials and subsequently verify Hooke's Law relating to elasticity by solving practical problems (12)   ❑

C Motion and Energy

C6   Constructs velocity/time graphs from given data, calculates the gradient, interprets the slope as acceleration and solves simple problems using graphical and calculation techniques
- definition of acceleration (6)   ❑
- Distance = Average Velocity x Time (6)   ❑

C8   Carries out tests and solves problems associated with energy
- work in terms of force applied and distance moved (4)   ❑

- graphs (4)
- identification of forms of energy (4)

Information Technology Studies

A Introduction to Information Technology

A1 Explain information technology using suitable examples
- quality of information (6)

A2 Identifies practical examples of information technology, and explains their functions
- the office eg typewriters, telephones, reprographic equipment, calculators, dictating machines, in-house exchanges, electronic mail (4)

B Computing

B4 Investigates types of digital computer and their function and prepares a report
- typical fields of application for digital computers in both real time and batch processing modes (10)

B6 Analyse programming tasks by the use of flowcharts and identifies the standard flow symbols
- input/output operations (10)
- terminal point (10)
- connector (10)

C Information Technology Applications in the Office

C11 Outlines the basic characteristics of document preparation, and compare their cost effectiveness
- typewriters with no memory (8)
- typewriters with limited memory (10)

Task No. 2 – Design & Manufacture

Suggested learning support time – 33 hrs 30 min

Common Skills – Competence Objectives & Performance Criteria

A Managing and Developing People

A4 Transfer skills gained to new and changing situations and contexts
- prior skills and knowledge needed, identified and valued

B Working with and Relating to Others

B7 Work effectively as a member of a team
- help and support offered to and received from others as appropriate

C Communicating

C11 Participate in oral and non-verbal communication
- body language used to support and receive messages

G Applying Design and Creativity

G17 Apply a range of skills and techniques to develop a variety of ideas in the creation of new/modified products, services or situations
- creative design ideas produced and evaluated

Vocational – Competence Objectives & Indicative Content

Engineering Fundamentals

A Safety Hazards

A1 Studies the 'Health and Safety at Work Act', using practical situations and layouts in the workshop/laboratory to identify the major responsibilities of the employee and hazards
- dangers associated with unsuitable clothing and hair (1)
- importance of machine guards (1)

A2   Simulates the appropriate procedures which should be adopted in the event of workshop accidents
- various types of fire – oil, electrical and chemical (1)

A3   Recognises the importance of safe electrical working in protecting life and property
- effect of shock and burns on the human body (1)

B Hand and Machine Processes

B5   Performs marking out exercises on plane surfaces, selects the relevant hand tools for a task
- which equipment is required for simple tasks to mark out profiles (3)
- the relative merits of powered and non-powered tools, in terms of speed of production, cost, accuracy, human fatigue (3)
- how to maintain hand tools in good condition (3)

B6   Uses suitable equipment to measure components, explains the principles and identifies limitations governed by accuracy, robustness, etc. Examines equipment including micrometers; verniers; plunger dial gauges; level type test indicators (4)

B7   Uses machines and outline problems and limitations which could arise, also identies design and operational features and safety precautions
- sensitive drilling machine, centre lathe (3)
- twist drills, trepanning tools, reamers, cutting angles, holding and clamping methods (3)
- three methods of taper turning (3)
- cutting speeds for common tool/workpiece material combinations (3)
- machine spindle speeds for turning, boring and drilling (3)

C Fastening and Joining of Materials

C9   Carries out various joining methods for materials, identifies their applications, advantages and disadvantages
- screws, bolts, nuts and washers commonly available and types of thread (4)
- techniques employed in various locking devices, such as spring washers, self-locking nuts, castle nuts (4)

D Working in Plastics

D10   Uses and describes the techniques available within conventional workshops to produce shapes in plastic materials and subsequently indicates applications, gives details of techniques used, associated problems and safety measures
- problems associated with the machining of plastics and the speeds and feeds necessary (7)

E Engineering Drawing

E11   Explains with the aid of drawings the meaning of orthographic projection, and produces neat and clear drawings including the use of hidden detail lines
- simple 3-dimensional objects (3)
- first angle projection (3)

E13   Draws, from given orthographic drawings and orthographic views
- isometric views with no isometric scale (3)
- oblique views to include rectilinear and curved objects (3)

G Electrical Connection and Termination

G19   Identifies different types of connection method, recognise their characteristics, and selects a method of connection for a given job, giving reasons for the choice
- soldered lug (4)
- mechanical clamping (4)

J Electronic Systems

J24   Demonstrates and compares different types of input and output waveforms and frequencies
- oscillators giving sinusoidal, square and sawtooth outputs (4)

Mathematics
A Arithmetic

A1 Evaluates expressions involving integer indices and use standard form
- standard form eg 1.234 x 10 to the power of 5 (5)

A2 Evaluates expressions involving negative and fractional indices and logarithms
- inverse of (a to the power x) = y as x = log (base a) of y (5)

A4 Understands and uses, tables and charts
- conversion tables (5)
- applications to practical problems (5)

A5 Performs basic arithmetic operations on a calculator
- four basic operations (5)
- reciprocals (5)
- checking of results (5)

B Algebra

B8 Solves, algebraically, simple equations and linear simultaneous equations
- linear equations with one unknown (5)
- construction of equations from derived data (5)

B9 Evaluate and transform formulae
- transformation to change subject of formula (5)

B10 Illustrates direct and inverse proportionality
- dependent and independent variables (5)

C Geometry and Trigonometry

C12 Calculates areas and volumes of plane figures and common solids using given formulae
- surface area of cubes, prisms, cylinders (8)

C13 Recognises the types and properties of triangles
- acute-angled, right-angled, obtuse-angled, equilateral, isosceles (8)
- complementary angles (8)

C15 Solves right-angled triangles for angles and lengths of sides using sine, cosine and tangent functions
- construction of right-angled triangles (8)
- use of tables or calculators (8)

Science
C Motion and Energy

C5 Determines experimentally distance/time data (including average speed), plot distance/time graphs, determine gradients of such graphs and interprets the slopes as speeds, explaining why speed is a scalar quantity and velocity is a vector quantity (23)

C6 Constructs velocity/time graphs from given data, calculates the gradient, interprets the slope as acceleration and solves simple problems using graphical and calculation techniques
- effect of force on acceleration (6)
- gravitational force (6)
- frictional resistance (6)

Information Technology Studies
A Introduction to Information Technolgy

A2 Identifies practical examples of information technology, and explains their functions
- industry eg design, manufacturing, planning, process automation, monitoring and control (4)
- the Home, for entertainment, personal information handling, security and as an aid to learning (4)

B Computing

B5   Demonstrates an understanding of the basic structure of a digital computer system and distinguishes between the control signal paths and data paths by illustrating the relationship between the central processor and peripheral equipment
- main store (8)
- control unit (8)

B6   Analyse programming tasks by the use of flowcharts and identifies the standard flow symbols
- processing functions (10)

B7   Identifies the relative merits of machine level coding and high level language programming and explains the need within an instruction for an address and a function. Writes a simple program, using a flow chart and employing a simple instruction set containing up to 8 instructions such as Load, Store, Add, Decrement, Halt, Conditional and Unconditional Jump, Compare. Enter and execute the program (10)

B8   Distinguishes between types of storage and recognises their role within the computer system
- characteristics of devices used in main store (10)
- characteristics (eg latency time and capacity) of backing store (10)

C Information Technology Applications in the Office

C13 Identifies the components of a communicating word processing system as being processor, disk stores, switching system and control printer, and explains the function of each (10)

C14 Outlines the operation and compares the characteristics of the main types of printer in common use. Select the appropriate printer for a specified application, showing an awareness of cost factors and print quality (10)

C16 Outlines the basic characteristics of document storage and retrieval, comparing such factors as cost, ease of use and storage space
- microform (microfilm and microfiche) (3)

Task No. 3 – Sensors & Measurement

Suggested learning support time – 45 hrs 30 min

Common Skills – Competence Objectives & Performance Criteria

B Working with and Relating to Others

B5   Treat other's values, beliefs and opinions with respect
- dealings with those of differing values, beliefs and opinions undertaken sensitively

D Managing Tasks and Solving Problems

D13 Deal with a combination of routine and non-routine tasks
- appropriate tasks completed accurately and on time under supervision

F Applying Technology

F16 Use a range of technological equipment and systems
- basic errors rectified and more complex errors reported appropriately

Vocational – Competence Objectives & Indicative Content
Engineering Fundamentals

A Safety Hazards

A1   Studies the 'Health and Safety at Work Act', using practical situations and layouts in the workshop/laboratory to identify the major responsibilities
- danger associated with electricity in the workshop (1)
- the need for eye protection against sparks and dust (1)

A2   Simulates the appropriate procedures which should be adopted in the event of workshop accidents
- physical injury (1)

A3   Recognises the importance of safe electrical working in protecting life and property
- likely sources of electrical danger (1)   ❑

B Hand and Machine Processes

B6   Uses suitable equipment to measure components, explains the principles and identifies limitations governed by accuracy, robustness, etc. Examines equipment including micrometers; verniers; plunger dial gauges; level type test indicators (4)   ❑

B7   Uses machines and outline problems and limitations which could arise, also identies design and operational features and safety precautions
- grabbing, lobed holes (3)   ❑

B8   Selects appropriate tools and cutting fluids for various machining operations and describes suitable tool maintenance
- identification of relevant angles on common cutting tools (8)   ❑
- the advantages of using cutting fluids (8)   ❑
- identification of drilling faults and reasons (10)   ❑

C Fastening and Joining Materials

C9   Carries out various joining methods for materials, identifies their applications, advantages and disadvantages
- riveting methods with particular emphasis on hollow riveting using a mandrel (4)   ❑
- silver-soldering; gas-and arc-welding; brazing (4)   ❑
- welding of thermoplastics (4)   ❑

E Engineering Drawing

E15 Uses conventions shown in appropriate standards to interpret and draw electrical circuit diagrams
- power supplies – battery, earth, a.c. mains, d.c. mains (4)   ❑
- connections, junctions, cables(twin-core, 3-core, screened) (4)   ❑
- lamps – filaments (4)   ❑
- switches, etc. – single-pole, two-pole, relay and contacts (4)   ❑

F Electrical Measuring Instruments

F16 Carries out tests/measurements
- insulation resistance using IR tester (multi-meter) (3)   ❑
- continuity using a lamp and battery (3)   ❑
- resistance (in the region 10 to 100 ohms) using a voltmeter and an ammeter (3)   ❑
- resistance, voltage and current, for continuity using multi-range instruments (3)   ❑

F17 Uses a cathode ray oscilloscope to measure the amplitude and frequency of sinusoidal signals and for a regular train of pulses
- x and y gain (3)   ❑
- time base (3)   ❑
- focus (3)   ❑
- brilliance (3)   ❑

G Electrical Connection and Termination

G18 Produces soldered joints and explains limitations and precautions (eg close clean surfaces; non-corrosive flux; correct heat from clean source; quality solder; surface flow for tinning) (10)   ❑

G19 Identifies different types of connection method, recognise their characteristics, and selects a method of connection for a given job, giving reasons for the choice
- crimped lug (4)   ❑

G20 Carries out an electrical jointing and connection assignment (15)   ❑

I Electrical Protection

I23   Prepares explanatory notes from given references concerned with adequate protection of electrical installations
- reasons for protection against excess current and earth leakage current (4)
- reliability, discrimination, low maintenance costs, protection of the smallest conductor in the circuit, as protection equipment criteria (4)

J Electronic Systems

J24   Demonstrates and compares different types of input and output waveforms and frequencies
- amplifiers,voltage amplifiers, current amplifiers, power amplifiers, d.c. and a.c. amplifiers (4)
- using, for example a CRO and in addition measures the gain of a simple a.c. amplifier (4)

Mathematics

A Arithmetic

A1   Evaluates expressions involving integer indices and use standard form
- base, index, power. reciprocal in terms of a to the power of n (5)

A2   Evaluates expressions involving negative and fractional indices and logarithms
- logarithms of numbers (5)

A5   Performs basic arithmetic operations on a calculator
- checking of calculations (5)

B Algebra

B6   Uses basic notation and rules of algebra
- four basic operations, commutative, associative and distributive, precedence laws (4)

B7   Multiplies and factorises algebraic expressions involving brackets
- factorising as a reverse of the above (5)
- grouping for factorisation (5)

B9   Evaluate and transform formulae
- algebraic expressions involving whole number indices, negative indices, fractional and decimal indices (5)

B11 Determines the equation of a straight-line graph
- three or more points from coordinates of equation of form $y = mx + c$ (4)
- gradient of the straight line graph (4)

C Geometry and Trigonometry

C12 Calculates areas and volumes of plane figures and common solids using given formulae
- area of triangle, square, rectangle, parallelogram, circle, semi-circle (7)

D Statistics

D16 Collects, tabulates and summarise statistical data and interprets it descriptively
- data collection (6)
- range and density (6)
- pictorial presentation – bar charts, component bar charts, pie charts, pictograms (8)

Science

B Statics

B4   Establishes by experiments that fluid pressure at any level is equal in all directions, is normal to its containing surface, and is dependent on density and head of liquid
- measurement of pressure (12)
- application to simple problems (including gas pressure) (12)

C Motion and Energy

C7   Describes wave motion and solves problems involving wave velocity
- wavelength (5)

- frequency (5)
- v = f (5)

D Electricity

D11 Solves problems related to current, potential difference and resistance for simple resistive circuits in parallel and series
- use of ammeters and voltmeters (13)

D12 Calculates power in simple electrical circuits
- $P = I\,V = I^2\,R = V^2/R$ (13)

D13 Uses practical examples to explain the chemical effects of electricity
- construction of a simple cell (13)

D14 Establishes, by experiments, electro-magnetic effects and illustrates simple, practical applications of these
- field patterns produced by bar magnet and solenoid (12)
- effects on current carrying conductors (12)
- electromagnetic induction (12)

Information Technology Studies

A Introduction to Information Technology

A2 Identifies practical examples of information technology, and explains their functions
- finance and commerce eg bar codes on goods in shops, computer controlled stock, electronic payment services, debit-card terminals, cash points (4)

B Computing

B4 Investigates types of digital computer and their function and prepares a report
- differences between user programmable and stored program machines (10)

B5 Demonstrates an understanding of the basic structure of a digital computer system and distinguishes between the control signal paths and data paths by illustrating the relationship between the central processor and peripheral equipment
- input unit (8)
- output unit (8)
- arithmetic unit (8)

B7 Identifies the relative merits of machine level coding and high level language programming and explains the need within an instruction for an address and a function. Writes a simple program, using a flow chart and employing a simple instruction set containing up to 8 instructions such as Load, Store, Add, Decrement, Halt, Conditional and Unconditional Jump, Compare. Enter and execute the program (10)

Task No. 4 – Properties of Materials

Suggested learning support time – 15 hrs

Common Skills – Competence Objectives & Performance Criteria

B Working with and Relating to Others

B6 Relate to and interact effectively with individuals and groups
- personal behaviour adjusted in response to constructive feedback

C Communicating

C8 Receive and respond to a variety of information
- appropriate method of response selected and used

D Managing Tasks and Solving Problems

D13 Deal with a combination of routine and non-routine tasks
- own performance reviewed and modified as necessary ❑

Vocational – Competence Objectives & Indicative Content

Engineering Fundamentals

B Hand and Machine Process

B6 Uses suitable equipment to measure components, explains the principles and identifies limitations governed by accuracy, robustness, etc. Examines equipment including micrometers; verniers; plunger dial gauges; level type test indicators (5) ❑

B7 Uses machines and outline problems and limitations which could arise, also identies design and operational features and safety precautions
- clogging, overheating and toxic fumes when producing holes in plastic (3) ❑

C Fastening and Joining Materials

C9 Carries out various joining methods for materials, identifies their applications, advantages and disadvantages
- adhesives, resins and solvents, with particular attention to safety hazards (4) ❑

D Working in Plastics

D10 Uses and describes the techniques available within conventional workshops to produce shapes in plastic materials and subsequently indicates applications, gives details of techniques used, associated problems and safety measures
- the use of casting to form plastic materials with special reference to encapsulation techniques for electrical components (7) ❑

K Materials

K25 Uses laboratory tests and given reference sources to indicate the general composition, properties of certain engineering materials. The properties should be compared in terms such as strength, rigidity, hardness, elasticity toughness, electrical conductivity, temperature stability, ease of processing and costs
- low, medium and high carbon steel and cast iron (1) ❑
- aluminium alloys (1) ❑
- magnesium alloys (1) ❑
- copper (1) ❑

K26 Carries out examples of heat treatment and records the individual stages of annealing; normalising; hardening and tempering as applied to commonly used metals and alloys; identifying their effects on the properties (2) ❑

K27 Identifies the bearing properties of phospher bronze, cast iron, PTFE, nylon and graphite (2) ❑

K28 Carries out simple tests to discover the differences between thermoplastics and thermo-setting plastics, uses reference sources to list engineering applications and properties of these materials (2) ❑

Mathematics

A Arithmetic

A1 Evaluates expressions involving integer indices and use standard form
- four basic operations using standard form (5) ❑

A3 Ensures the answers to numerical problems are reasonable
- significant figures, validity and feasibility of solutions, approximations, checking results (5) ❑

B Algebra

B9 Evaluate and transform formulae
- algebraic expressions involving whole number indices, negative indices, fractional and decimal indices (5) ❑

B10 Illustrates direct and inverse proportionality
- applications eg Boyle's Law, Charles' Law, Hooke's Law, Ohm's Law (5) ❏

B11 Determines the equation of a straight-line graph
- intercept with the y axis (4) ❏
- positive, negative and zero gradients (4) ❏

C Geometry and Trigonometry

C12 Calculates areas and volumes of plane figures and common solids using given formulae
- proportionality (8) ❏

C14 Identifies the geometric properties of a circle
- radius, diameter, circumference, chord, tangent, secant, sector, segment, arc (8) ❏

D Statistics

D16 Collects, tabulates and summarise statistical data and interprets it descriptively
- discrete and continuous data (6) ❏
- frequency and relative frequency (8) ❏
- tally counts (8) ❏

Science

B Statics

B2 Produces graphs from results obtained experimentally to determine the relationship between force and extension for different given materials and subsequently verify Hooke's Law relating to elasticity by solving practical problems (12) ❏

C Motion and Energy

C8 Carries out tests and solves problems associated with energy
- efficiency in terms of energy input and output (4) ❏
- power (2) ❏

Information Technology Studies

A Introduction to Information Technology

A1 Explain information technology using suitable examples
- information Technology (6) ❏

A2 Identifies practical examples of information technology, and explains their functions
- document storage and retrieval eg computer systems, microfiche (4) ❏

B Computing

B4 Investigates types of digital computer and their function and prepares a report
- advantages and disadvantages of stored program machines (10) ❏

Task No. 5 – Report & Recommendations

Suggested learning support time – 19 hrs

Common Skills – Competence Objectives & Performance Criteria

B Working with and Relating to Others

B7 Work effectively as a member of a team
- own tasks completed to required standards and deadlines ❏

C Communicating

C10 Communicate in writing
- relevant information presented in a clear, easily assimilated manner and format appropriate for its intended use ❏

E Applying Numeracy

E15 Apply numerical skills and techniques
- valid conclusions drawn ❑

Vocational – Competence Objectives & Indicative Content
Engineering Fundamentals
A Safety Hazards

A3 Recognises the importance of safe electrical working in protecting life and property
- personal safety precautions regarding clothing, dampness, tools (1) ❑

E Engineering Drawing

E11 Explains with the aid of drawings the meaning of orthographic projection, and produces neat and clear drawings including the use of hidden detail lines
- third angle projection (3) ❑

E13 Draws, from given orthographic drawings and orthographic views
- isometric views (3) ❑

E14 Uses the conventions shown in the British Standards to produce sectioned and dimensioned working drawings
- fastenings, locking devices, threads, knurling, square on shaft, related holes, bearings, springs, gears, matching symbols, welding symbols (3) ❑

E15 Uses conventions shown in appropriate standards to interpret and draw electrical circuit diagrams
- circuit elements - resistor (fixed, variable, potential divider), capacitor (fixed, variable), inductor (air-cooled, iron-cored), transformer(double-wound) (4) ❑
- electronic devices – semiconductor diode, transistor, LEDs and Zener diode (5) ❑

I Electrical Protection

I23 Prepares explanatory notes from given references concerned with adequate protection of electrical installations
- construction advantages and disadvantages of rewireable fuses and cartridge fuse element (4) ❑
- inherent time lag in fuses (4) ❑
- minimising danger from shock and fire by isolating circuits through earth leak protection (4) ❑
- reasons for non-current carrying metal being earthed (4) ❑

K Materials

K25 Uses laboratory tests and given reference sources to indicate the general composition, properties of certain engineering materials. The properties should be compared in terms such as strength, rigidity, hardness, elasticity toughness, electrical conductivity, temperature stability, ease of processing and costs
- copper alloys (1) ❑
- tin/lead soldering alloys (1) ❑

K29 Uses given reference sources to list the engineering application
- ceramics (2) ❑

K30 Discusses the safety hazards in the use of asbestos (2) ❑

K31 Distinguishes between the electrical properties of conductors and insulators and gives examples of materials in each class of material (2) ❑

K32 Discovers the reason for and methods of protecting materials from atmospheric attack
- how painting, anodising, plating can be used to protect against atmospheric corrosion (2) ❑

Mathematics
A Arithmetic

A2 Evaluates expressions involving negative and fractional indices and logarithms
- combination of positive, negative and fractional indices (5) ❑

A4   Understands and uses, tables and charts
- conversion tables (5)   ☐

B Algebra

B9   Evaluate and transform formulae
- substitution of given data (5)   ☐
B11 Determines the equation of a straight-line graph
- positive, negative and zero gradients (4)   ☐

D Statistics

D16 Collects, tabulates and summarise statistical data and interprets it descriptively
- histogram, frequency polygon, ogive-interpretation (8)   ☐

Science

A Oxidation

A1   Establishes through experiments, the basic chemical processes involved in burning and rusting as examples of chemical reactions (interactions between substances which result in a rearrangement of their atoms) and applies this knowledge to a variety of practical situations
- preventative treatments (25)   ☐

B Statics

B2   Produces graphs from results obtained experimentally to determine the relationship between   ☐ force and extension for different given materials and subsequently verify Hooke's Law relating to elasticity by solving practical problems (12)
B3   Establishes the effect of a force rotating about a point and solves simple problems related to static equilibrium
- principle of moments (12)   ☐
- use of calculation, practical and vector diagram techniques (12)   ☐

C Motion and Energy

C8   Carries out tests and solves problems associated with energy
- power (2)   ☐

Information Technology Studies

C Information Technology Applications in the Office

C11 Outlines the basic characteristics of document preparation, and compare their cost effectiveness
- word processor systems (10)   ☐
C15 Plans the layout of a document and uses a word processor to prepare it (10)   ☐
C16 Outlines the basic characteristics of document storage and retrieval, comparing such factors as cost, ease of use and storage space
- paper (3)   ☐
- computerised systems (4)   ☐

Module Specifications and Profile

Competence Objectives & Performance Criteria Check List

Common Skills

A Managing and Developing People

A1 Manage own roles and responsibilities
- personal and work roles and responsibilities to be managed, agreed and accepted ☐
- constraints of roles and responsibilities identified ☐
- given criteria for achievement accepted, monitored and adjustments agreed ☐
- opportunities for developing own roles and responsibilities agreed ☐

A2 Manage own time in achieving objectives
- plan provided for achieving objectives accepted and implemented ☐
- prescribed techniques used and planned objectives achieved within an agreed timescale ☐

A3 Undertakes personal and career development
- areas for development identified and an action plan agreed and produced ☐
- own performance improved in line with action plan ☐

A4 Transfer skills gained to new and changing situations and contexts
- prior skills and knowledge needed, identified and valued ☐
- existing skills and concepts applied to differing situations and contexts ☐
- new skills and knowledge to be developed identified in cooperation with others ☐

B Working with and relating to others

B5 Treat other's values, beliefs and opinions with respect
- own values, beliefs and opinions identified, reflected upon and described ☐
- other's values, beliefs and opinions identified, reflected upon and described. ☐
- dealings with those of differing values, beliefs and opinions undertaken sensitively. ☐

B6 Relate to and interact effectively with individuals and groups
- experience, skills and knowledge of others identified and valued ☐
- others listened to and observed appropriately ☐
- help and support offered to and received from others ☐
- personal behaviour adjusted in response to constructive feedback ☐

B7 Work effectively as a member of a team
- importance of teamwork recognised and accepted ☐
- strengths and weaknesses of team members identified ☐
- participation in allocation of team tasks ☐
- accuracy of own interpretation of brief/allocated tasks agreed with team ☐
- own tasks completed to required standards and deadlines ☐
- help and support offered to and received from others as appropriate ☐
- personal contribution is adjusted in response to constructive feedback ☐

C Communicating

C8 Receive and respond to a variety of information
- information clarified as necessary through questioning and enquiry ☐
- received information accurately interpreted and summarised ☐
- appropriate method of response selected and used ☐

C9   Present information in a variety of visual forms
- appropriate visual methods of presentation identified and selected ☐
- relevant visual information presented in a clear and easily assimilated manner ☐

C10   Communicate in writing
- correct sources of information identified and consulted ☐
- relevant information extracted from a variety of sources ☐
- relevant information presented in a clear, easily assimilated manner and format appropriate for its intended use ☐

C11   Participate in oral and non-verbal communication
- others listened to and observed without unnecessary interruption ☐
- appropriate vocabulary, language, tone and techniques used to give and receive messages ☐
- body language used to support and receive messages ☐

D   Managing Tasks and Solving Problems

D12   Use information sources
- information located and collected from appropriate sources ☐
- information sorted into a useable and effective format ☐

D13   Deal with a combination of routine and non-routine tasks
- routine and non-routine tasks identified ☐
- tasks prioritised and sequenced ☐
- where appropriate, advice identified, sought and used ☐
- appropriate tasks completed accurately and on time under supervision ☐
- own performance reviewed and modified as necessary ☐

D14   Identify and solve routine and non-routine problems
- nature and extent of problem correctly identified ☐
- plan of action devised and implemented using suitable problem solving techniques ☐
- realistic solution selected and used ☐
- solution checked and action adjusted as necessary ☐

E   Applying Numeracy

E15   Apply numerical skills and techniques
- use and application of numerical techniques identified ☐
- appropriate techniques selected and applied ☐
- numerical information correctly interpreted ☐
- valid conclusions drawn ☐

F   Applying Technology

F16   Use a range of technological equipment and systems
- appropriate equipment for task identified ☐
- initial preparation procedures for equipment completed ☐
- equipment used effectively ☐
- basic errors rectified and more complex errors reported appropriately ☐
- operating, safety and security procedures followed at all times ☐

G   Applying Design and Creativity

G17   Apply a range of skills and techniques to develop a variety of ideas in the creation of new/modified products, services or situations
- given opportunities for innovation and creativity recognised ☐
- use and combination of skills and techniques explored ☐
- creative design ideas produced and evaluated ☐

G18 Use a range of thought processes
- ways of thinking identified and stated
- ideas mixed in usual and unusual ways to provide creative approaches and solutions
- use of ideas and results produced, reviewed and evaluated

Engineering Fundamentals BTEC 2861B F

A Safety hazards

A1 Studies the 'Health and Safety at Work Act', using practical situations and layouts in the workshop/laboratory to identify the major responsibilities of the employee and hazards
- the need for personal hygiene, cleanliness and tidiness in the working situation, highlighting possible hazards arising from untidy working conditions
- dangers associated with unsuitable clothing and hair
- importance of machine guards
- dangers associated with electricity in the workshop
- possible dangers from: compressed air; noxious fumes and liquids; explosive gases and dust
- the need for eye protection against sparks and dust

A2 Simulates the appropriate procedures which should be adopted in the event of workshop accidents
- mouth to mouth resuscitation, using dummies
- various types of fire – oil, electrical and chemical
- physical injury

A3 Recognises the importance of safe electrical working in protecting life and property
- likely sources of electrical danger
- personal safety precautions regarding clothing, dampness, tools
- effect of shock and burns on the human body
- likely damage to property

A4 Carries out simulation exercises successfully and outlines procedures to be followed in cases of electric shock, respiratory or cardiac failure; outlines likely effects, identifying symptoms. Explains procedure when a person is in contact with a live line

B Hand and machine processes

B5 Performs marking out exercises on plane surfaces, selects the relevant hand tools for a task and uses them. Explains the following:
- the function of datum lines and centre lines
- which equipment is required for simple tasks to mark out profiles
- the relative merits of powered and non-powered tools, in terms of speed of production, cost, accuracy, human fatigue
- how to maintain hand tools in good condition

B6 Uses suitable equipment to measure components, explains the principles and identifies limitations governed by accuracy, robustness, etc. Examines equipment including micrometers; verniers; plunger dial gauges; level type test indicators

B7 Uses machines and outlines problems and limitations which could arise, also identies design and operational features and safety precautions.
The following machines and processes should be included:
- sensitive drilling machine, centre lathe
- twist drills, trepanning tools, reamers, cutting angles, holding and clamping methods
- grabbing, lobed holes
- clogging, overheating and toxic fumes when producing holes in plastic
- three methods of taper turning
- cutting speeds for common tool/workpiece material combinations

- machine spindle speeds for turning, boring and drilling

B8   Selects appropriate tools and cutting fluids for various machining operations and describes suitable tool maintenance
- identification of relevant angles on common cutting tools
- the advantages of using cutting fluids
- identification of drilling faults and reasons

C Fastening and Joining of Materials

C9   Carries out various joining methods for materials, identifies their applications, advantages and disadvantages, and describes any process involved
- screws, bolts, nuts and washers commonly available and types of thread
- techniques employed in various locking devices, such as spring washers, self-locking nuts, castle nuts
- riveting methods with particular emphasis on hollow riveting using a mandrel.
- adhesives, resins and solvents, with particular attention to safety hazards
- silver-soldering; gas-and arc-welding; brazing
- welding of thermoplastics

D Working in Plastics

D10   Uses and describes the techniques available within conventional workshops to produce shapes in plastic materials and subsequently indicates applications, gives details of techniques used, associated problems and safety measures
- problems associated with the machining of plastics and the speeds and feeds necessary
- the use of casting to form plastic materials with special reference to encapsulation techniques for electrical components

E Engineering Drawing

E11   Explains with the aid of drawings the meaning of orthographic projection, and produces neat and clear drawings including the use of hidden detail lines
- principle planes of projection
- points
- lines
- areas
- simple 3-dimensional objects
- first angle projection
- third angle projection

E12   Produces neat and clear drawings using pictorial projection
- isometric projection
- oblique projection

E13   Draws, from given orthographic drawings and orthographic views
- isometric views with no isometric scale
- oblique views to include rectilinear and curved objects
- isometric views
- oblique views

E14   Uses the conventions shown in the British Standards to produce sectioned and dimensioned working drawings:
- components from electrical/mechanical devices
- assemblies (not more than 6 parts)
- functional and non-functional dimensions

- fastenings, locking devices, threads, knurling, square on shaft, related holes, bearings, springs, gears, machining symbols, welding symbols ❏

E15 Uses conventions shown in appropriate standards to interpret and draw electrical circuit diagrams
- power supplies – battery, earth, a.c. mains, d.c. mains ❏
- connections, junctions, cables(twin-core, 3-core, screened) ❏
- lamps – filaments ❏
- switches, etc. – single-pole, two-pole, relay and contacts ❏
- circuit elements – resistor (fixed, variable, potential divider), capacitor (fixed, variable), inductor (air-cooled, iron-cored), transformer(double-wound) ❏
- electronic devices – semiconductor diode, transistor, LEDs and Zener diode ❏

F Electrical Measuring Instruments

F16 Carries out tests/measurements for:
- insulation resistance using IR tester (multi-meter) ❏
- continuity using a lamp and battery ❏
- resistance (in the region 10 to 100 ohms) using a voltmeter and an ammeter ❏
- resistance, voltage and current, for continuity using multi-range instruments ❏

F17 Uses a cathode ray oscilloscope to measure the amplitude and frequency of sinusoidal signals and for a regular train of pulses, and demonstrates the purposes of the following controls:
- x and y gain ❏
- time base ❏
- focus ❏
- brilliance ❏
- trigger ❏

G Electrical Connection and Termination

G18 Produces soldered joints and explains limitations and precautions (eg close clean surfaces; non-corrosive flux; correct heat from clean source; quality solder; surface flow for tinning) ❏

G19 Identifies different types of connection method, recognises their characteristics, and selects a method of connection for a given job, giving reasons for the choice. Types of connection method should include:
- pinched screw ❏
- soldered lug ❏
- crimped lug ❏
- bolted connections ❏
- mechanical clamping ❏

G20 Carries out an electrical jointing and connection assignment involving a number of techniques ❏

H Lighting and Power Circuits

H21 Demonstrates an understanding of the layout of lighting and power circuits by:
- defining a final sub-circuit as an assembly of conductors and accessories emanating from a final distribution board ❏
- sketching the circuit diagrams for one-way and two-way lighting circuits ❏
- studying and listing the IEE Regulations for the limitations of the number of lighting points and circuit ratings ❏
- describing the following circuit arrangements – 15 amp radial circuit – 30 amp ring circuit supplying 13 amp socket outlets ❏

H22 Carries out an assignment involving the building and testing of a lighting circuit: (For safety reasons the circuit **must not** be connected to the mains supply) ❏

I Electrical Protection

I23   Prepares explanatory notes from given references concerned with adequate protection of electrical installations.
- reasons for protection against excess current and earth leakage current
- reliability, discrimination, low maintenance costs, protection of the smallest conductor in the circuit, as protection equipment criteria
- construction advantages and disadvantages of rewireable fuses and cartridge fuse elements
- inherent time lag in fuses
- minimising danger from shock and fire by isolating circuits through earth leak protection
- reasons for non-current carrying metal being earthed

J Electronic Systems

J24   Demonstrates and compares different types of input and output waveforms and frequencies on examples of each of the following systems
- d.c. supply operating from an a.c. mains
- oscillators giving sinusoidal, square and sawtooth outputs
- amplifiers,voltage amplifiers, current amplifiers, power amplifiers, d.c. and a.c. amplifiers
- using, for example a CRO and in addition measures the gain of a simple a.c. amplifier

K Materials

K25   Uses laboratory tests and given reference sources to indicate the general composition, properties of certain engineering materials. The properties should be compared in terms such as strength, rigidity, hardness, elasticity toughness, electrical conductivity, temperature stability, ease of processing and costs
- low, medium and high carbon steel and cast iron
- aluminium alloys
- magnesium alloys
- copper
- copper alloys
- tin/lead soldering alloys

K26   Carries out examples of heat treatment and records the individual stages of annealing; normalising; hardening and tempering as applied to commonly used metals and alloys; identifying their effects on the properties

K27   Identifies the bearing properties of phospher bronze, cast iron, PTFE, nylon and graphite

K28   Carries out simple tests to discover the differences between thermoplastics and thermo-setting plastics, uses reference sources to list engineering applications and properties of these materials

K29   Uses given reference sources to list the engineering application
- rubber
- ceramics

K30   Discusses the safety hazards in the use of asbestos

K31   Distinguishes between the electrical properties of conductors and insulators and gives examples of materials in each class of material

K32   Discovers the reason for and methods of protecting materials from atmospheric attack
- the need for the protection of metallic materials from atmospheric corrosion
- how painting, anodising, plating can be used to protect against atmospheric corrosion

L Integrative Assignments

L33   Completes both independently and as a member of a team, several vocationally related assignments involving topic areas covered in this unit and using related topics from other units in the course. These could be based on designing and producing simple items/assemblies from

drawing to tested product stage, or similar industrially relevant tasks involving problem-solving and other process skills
- translates the circuit diagram into a physical layout
- designs and etches a simple printed circuit board for the device
- wires up the circuit
- tests the circuit

Mathematics BTEC 2862B F

A Arithmetic

A1 Evaluates expressions involving integer indices and use standard form
- base, index, power. reciprocal in terms of a to the power of n ☐
- indices – multiplication, division, power, reciprocal ☐
- standard form eg 1.234 x 10 to the power of 5 ☐
- four basic operations using standard form ☐

A2 Evaluates expressions involving negative and fractional indices and logarithms
- index rules for negative and fractional indices ☐
- combination of positive, negative and fractional indices ☐
- inverse of (a to the power x) = y as x = log (base a) of y ☐
- logarithms of numbers ☐

A3 Ensures the answers to numerical problems are reasonable
- significant figures, validity and feasibility of solutions, approximations, checking results ☐

A4 Understands and uses, tables and charts
- logarithms, squares, cubes, square roots, cube roots, sine, cosine, tangent, reciprocals ☐
- conversion tables ☐
- applications to practical problems ☐

A5 Performs basic arithmetic operations on a calculator
- four basic operations ☐
- numbers to a power ☐
- reciprocals ☐
- checking of calculations ☐
- checking of results ☐

B Algebra

B6 Uses basic notation and rules of algebra
- numbers and letters ☐
- four basic operations, commutative, associative and distributive, precedence laws ☐
- simplification of expressions ☐

B7 Multiplies and factorises algebraic expressions involving brackets
- multiplying expressions inside brackets by numbers, symbols or expressions within brackets eg $3a(2 + b) = 6a + 3ab, (a + b)(2 + c) = 2a + ac + 2b + bc$ ☐
- factorising as a reverse of the above ☐
- grouping for factorisation ☐

B8 Solves, algebraically, simple equations and linear simultaneous equations
- maintenance of equality ☐
- linear equations with one unknown ☐
- construction of equations from derived data ☐
- simultaneous equations with two unknowns ☐

B9 Evaluates and transforms formulae
- substitution of given data ☐

- transformation to change subject of formula
- algebraic expressions involving whole number indices, negative indices, fractional and decimal indices

B10 Illustrates direct and inverse proportionality
- dependent and independent variables
- coefficient of proportionality from given data
- applications eg Boyle's Law, Charles' Law, Hooke's Law, Ohm's Law

B11 Determines the equation of a straight-line graph
- three or more points from coordinates of equation of form $y = mx + c$
- intercept with the y axis
- gradient of the straight line
- positive, negative and zero gradients

C Geometry and Trigonometry

C12 Calculates areas and volumes of plane figures and common solids using given formulae
- area of triangle, square, rectangle, parallelogram, circle, semi-circle
- volume of cubes, prisms, cylinders
- surface area of cubes, prisms, cylinders
- proportionality

C13 Recognises the types and properties of triangles
- acute-angled, right-angled, obtuse-angled, equilateral, isosceles
- complementary angles
- Pythagoras – 3, 4, 5 and 5, 12, 13 triangles
- similarity or congruency – applications to find one side or one angle
- construction of triangle given limited information

C14 Identifies the geometric properties of a circle
- radius, diameter, circumference, chord, tangent, secant, sector, segment, arc
- applications relating radius, circumference and diameter
- relationship of angles

C15 Solves right-angled triangles for angles and lengths of sides using sine, cosine and tangent functions
- construction of right-angled triangles
- trigonometric functions
- use of tables or calculators
- standard triangles ($60°\ 30°\ 90°$ and $45°\ 45°\ 90°$ trigonometric properties)
- trigonometric relationships [$\cos \theta = \sin(90-\theta)$, $\sin \theta = \cos(90-\theta)$]
- applications to technical problems

D Statistics

D16 Collects, tabulates and summarise statistical data and interprets it descriptively
- data collection
- discrete and continuous data
- sample and population
- range and density
- frequency and relative frequency
- tally counts
- pictorial presentation – bar charts, component bar charts, pie charts, pictograms
- histogram, frequency polygon, ogive-interpretation

Science BTEC 2863B F

A Oxidation

A1   Establishes through experiments, the basic chemical processes involved in burning and rusting as examples of chemical reactions (interactions between substances which result in a rearrangement of their atoms) and applies this knowledge to a variety of practical situations
  - composition of air
  - mass gain of metals such as copper, brass, iron and steel
  - analysis of oxides
  - effects of oxygen and water
  - examples of damage caused by rusting
  - preventative treatments

B Statics

B2   Produces graphs from results obtained experimentally to determine the relationship between force and extension for different given materials and subsequently verify Hooke's Law relating to elasticity by solving practical problems

B3   Establishes the effect of a force rotating about a point and solves simple problems related to static equilibrium
  - co-planar forces
  - scalar and vector quantities
  - principle of moments
  - centre of gravity
  - use of calculation, practical and vector diagram techniques

B4   Establishes by experiments that fluid pressure at any level is equal in all directions, is normal to its containing surface, and is dependent on density and head of liquid
  - definition of pressure
  - absolute and gauge pressure
  - measurement of pressure
  - application to simple problems (including gas pressure)

C Motion and Energy

C5   Determines experimentally distance/time data (including average speed), plot distance/time graphs, determine gradients of such graphs and interprets the slopes as speeds, explaining why speed is a scalar quantity and velocity is a vector quantity

C6   Constructs velocity/time graphs from given data, calculates the gradient, interprets the slope as acceleration and solves simple problems using graphical and calculation techniques
  - definition of acceleration
  - Distance = Average Velocity x Time
  - effect of force on acceleration
  - gravitational force
  - frictional resistance

C7   Describes wave motion and solves problems involving wave velocity
  - wavelength
  - frequency
  - $v = f\lambda$

C8   Carries out tests and solves problems associated with energy
  - work in terms of force applied and distance moved
  - graphs
  - identification of forms of energy

- efficiency in terms of energy input and output ☐
- power ☐

C9 Solves problems associated with mass, specific heat capacity and temperature change, showing how materials expand or contract with temperature change, and illustrates positive and negative effects in practical situations

- temperature/time graphs for change of state ☐
- sensible and latent heat ☐
- coefficient of linear expansion ☐
- single and composite materials ☐

D Electricity

D10 Uses waveform diagrams to illustrate the difference between direct current (d.c.) and alternating current (a.c.) ☐

D11 Solves problems related to current, potential difference and resistance for simple resistive circuits in parallel and series

- electromotive force (e.m.f.) ☐
- potential difference ☐
- current flow ☐
- use of ammeters and voltmeters ☐
- Ohm's law ☐
- temperature effect ☐
- practical applications ☐

D12 Calculates power in simple electrical circuits

- P = I V = I(to power 2) R = V(to power 2)/R ☐
- power dissipation ☐
- calculation of fuse values given power rating and voltage of an appliance ☐

D13 Uses practical examples to explain the chemical effects of electricity

- good and bad conductors ☐
- electrolytes ☐
- electrodeposition ☐
- construction of a simple cell ☐
- primary and secondary cells ☐
- effect of internal resistance ☐

D14 Establishes, by experiments, electro-magnetic effects and illustrates simple, practical applications of these

- magnetic field ☐
- field patterns produced by bar magnet and solenoid ☐
- effects on current carrying conductors ☐
- moving coil meter ☐
- electromagnetic induction ☐
- generators ☐

Information Technology Studies BTEC 2864B F

A Introduction to Information Technology

A1 Explain information technology using suitable examples

- information ☐
- message transmission ☐
- quality of information ☐
- Information Technology ☐

A2 Identifies practical examples of information technology, and explains their functions
- the office eg typewriters, telephones, reprographic equipment, calculators, dictating machines, in-house exchanges, electronic mail ❑
- document storage and retrieval eg computer systems, microfiche ❑
- publishing and printing eg author editing-printing-warehousing-marketing, electronic publishing ❑
- finance and commerce eg bar codes on goods in shops, computer controlled stock, electronic payment services, debit-card terminals, cash points ❑
- communications eg telephone service, broadcasting, cellular radio ❑
- industry eg design, manufacturing, planning, process automation, monitoring and control
- the home, for entertainment, personal information handling, security and as an aid to learning ❑

A3 Considers the present and likely future effects of information technology
- patterns of employment ❑
- domestic and leisure activities ❑

B Computing

B4 Investigates types of digital computer and their function and prepares a report
- differences between user programmable and stored program machines ❑
- advantages and disadvantages of stored program machines ❑
- typical fields of application for digital computers in both real time and batch processing modes ❑

B5 Demonstrates an understanding of the basic structure of a digital computer system and distinguishes between the control signal paths and data paths by illustrating the relationship between the central processor and peripheral equipment
- main store ❑
- input unit ❑
- output unit ❑
- control unit ❑
- arithmetic unit ❑

B6 Analyse programming tasks by the use of flowcharts and identifies the standard flow symbols
- processing functions ❑
- input/output operations ❑
- decision ❑
- terminal point ❑
- connector ❑

B7 Identifies the relative merits of machine level coding and high level language programming and explains the need within an instruction for an address and a function. Writes a simple program, using a flow chart and employing a simple instruction set containing up to 8 instructions such as Load, Store, Add, Decrement, Halt, Conditional and Unconditional Jump, Compare. Enter and execute the program

B8 Distinguishes between types of storage and recognises their role within the computer system
- basic characteristics of stores ie access and cycle time ❑
- need for main stores and immediate access stores ❑
- volatile and non-volatile storage ❑
- destructive and non-destructive read output ❑
- use of the main categories of storage ie scratchpad, main store, backing store ❑
- characteristics of devices used in main store ❑
- characteristics (eg latency time and capacity) of backing store ❑

B9 Identifies the range and differences between current computer system hardware devices and categories of software
- mainframe, mini and micro computers ❑

- user application software, support software, system software ☐
- data input/output, image, sound and text ☐
- importance of man-machine interface and the demands that input/output make on the user ☐

B10 Explains the need for data protection and distinguishes between privacy and security with respect to data, giving an example of each to show how unauthorised access to computerised information can be prevented using codes ☐

C Information Technology Applications in the Office

C11 Outlines the basic characteristics of document preparation, and compares their cost effectiveness
- typewriters with no memory ☐
- typewriters with limited memory ☐
- word processor systems ☐

C12 Identifies the components of a stand-alone word processor system as being processor, printer and disk store and explains the function of each ☐

C13 Identifies the components of a communicating word processing system as being processor, disk stores, switching system and control printer, and explains the function of each ☐

C14 Outlines the operation and compares the characteristics of the main types of printer in common use. Selects the appropriate printer for a specified application, showing an awareness of cost factors and print quality ☐

C15 Plans the layout of a document and uses a word processor to prepare it ☐

C16 Outlines the basic characteristics of document storage and retrieval, comparing such factors as cost, ease of use and storage space
- paper ☐
- microform (microfilm and microfiche) ☐
- computerised systems ☐

C17 Identifies the functions required of any form of filing system and suggests a possible filing system for a given situation, bearing in mind the forms of retrieval required. Retrieve specified information from a database

D Integrative Assignments

D18 Completes, individually or as a member of a team, work-related assignments incorporating topics in other units in the course and focusing on the technology (eg Engineering Fundamentals F). The philosophy outlined in Vocational Assignments F should be adopted ☐

Index